FLANNERY O'CONNOR'S
RELIGION OF THE GROTESQUE

FLANNERY
O'CONNOR'S

University Press of Mississippi
Jackson and London

RELIGION
of the
GROTESQUE

Marshall Bruce Gentry

The University Press of Mississippi thanks:
Robert Giroux, Flannery O'Connor's literary executor, for
permission to quote from unpublished material;
Farrar, Straus, and Giroux, Inc., for permission to quote from
the following works: *The Complete Stories,*
© 1971; *The Habit of Being,* © 1979; *Mystery and Manners,* © 1969;
The Violent Bear it Away, © 1960, and *Wise Blood,* © 1962;
Harold Matson Company, Inc., for permission to reprint excerpts
from the above mentioned works;
and *Modern Fiction Studies* for permission to use the material
that appeared as "The Eye vs. the Body: Individual and
Communal Grotesquerie in *Wise Blood*" (Autumn 1982),
copyright by the Purdue Research Foundation.

Library of Congress Cataloging-in-Publication Data

Gentry, Marshall Bruce.
  Flannery O'Connor's religion of the grotesque.

  Bibliography: p.
  Includes index.
  1. O'Connor, Flannery—Criticism and interpretation.
2. Grotesque in literature. 3. Redemption in
literature. 4. Narration (Rhetoric) I. Title.
PS3565.C57Z675 1986   813'.54   85-20267
ISBN 0-87805-285-2

*To Robert Bruce Gentry
and Daisy Belle Gentry*

CONTENTS

PREFACE

THIS STUDY presents fresh approaches to Flannery O'Connor's use of the grotesque and to her narration. I hope that this study also shows that there are areas of O'Connor's works which we have not yet begun to understand.

I owe thanks to many people. Professor Joseph J. Moldenhauer, of the University of Texas at Austin, has been encouraging, painstaking, patient. Professors Walter Reed, Anthony Hilfer, Wayne Lesser, and Thomas Philpott, also of the University of Texas, have all given me valuable ideas and encouragement. I am grateful to Professor Susan Blalock, of Virginia Polytechnic Institute and State University, and to William Meyer, Jr., of Beaumont, Texas, for inspiring conversation and friendship. Evelyn Sweet-Hurd and Professor Mark Busby, of Texas A&M University, have helpfully suggested revisions. My thanks also go to Vernon McGee, of the University of Texas, for allowing me to examine a draft of his forthcoming translation of an essay by Mikhail Bakhtin. Seetha Srinivasan of the University Press of Mississippi encouraged and guided me through the preparation of the final text of this study.

In the summer of 1981 I worked with O'Connor's typescripts at Georgia College, in Milledgeville; I am grateful to the staff of the Ina Dillard Russell Library for making my time in Milledgeville enjoyable. I would also like to thank the Graduate School of the University of Texas at Austin for a research grant for my trip to Georgia College.

Viven Weems has my thanks for typing this study.

Finally, I want to thank my parents and the rest of my family for their love, encouragement, and patience.

Parts of this study have appeared in a different form as "The Eye vs. the Body: Individual and Communal Grotesquerie in *Wise Blood*," *Modern Fiction Studies* 28 (1982): 287–93.

ABBREVIATIONS

CS   *The Complete Stories* (New York: Farrar, 1971)

HB   *The Habit of Being,* ed. Sally Fitzgerald (New York: Farrar, 1979)

MM   *Mystery and Manners,* ed. Sally and Robert Fitzgerald (New York: Farrar, 1969)

V   *The Violent Bear It Away* (New York: Farrar, 1960)

WB   *Wise Blood,* 2d ed. (New York: Farrar, 1962)

FLANNERY O'CONNOR'S
RELIGION OF THE GROTESQUE

TRACKS TO THE OVEN OF REDEMPTION

I am come to cast fire on the earth: and what will I, but that
it be kindled?

—Luke 12:49

ROBERT E. GOLDEN correctly identifies the foremost issue in
O'Connor criticism as "the relation between O'Connor's stated
religious intent and the realization of that intent within the fiction."[1] The first of the four critical schools to appear denies the
realization of theological intent. Many early reviews reflect this
view; a recent, thoughtful argument that "nothing" in the works
"compels a theological reading" is by Carol Shloss.[2] The two
largest schools of O'Connor criticism today agree that her intent
does manifest itself in the fiction; these schools differ on the quality
of her religious vision. The second school includes such critics as
Carter Martin and Kathleen Feeley,[3] who consider O'Connor's
outlook to be orthodoxly Catholic. The third school of critics
suspects O'Connor's religious outlook of being overly harsh; this
school includes such critics as Martha Stephens and Miles Orvell.[4]
The fourth school questions whether O'Connor's intent is actually
religious; such critics sometimes even assert that O'Connor's art-
istry is demonic. Josephine Hendin, John Hawkes, and Claire Katz
Kahane belong to this school.[5]

O'Connor herself describes her work as deeply Catholic, insisting, "I see from the standpoint of Christian orthodoxy. This means
that for me the meaning of life is centered in our Redemption by
Christ" (*MM*, 32). She describes the subject of her fiction as "the
action of grace in territory held largely by the devil" (*MM*, 118).
Most critics, whatever their school, assume that the narrator of
every work by O'Connor is O'Connor herself, authoritatively

pronouncing the truth about event and character. O'Connor's characters, inhabitants of that "territory held largely by the devil," are generally considered to be grotesque in an entirely negative sense: their grotesquerie reflects and increases the characters' separation from spiritual well-being. Most critics who agree that O'Connor characters sometimes achieve redemption (usually these are critics in the second or third school) see such events as the result of grace that the characters have done everything possible to avoid. Although I agree that theology is relevant to O'Connor's fiction, I also think that most critics who discuss theology have underestimated her reinterpretations of dogma. The individualistic, judgmental tone of her narrators conflicts with the communal feeling that the stories usually contain; therefore, to consider the narrators authoritative often makes O'Connor's religious outlook seem exceedingly harsh by the standards of her own fiction. Furthermore, to consider her characters thoroughly corrupt makes the redemption of many of them seem dramatically (if not theologically) absurd.

The title of this introduction refers to a shared fantasy and a pattern of imagery that suggest an explanation for O'Connor characters' redemptive experiences. Frequently these characters imagine themselves transported toward the site of their death. In the most suggestive versions of this fantasy, the character imagines traveling in a boxcar to join a pile of dead bodies or to be burned in an oven. This study explores how characters themselves lay the tracks for their transport toward a redemptive experience that they perceive as a physical annihilation. Along the way, the characters come to rival the narrators in authority.

It may seem unorthodox for a character to experience redemption by annihilating the self. *The Catholic Encyclopedia* defines redemption as "the restoration of man from the bondage of sin to the liberty of the children of God through the satisfactions and merits of Christ."[6] In the traditional definition, redemption results from the actions of Christ and of grace (the individual's role being merely to cooperate); redemption is experienced consciously; and the moment of redemption is a natural conclusion to a sequence of preparations. O'Connor dramatizes such redemptions in a few stories: the most famous character who appears to undergo such a redemption is the grandmother in "A Good Man Is Hard to Find." Most of the time, however, in order to make them aesthetically convincing, O'Connor makes her redemptions untraditional. Usually, they result primarily from the action of the individual's unconscious; the consciousness of the individual is nearly irrelevant to redemption;

and redemption is a momentary state in a process that has no natural end. What is traditional about O'Connor's redemptions is that they involve a return to a prior, ideal state, and that they involve the discovery of freedom in the communal ("the liberty of the children of God"). As they join the community of the redeemed, most O'Connor characters give up their selfhood, thus freeing themselves from what has oppressed them.

To show what connects the apparently "untraditional" and "traditional" qualities of O'Connor's redemptions, I should explain the significance I attach to the words "ideal" and "community." O'Connor characters constantly make us aware of their connection to ideals, most often religious truths shared by all the "children of God." At the same time, the ideals are wed to misunderstanding, banality, even cruelty, so that the characters are oppressed by degraded ideals. Similarly, the communities of which we are most aware seem degraded: small-minded farms or towns, hateful families, even groups of dead bodies. As a result of these degradations, the terms "ideal" and "community" are two-faced; while pointing to something ultimate and desirable, ideals and communities can also be mechanical and arbitrary. The point to keep in mind, however, is that the honorific and pejorative senses of these two words are always linked. Redemption is the moment when oppression lapses or is unfelt, but O'Connor's characters repeatedly move beyond the ideal community they rejoin. When Tarwater has his redemptive vision of a multitude feeding on loaves and fishes, he sets out again "toward the dark city, where the children of God lay sleeping" (*V*, 243).

Those passages with explicit imagery of tracks toward physical annihilation indicate that the site of the redemptive oven is primarily psychological. The characters in whom the pattern works itself out most fully consciously locate the oven in another continent, but they send themselves toward an oven in familiar surroundings. Mrs. Shortley of "The Displaced Person" is deeply affected by a newsreel from Europe of "a small room piled high with bodies of dead naked people all in a heap, their arms and legs tangled together, a head thrust in here, a head there, a foot, a knee, a part that should have been covered up sticking out, a hand raised clutching nothing" (*CS,* 196). Later she uses the newsreel when she constructs the prophecy she consciously expects the displaced people from Poland to suffer: " 'The children of wicked nations will be butchered,' she said in a loud voice. 'Legs where arms should be, foot to face, ear in the palm of hand. Who will remain whole? Who will remain whole? Who?' " (p. 210). When Mrs. Shortley finally has a stroke, her own actions recall the newsreel's pile of bodies; I shall argue that through her unconscious strategies she experiences a kind of redemption.

Ruby Turpin, of "Revelation," dreams repeatedly that all the social classes are "crammed in together in a box car, being ridden off to be put in a gas oven" (*CS*, 492), and in her final vision she manages to see herself on a fiery pathway to heaven. Mrs. Cope, of "A Circle in the Fire," who has a dread of fire on her farm, says that she is thankful she is not one of "those poor Europeans" who were "put in boxcars like cattle" and "rode . . . to Siberia" (*CS*, 178). When three delinquent boys set fire to the woods around the farm, however, their voices sound "a few wild high shrieks of joy as if the prophets were dancing in the fiery furnace, in the circle the angel had cleared for them" (p. 193). Mrs. Cope's breakthrough to a communal identity is experienced as pain; her face looks to her daughter "as if it might have belonged to anybody, a Negro or a European or to Powell [a delinquent boy] himself." Mrs. Cope unconsciously combines for herself the horrific and religious implications of holocaust.

Even works that do not use this image pattern extensively suggest its relevance. In "The Enduring Chill," when the failed writer Asbury Fox arrives home after a train trip, his sister maliciously says, "The artist arrives at the gas chamber" (*CS*, 363). In "Good Country People," Joy Hopewell's new name—Hulga—reminds her of the "ugly sweating Vulcan who stayed in the furnace" (*CS*, 275); when she and Manley Pointer head for the barn where she intends to seduce him, the narrator says, "They made for it rapidly as if it might slide away like a train" (p. 286).

This pattern of imagery suggests that it is the characters themselves who prepare for and bring about the revelatory religious experiences they undergo. Although consciously these characters consider the prospect of such an experience to be very threatening, unconsciously they desire it and bring it about—figuratively, they lay the tracks for their trip to the oven in which individuality is burned away. To understand the necessity and significance of such maneuvers on the part of O'Connor's characters, one needs to examine her narration and the strategies by which a character's experience acquires meaning.

O'Connor's Narration and the Problem of Grace

Most of O'Connor's narrators use the techniques at the disposal of any narrator—structuring the story to provide emphasis, describing setting, character, action, etc.—in a manner that reflects the outlook of an authoritarian religion. Even though virtually every story focuses on one character, the narration typically emphasizes a protagonist's consistent wrongheadedness, which can only be transformed by the intervention of an outside force. The typical O'Connor narrator, in other words, emphasizes the main character's need for grace.[7]

Although O'Connor's narrators are often taken as mouthpieces for her own views, the characters consistently refuse to remain merely isolated individuals incapable of bringing about their own redemption. However peculiar they seem individually, many of her characters achieve a return to community. Although the maneuvers by which they transform themselves are individualistic, "protestant" in more than the religious sense, their destinations are remarkably similar. One significant suggestion of the boxcars on tracks to the oven in a concentration camp is, as David Eggenschwiler says, "mankind's essential oneness."[8] The question whether O'Connor's characters transform themselves or are transformed by an external force relates, of course, to the contrast between Catholicism and Protestantism in her works. I do not intend to dwell on the relationship between Catholicism and Protestantism in O'Connor's works, but two broad Catholic/Protestant issues are important to this study: redemption through the individual's works versus redemption through grace, and the importance of the community versus the importance of the individual.

Most O'Connor critics accept the notion that her characters need grace, in part because grace can take many forms. Grace can be described as entirely supernatural, or as working through the unconscious, or as working in the demonic, or as working in all the physical world. It is even possible to consider grace responsible for everything, physical and spiritual, in the entire universe. This last, all-inclusive description, however, makes the concept nearly useless when one wishes to compare the relative importance of forces. One aesthetic problem with the notion that O'Connor's characters can be transformed only by an external force is that it raises doubts about whether many of them are transformed. Not every work by O'Connor ends unambiguously, or should, but if the ultimate state of a character's soul depends upon a momentary acceptance of grace, an action impossible to dramatize completely, then the climax of virtually every work by O'Connor occurs, as it were, offstage. This problem with the endings of her stories has led to much unnecessary speculation on the final state of the soul of most O'Connor protagonists. By exploring the extent to which characters unconsciously bring about their own transformation rather than passively accepting transformation by an external force, this study attempts to alter the context in which we interpret her endings. Insofar as we can see characters transforming themselves, we avoid problems of the representation of divine grace and of characters' momentary receptions of grace in fiction, and we focus instead upon the nature of the transformation that her characters prepare for themselves. Only when we redefine "grace" as a force characters control, even as they sin (see the Conclusion), do I consider the term helpful in describing O'Connor's works.

The conflict I see between the characters' actions and the narration leads me to propose a new perspective on O'Connor's texts. Rather than accepting them as rigid works with clear narrative authority, I suggest a perspective that gives more importance to individual characters' world views and emphasizes the ways in which those views rival the narrators'. What I have in mind, specifically, is Mikhail Bakhtin's model of the novelistic literary text as a battleground, where rebellious characters fight for what they sense is the truth, in opposition to the standards supported weakly, most of the time, by the narrator's authoritarianism. What makes the novel unique, according to Bakhtin, is that it combines and systematizes a variety of "unities," "styles," "languages," and these various forms of language remain "relatively autonomous"[9] despite their systematization. In such a model, the narrator's voice becomes one voice in a shouting match. The narrator's highly authoritarian tone does not prevent its demotion; the more authoritarian and complete the narration presents itself as, the more conspicuous the narrator's incompletions, failures, and distortions appear. The language and consciousness of characters find a way into works of fiction not only through direct quotations of their speech, says Bakhtin, but also through "character zones," which are made up of "fragments of character speech," "various forms for hidden transmission of someone else's word," "scattered words and sayings belonging to someone else's speech," and "those invasions into authorial speech of others' expressive indicators."[10] In such zones, characters can rival the author/narrator: "A character zone is the field of action for a character's voice, encroaching in one way or another upon the author's [narrator's] voice."[11]

Bakhtin's theory of novelistic narration may seem quite alien to many readers, particularly those who believe that "omniscient" narrators like O'Connor's should provide the authoritative perspective on events and characters. O'Connor indicated that she did not fully accept such a simple theory of narration by consistently asserting that handling point of view was among her most difficult tasks. The potential complexity of the rivalry between character and author/narrator is such that we can understand why, in a letter dated 27 August 1957, O'Connor said, "Point of view runs me crazy when I think about it but I believe that when you are writing well, you don't think about it. I seldom think about it when I am writing a short story" (*HB*, 239). Bakhtin considers it unusual for a character to rival the author/narrator, but his idea of "dialogism" is relevant to more literature than he says. As Roger Fowler argues, languages associated with different social levels always start a dialogue:

> Fictional presentations of criminals, perverts, junkies, political extremists, idiots, children, deities, and other figures beyond the range of accepted experience of the bourgeoisie are potential illustrations of Bakhtin's theory. However, the hero as subject with his own effective voice need not by any means be a deviant; all that is necessary is that s/he should articulate a world-view which is different from the implied author's and which is perceptible as in principle valid, which is not just depicted and dismissed by the author: which is *alien* but *possible*.[12]

I would like to expand further this idea of dialogism, for the notion that the author/narrator can easily discredit a character's world view is suspect. When a narrator seems *most* intent upon dismissing a character's perspective, a reader may feel an increased desire to investigate that world view thoroughly, and may notice points at which the character's perspective seems to be unfairly dismissed. Dorrit Cohn discusses most if not all of the contents of Bakhtin's character zone, and Cohn says that even when the style is "psycho-narration," in which the narrator tells the reader what goes on in the mind of a character, one need not accept the narrator's attitude.[13] In "narrated monologue" (Cohn's term, which closely corresponds to "free indirect style"), the matter is equally complicated. Narrated monologue reduces the distance between the narrator and the character whose consciousness is narrated, but the narrator's attitude toward that character may be sympathetic, ironic, or both. Even when the narration is most ironic, it cannot completely subordinate the character's consciousness. In such narrated monologue, more than elsewhere, the character's own words are transmitted to the reader, who may well discover more meaning in them than the narrator's general treatment of the character would lead one to expect. Once their grotesqueries have been presented, it may seem that O'Connor's characters are hardly fit to rival the narrator; consequently, O'Connor's use of the grotesque needs reexamination.

O'Connor's Grotesque and the Unconscious

On a basic level, the term "grotesque" describes images of degraded physicality with an effect at once humorous and disturbing. The notion of degradation, of descent from a higher to a lower grade, separates the "grotesque," as I shall use it, from related terms such as "absurd" or "bizarre," for the grotesque always depends upon an attraction to the ideals that the grotesque declines from. Even as the grotesque attacks a hierarchy, turning the elevated or self-important into animals or objects, it maintains an attachment to that hierarchy, and one may find horror or pleasure in the attachment. The mixed effect of the grotesque is important in at least two ways: the instability of effect separates the grotesque from the comic (which is only occasionally disturbing) or the macabre (which is rarely humorous), and marks it as essentially transitional, transformative. Although it may seem that grotesquerie is primarily a state of being in O'Connor (as with the hermaphrodite in "A Temple of the Holy Ghost," for example), this version of the grotesque is relatively unimportant to this study. The more important forms of the grotesque are its uses as a mode of representation and as a mode of perception. These two forms are most commonly found in the actions, respectively, of the narrator (who creates grotesque comparisons to represent the characters) and of the characters (who frequently perceive themselves as degraded or perceive the world around them in ways the reader recognizes as degraded). When I refer to characters as grotesque, then, I may mean that they are physically degraded, but often I also mean that they are described as degraded or see themselves or the world as degraded.

By far the most common critical attitude toward O'Connor's grotesque is that it expresses a negative judgment, that the grotesque reflects a character's fallen state. The only positive purpose the grotesque can serve, according to this view, is to indicate a need for change, although the character who is grotesque may seem incapable of change. The notion that O'Connor's grotesque expresses a fixed judgment leads some critics to argue that O'Connor has disgust for the body. Such arguments suggest a serious problem in regarding O'Connor's grotesquerie as religious; the logic behind these statements tends to cut characters off from religion entirely. Josephine Hendin, who extends this approach forcefully, considers the grotesquerie of O'Connor's writing essentially reductive: "There is very little emphasis on the soul, the mind, or any other form of transcendent reality in O'Connor's work."[14]

Another reflection of critics' inclination to see the grotesque as negative is the fact that when a character gains a critic's approval, the critic tends to deny that the character is actually grotesque. A related problem is that if one sees the grotesque as entirely negative and wishes to evaluate a character positively, one is forced to use standards imported from outside the text. Carol Shloss attacks O'Connor's use of the grotesque for requiring a religious standard not in the text; and Shloss has a valid complaint, if most of the commentators on O'Connor's use of the grotesque are to be believed.[15] Actually, however, the grotesquerie of the O'Connor character is usually a result of the degradation of an ideal, rather than merely a departure from an ideal. The ideal can be inferred from its degraded form in O'Connor's text, and this ideal provides the standard by which a character is to be understood. The readings of O'Connor's works presented in this study will identify a variety of degraded ideals, all of which ultimately relate to religion.

At times, it is true, O'Connor speaks about the grotesque in thoroughly negative terms. She quotes Wyndham Lewis's statement, "If I write about a hill that is rotting, it is because I despise rot" (*MM,* 31), to imply that she despises her grotesques. Christian writers, she says, have "the sharpest eyes for the grotesque, for the perverse, and for the unacceptable" (p. 33), as if the grotesque were the same as the merely perverse and as if both were always unacceptable. But O'Connor's comments about the negative grotesque seem partially rhetorical. She complains, on the other hand, that "the general reader has managed to connect the grotesque with the sentimental" (p. 43); for a more valid view, O'Connor mentions Thomas Mann's notion that "the grotesque is the true anti-bourgeois style." Perhaps the reason O'Connor considers the grotesque to work in opposition to bourgeois values is provided by her statement that grotesque characters "have an inner coherence, if not always a coherence to their social framework" (p. 40). The implication here that O'Connor sensed positive qualities in her use of the grotesque is an idea I shall return to.

The primary critic who argues that the grotesquerie of a character can suggest that character's positive qualities is Bakhtin, who says in *Rabelais and His World* that the grotesque degrades ideal and abstract qualities to a physical level. The grotesque thus produces a "regenerating ambivalence"[16] leading to a sense of communal wholeness, to a new way of seeing, to a rebirth of the spirit and the body. According to Bakhtin, the grotesque "liberates the world from all that is dark and terrifying" and "takes away all fears and is therefore completely gay and bright."[17] Bakhtin challenges the negative version of the grotesque, described by Wolfgang Kayser, who says the grotesque "instills fear of life" by causing an "awareness that the familiar and apparently harmonious world is alienated under the impact of abysmal forces, which break it up and shatter its coherence."[18] Bakhtin goes beyond Kayser most clearly by saying that in the grotesque, even death is "always related to birth; the grave is related to the earth's life-giving womb."[19] Bakhtin explains the difference between his view of the grotesque and Kayser's by saying that Kayser's book "offers the theory of the Romantic and modernist forms only, or, more strictly speaking, of exclusively modernist forms," while Bakhtin claims that his approach accounts for "the thousand-year-long development of the pre-Romantic era: that is, the archaic and antique grotesque . . . and the medieval and Renaissance grotesque, linked to the culture of folk humor."[20] My claims about O'Connor's grotesque, of course, call into question Bakhtin's restriction of the positive grotesque to "archaic and antique" literature and folklore; although one might agree with Bakhtin that the positive grotesque has been almost dead for well over a century, O'Connor revives the possibility of the positive grotesque.[21] I do not propose to substitute Bakhtin's positive view of the grotesque for Kayser's negative view and thus turn O'Connor's grotesque into Bakhtin's "carnivalesque" joy. Rather than choose between Bakhtin's and Kayser's versions of the grotesque, one needs to see the connections between these versions and to develop a larger view of the possibilities in the grotesque.

Although the emphasis in Western literature may have shifted, as Bakhtin says, from the positive grotesque in medieval times toward the negative grotesque in modern times, both forms of the grotesque have been achieved in each period. Let us examine an obviously grotesque theme—the massacre of the innocents—to compare the achievements of grotesque literature in medieval times and our own. In the medieval plays on the massacre from the N Town and Chester cycles, we can identify two quite different emphases in the use of the grotesque. The N Town plays *The Massacre of the Innocents* and *The Death of Herod* stress the negative grotesque. The massacre scene in the first play consists merely of a stage direction for soldiers to kill the innocents, whereupon two mothers deliver laments in speeches of eight lines each. The emphasis in the N Town plays is on the wild ranting of Herod, the degraded king who begins *The Massacre of the Innocents* by talking about physical violence.[22] Herod's downfall is both sudden and laughable; in one of the cycle's most startling reversals, the character Death enters, kills Herod at his proudest moment, and quickly turns him over to the

Devil. In the N Town cycle, the grotesque degradation of the king reduces the threat posed by malevolent forces; the complementary, positive function of the grotesque, a function easier to detect in the Chester cycle, is to give the audience a renewed sense of the Christian message of redemption. The element that distinguishes the Chester play of *The Slaughter of the Innocents*[23] from the N Town plays is the use of the positive grotesque in the massacre scene. The mothers whose children are eventually killed fight the massacring soldiers both verbally and physically, and they manage temporary success. They call the soldiers degrading names and make scatological references while beating up the soldiers. One desperate mother even resorts to insisting graphically that her boy is a girl: "Hit hath two hooles under the tayle; / kysse and thou may assaye." The vitality of the positive grotesquerie in the Chester play suggests movement toward rebirth and redemption even in moments of destruction.

Today it might seem that the representation of mass infanticide could produce only feelings of horror and guilt. Such is the case in Camus's *The Fall*. The protagonist explains that Christ was crucified because

> *he* knew he was not altogether innocent. If he did not bear the weight of the crime he was accused of, he had committed others—even though he didn't know which ones. Did he really not know them? He was at the source, after all; he must have heard of a certain Slaughter of the Innocents. The children of Judea massacred while his parents were taking him to a safe place—why did they die if not because of him? Those blood-spattered soldiers, those infants cut in two filled him with horror.[24]

O'Connor herself refers to this speaker to illustrate "one of the tendencies of our age" (*MM*, 226). The "tenderness" of such a character, "long since cut off from the person of Christ, is wrapped in theory. When tenderness is detached from the source of tenderness, its logical outcome is terror. It ends in forced-labor camps and in the fumes of the gas chamber" (p. 227). O'Connor's point is that the secular quality of the modern mind leads away from genuine concern for humanity and toward not only sentimental humanism but also concentration camps and ovens. O'Connor took it as her artistic enterprise, I would suggest, to transform these images of negative modern grotesquerie into part of a redemptive process.

In *The Violent Bear It Away*, Rayber has a vision of the massacre of the innocents, and again, as in *The Fall*, Christ is guilty. As Lucette Carmody, the child evangelist, preaches about the massacre of the innocents, Rayber finds nothing positive in it and sees himself as Christ's antagonist. As Lucette refers to Jesus raising the dead, "Rayber felt his spirit borne aloft. But not those dead! he cried, not the innocent children, not you, not me when I was a child, not Bishop, not Frank! and he had a vision of himself moving like an avenging angel through the world, gathering up all the children that the Lord, not Herod, had slain" (*V*, 132). The difference in O'Connor's text is that Rayber deserves criticism precisely because he fails to see the positive qualities in the grotesque. Throughout O'Connor's works we are reminded of piles of innocent dead whose grotesquerie is potentially redemptive. Nor does O'Connor stop there. In addition to presenting negative grotesquerie (some characters feel degraded by physical deformity and isolated from their society) and positive grotesquerie (some characters achieve a transformation of themselves and of a community), O'Connor often sets up a causal connection between the two sides of the grotesque. It is because of their negative grotesquerie (their sense that they are degraded and oppressed) that her characters sometimes are able to effect reform of degraded ideals.

One indication that O'Connor knew of the positive grotesque is Kathleen Feeley's report that O'Connor marked a passage in Mircea Eliade's *Patterns in Comparative Religion* that discusses the holiness appearing in connection with the peculiar: "This setting-apart sometimes has positive effects; it does not merely isolate, it elevates. Thus ugliness and deformities, while marking out those who possess them, at the same time make them sacred."[25] Perhaps the best indication that O'Connor was aware of the positive qualities in the grotesque is her statement in the introduction to *A Memoir of Mary Ann* that "a new perspective on the grotesque" had occurred to her as she learned about the child, who had a tumor on the side of her face:

> Most of us have learned to be dispassionate about evil, to look it in the face and find, as often as not, our own grinning reflections with which we do not argue, but good is another matter. Few have stared at that long enough to accept the fact that its face too is grotesque, that in us the good is something under construction. The modes of evil usually receive worthy expression. The modes of good have to be satisfied with a cliché or a smoothing-down that will soften their real look. When we look into the face of good, we are liable to see a face like Mary Ann's, full of promise. (*MM*, 226)

At this point I would like to summarize the principles by which many of O'Connor's major characters make positive use of the grotesque. The typical O'Connor protagonist is oppressed by degradations of the society's ideals: by the economy of the South, by ignorance, by physical deformity and disease, by systems of class and race, and by the strictures of religion. All these forms of oppression make O'Connor characters perceive themselves as grotesque in a negative sense, and on the conscious level, the typical O'Connor character sees no prospect for anything but continued and increasing degradation. Within this desperate context, the positive use of the grotesque becomes a way to escape some (although not all) oppression. The protagonist may realize that not all the forces of oppression can be banished; the protagonist can, however, take control of one form of degradation, make it more important than other forms, and then transform that grotesquerie into a force for redemption. Consciously the character may perceive the relationship between the ideal and the grotesque as one of absolute opposition, but on an unconscious level the character constructs (or discovers) a relationship between the opposing terms that makes the negative grotesque lead back toward the ideal. I will show in chapter 1 that Mrs. Shortley feels so oppressed by the Displaced Person that, by exercising control over her relationship to him, she is able to bring about her own redemptive displacement. Other examples of negatively grotesque figures that characters connect to the ideal are Mrs. May's scrub bull in "Greenleaf" and Hazel Motes's sexual partners in *Wise Blood*. The construction of such a relationship between the grotesque and an ideal is typically made apparent to the reader through banality taken seriously or through slips in the character's logic; ignorance and banality themselves become tools for redemption. Mrs. Cope's trite expressions in "A Circle in the Fire" and Hulga/Joy Hopewell's thoughts on Vulcan in "Good Country People" are examples.

It is probably apparent that this notion of the positive grotesque differs significantly from Bakhtin's. In O'Connor the grotesque becomes positive through individual action rather than through mass effort, and—unlike Bakhtin's grotesque, where all forms of oppression are overcome—O'Connor's grotesque produces redemption in one area, which becomes the focus of the character's life. The diverse oppressions her characters suffer are overcome only in the sense that they are ignored as the character becomes more and more obsessive about one oppression. The peculiarity of each protagonist's path toward redemption suggests that individuals themselves construct those paths; unlike Bakhtin's grotesque, which is a sort of institutionalized anti-institutionalism, O'Connor's positive grotesque requires a contribution by the individual. Of course, no individual uses the grotesque in a vacuum; the community's ideals always provide a starting point for a protagonist's maneuvers. But O'Connor insists that without the contribution of the individual's unconscious, the grotesque remains merely negative.

It may seem peculiar that the character's consciousness of the positive operation of the grotesque is almost irrelevant. O'Connor's protagonists sometimes seem to become partially conscious (often at the last possible instant) of their redemption, but O'Connor typically treats the unconscious as the essence of a human being, so that a character's conscious awareness of redemption is not necessary in order for the reader to see the redemption. One of the strongest arguments for the notion that redemption is valuable in O'Connor's fiction is that the characters must overcome so much conscious disgust for the actions that promise redemption; behind conscious disgust, we infer, there lies a stronger unconscious desire. Another peculiarity, the value of physical annihilation in O'Connor, can be explained by the observation that as characters bring about their death, they conclude their grotesque process of perception at the most positive moment. Most of O'Connor's works obscure the fact that, like Bakhtin's grotesque, the grotesque for O'Connor is essentially a process, as I will demonstrate particularly in chapter 3; one reason O'Connor's stories frequently end with the protagonist's death is that the process that drives the story can be stopped only by killing the character. In these various untraditional qualities of O'Connor's redemptions we see her led not so much by dogma as by art.

A number of critics have connected the grotesque to subconscious and/or unconscious levels of the psyche, but they are often skeptical about the value of the connection. Some have sensed that O'Connor's grotesque draws on non-Christian origins, and they tend to find her primitive grotesquerie nonreligious as a result. There is evidence, however, that O'Connor saw the unconscious as a positively religious force. Certainly she was aware of such a possibility: she underlined a passage by Jung that follows the statement that important innovation always comes from the people of the land. It reads in part as follows: "And it is just people of the lower social levels who follow the unconscious forces of the psyche; it is the much-derided, silent folk of the land. . . . All these people, looked at from above, present mostly a dreary or laughable comedy; and yet they are as impressively simple as those Galileans who were once called blessed."[26]

O'Connor's people may not impress us with their simplicity, but to O'Connor they are often closer to what is unconscious. O'Connor's most explicit and poetically appropriate reference to the unconscious is in *The Violent Bear It Away*. Rayber takes Tarwater fishing and explains the existence of the unconscious, but Tarwater rejects this information:

> "Do you know," he said, "that there's a part of your mind that works all the time, that you're not aware of yourself. Things go on in it. All sorts of things you don't know about."
>
> Tarwater looked around him as if he were vainly searching for a way to get out of the boat and walk off.
>
> "I think you're basically very bright," his uncle said. "I think you can understand the things that are said to you."
>
> "I never came for no school lesson," the boy said rudely. "I come to fish. I ain't worried what my underhead is doing. I know what I think when I do it and when I get ready to do it, I don't talk no words. I do it."
> (*V*, 171)

The term "underhead" is a brilliant stroke, for it keeps the unconscious secret, out of conscious control. By making the body (what is "under the head") more important than the head, and by making actions superior to words, Tarwater allows his unconscious to use the grotesque.

The characters' unconscious use of the grotesque is what makes the grotesque essentially a cyclical process. The grotesque degrades the ideal, but, as I have said, the ideal that is grotesquely degraded is not obliterated: the grotesque retains traces of the ideal. The retained connection between the ideal and the grotesque indicates that one "destination" of the grotesque is a reformation of the ideal. The process does not end there, however, for when the grotesque reestablishes an ideal, the ideal must again be desecrated. Some critics of the grotesque emphasize the problematic quality that they consider essential to the grotesque. For example, Philip Thomson considers the grotesque to be "the unresolved clash of incompatibles in work and response."[27] I would say that the grotesque achieves periodic resolutions, but I would agree that the grotesque process, once started, does not naturally end at moments of resolution.

Although the original impulse for the grotesque may ultimately come from within the community whose ideals are desecrated, it is the individual character who puts the grotesque in operation and who determines the change in the ideal as it is made grotesque and then reformed. That these determinations arise within the unconscious is one of the paradoxes of O'Connor's art. Such an emphasis may seem to imply that O'Connor treats her characters as important only as individuals, not as members of a community. I would say, however, that her art explores reinforcements between the individual and the communal. O'Connor characters appear to make unique contributions toward the rejuvenative operation of the grotesque, but if the ultimate source of these individual contributions is the unconscious, we are led back, perhaps, toward a version of the divine. It is common in O'Connor studies to consider psychological and religious readings completely irreconcilable. I prefer Joyce Carol Oates's conclusion, that O'Connor accepts "the divine origin of the unconscious."[28] Although she admits that O'Connor "would certainly refute me in saying this," Oates says that in O'Connor's works "the 'Christ' experience itself may well be interpreted as a psychological event that is received by the individual according to his private expectations."[29]

In the body of the present study, I investigate a series of variations on the handling of the grotesque. The first chapter examines Mrs. Shortley, of "The Displaced Person," and the grandmother of "A Good Man Is Hard to Find" as extreme examples of the two contrasting transformations O'Connor dramatizes—that which comes primarily from within, and that which comes primarily from without. The second, third, and fourth chapters examine stories in which characters unconsciously use the positive grotesque most successfully. Chapter 2 examines four major stories in which protagonists rival the O'Connor narrator for authority and bring about their own redemption. Chapter 3 investigates the two stories in which the positive grotesque is clearly cyclic. Chapter 4 concerns stories in which the operation of the positive grotesque is at once most apparent and simpler than usual; after outlining the pattern of the grotesque in each of the stories in this chapter, I explain what I take to be the uncharacteristic qualities of the narration in these stories. Chapter 5 discusses briefly the few stories in which, as with the grandmother in "A Good Man Is Hard to Find," transformation comes from outside. Chapter 6 returns to the stories considered in the first chapter, to discuss major characters—Mrs. McIntyre, of "The Displaced Person," and The Misfit, of "A Good Man Is Hard to Find"—who do not complete a grotesque self-redemption; these discussions introduce examinations of two other stories that present similar problems. Chapters 7 and 8 examine O'Connor's novels, which constitute her most complex involvement with the grotesque.

My intention in this study is not to deny the uniqueness of each work, but O'Connor's repetitiousness is essential to her art. As she produced work after work in which the grotesque reveals itself conclusively as redemptive, O'Connor aesthetically transformed the grotesque for herself. Her characters generally have to annihilate themselves to conclude the grotesque process in redemption, but O'Connor herself could use her art to return repeatedly to the redemptive moment. Redefined in her untraditional, literary manner, redemption could become at once a moment in a cyclical process and an object for her constant contemplation. For aesthetic and personal reasons, O'Connor desired a life lived in the moment when redemption and the grotesque are bound.

1. Golden and Sullivan, *O'Connor and Gordon,* p. 5. My description of critical schools modifies Golden's discussion, pp. 5–6.

2. Shloss, *O'Connor's Dark Comedies,* p. 8.

3. See Martin, *The True Country;* and Feeley, *Flannery O'Connor.*

4. See Stephens, *Question of O'Connor;* and Orvell, *Invisible Parade.*

5. See Hendin, *World of O'Connor;* Hawkes, "O'Connor's Devil"; and Katz [Kahane], "O'Connor's Rage of Vision."

6. J. F Sollier, "Redemption," *The Catholic Encyclopedia* (New York: Encyclopedia, 1913–14).

7. I wish to distinguish between the narrator's actions of structuring and describing, and the actions of "O'Connor" as an implied author actually responsible for *inventing* event and character.

8. Eggenschwiler, *Christian Humanism of O'Connor,* p. 42.

9. Bakhtin, "Discourse in the Novel," p. 262.

10. Ibid., p. 316. Bakhtin confuses the concepts of "author," "implied author," and "narrator," but he retains the concept of a figure who orchestrates the battling voices. In *Problems of Dostoevsky's Poetics,* for example, Bakhtin says, "The freedom of a character is an aspect of the author's design. A character's discourse is created by the author, but created in such a way that it can develop to the full its inner logic and independence. . . . As a result it does not fall out of the author's design, but only out of a monologic authorial field of vision" (p. 65).

11. Bakhtin, "Discourse in the Novel," p. 316.

12. Fowler, "Anti-Language in Fiction," p. 260.

13. Cohn, *Transparent Minds,* p. 29. Cohn also notes that psycho-narration with marked dissonance between narrator and character is often favored by theorists (most notably, Wayne C. Booth) who mistakenly expect such a style to produce explicit moral guidance.

14. Hendin, *World of O'Connor,* p. 19.

15. Shloss, *O'Connor's Dark Comedies,* p. 56.

16. Bakhtin, *Rabelais and His World,* p. 21.

17. Ibid., p. 47. Even as a form of neurosis, the grotesque involves a backlash against oppression. In "The Structure of the Grotesque-Comic Sublimation," *Bulletin of the Menninger Clinic* 13 (1949): 160–71, Annie Reich theorizes that the grotesque inherently combines self-punishment with aggression against rivals.

18. Kayser, *Grotesque in Art and Literature,* pp. 185, 37.

19. Bakhtin, *Rabelais and His World,* p. 50. Harpham, in *On the Grotesque,* feels that Bakhtin overemphasizes the positiveness of the grotesque. Harpham looks for a solution in "a system of decorum with indeterminacy or ambivalence as the norm" (p. 74). Such a system is Christianity, says Harpham, but he mistakenly considers Bakhtin's view of the grotesque incompatible with Christianity. The carnival (like the cycle plays to be discussed shortly) can be seen as the means by which the Church uses the grotesque to renew itself in the minds of the faithful. The grotesque is actually necessary to religion; as M. Conrad Hyers says in "The Dialectic of the

Sacred and the Comic," in *Holy Laughter: Essays on Religion in the Comic Perspective* (New York: Seabury, 1969), p. 223, "the profanation of the sacred is a necessity within the sacred itself."

20. Bakhtin, *Rabelais and His World*, p. 46. Bakhtin clearly relates the grotesque to narration when he describes the "carnival-grotesque form": grotesque literature works "to consecrate inventive freedom, to permit the combination of a variety of different elements and their rapprochement, to liberate from the prevailing point of view of the world" (p. 54).

21. Bakhtin describes the decline of the positive grotesque in *Rabelais and His World* as follows: "In the second half of the nineteenth century, the interest in the grotesque was considerably reduced both in literature and in literary thought and studies. If mentioned at all, it is either listed among the vulgar comic genres or interpreted as a peculiar form of satire, directed against isolated, purely negative objects. Because of such interpretation the deep and universal nature of grotesque images was completely obscured" (p. 45).

22. *Ludus Coventriae, or The Play Called Corpus Christi*, ed. K. S. Block (London: Oxford University Press, 1922), pp. 169–77.

23. *The Chester Mystery Cycle*, ed. R. M. Lumiansky and David Mills (New York: Oxford University Press, 1974), pp. 185–204. The quotation is from lines 367–68.

24. Camus, *The Fall*, trans. Justin O'Brien (New York: Vintage, 1956), p. 112.

25. Feeley, *Flannery O'Connor*, p. 24; the passage is from Eliade's *Patterns in Comparative Religion*, trans. Rosemary Sheed (New York: Sheed, 1958), p. 18. Kinney confirms Feeley's report in *O'Connor's Library*, p. 77.

26. Feeley, *Flannery O'Connor*, p. 150; the quotation is from Jung's *Modern Man in Search of a Soul*, trans. W. S. Dell and Cary F. Baynes (New York: Harcourt, 1933), p. 211. Kinney, *O'Connor's Library*, pp. 89–90, confirms Feeley's report.

27. Thomson, *The Grotesque*, p. 27.

28. Oates, *New Heaven, New Earth*, p. 151.

29. Ibid., p. 170.

1

MRS. SHORTLEY
AND THE GRANDMOTHER

The engine at this moment took its station in advance of the
cars, looking, I must confess, much more like a sort of
mechanical demon, that would hurry us to the infernal
regions, than a laudable contrivance for smoothing our way
to the Celestial City.

—Hawthorne,
"The Celestial Rail-road"

MRS. SHORTLEY, in "The Displaced Person," and the grandmother
in "A Good Man Is Hard to Find," despite the differences in their
social status, typify a banal self-righteousness shared by most
O'Connor characters. Because they both experience gruesome
deaths, and because both seem to experience some sort of awakening, one might imagine that their spiritual lives would be parallel.
Actually, however, they lie at opposite ends of O'Connor's scale of
characters undergoing religious experiences. The energy for Mrs.
Shortley's redemption comes primarily from within her own
psyche, while the grandmother's awakening is forced upon her. It is
also interesting that O'Connor dramatized Mrs. Shortley's peculiar
sort of redemption in many works; the grandmother's more traditional version of redemption—requiring a conscious response to
outside forces—appears rarely in O'Connor's fiction. Our understanding of each character's experience depends upon her relation to
the narrator of her story. The narrator of "The Displaced Person"
underemphasizes Mrs. Shortley's ability to change herself; the narrator's treatment of her reflects the oppressive, clichéd religious
standards from which Mrs. Shortley frees herself. Conversely, the
narrator of "A Good Man Is Hard to Find" consistently implies that
the grandmother is responsible for the massacre of her family by
The Misfit. But the narrator's misleading emphasis on the grand-

mother as the agent of catastrophe ultimately makes apparent just how little the grandmother has to do with bringing about even her own awakening.

While "The Displaced Person" is regularly called a tragic story,[1] no one considers Mrs. Shortley tragic. Our knowledge of the work's evolution complicates the issue of Mrs. Shortley's place in the story. In the first published version of the story, Mrs. Shortley is the central character; her displacement and death end the story.[2] And O'Connor was not satisfied with the sections centering on Mrs. McIntyre in the final, "complete" version of the story. In a letter dated 25 November 1955, O'Connor described the final version as a failure because it does not show what she wanted it to: that the Displaced Person, Mr. Guizac, achieves a sort of "redemption" of the McIntyre farm by destroying it and that he starts Mrs. McIntyre on the way to purgatorial suffering (*HB,* 118).[3]

The manner of description, the style in which the consciousness of characters is related, and the ordering of events all contribute to the narrator's portrait of Mrs. Shortley as grotesque in a negative sense. As the narrator's harsh criticism of her constantly reminds us, she is a mountainously overweight, ignorant woman for whom love consists of watching her corpselike husband pretend to swallow burning cigarette butts. She consistently seems isolated, tortured, absurd, even demonic. Even as this negative portrait takes form, however, the reader can discover considerable evidence for a different view of Mrs. Shortley. One need not ignore her grotesquerie in order to consider her a candidate for redemption; actually, Mrs. Shortley's negative grotesquerie reinforces her positive grotesquerie. She rivals her narrator for authority, and with Mrs. McIntyre's failure to achieve redemption (see chapter 6), Mrs. Shortley is left as the only character in the story who brings about her own redemption.

Mrs. Shortley is a good example of an "uppity" O'Connor character, so an examination of narrative situations in "The Displaced Person" as they relate to Mrs. Shortley should make clearer the status of O'Connor's characters in relation to her narrators. Consider the following passage, which follows Mrs. McIntyre's assertion that Mr. Guizac is her "salvation."

> Mrs. Shortley looked straight ahead as if her vision penetrated the cane and the hill and pierced through to the other side. "I would suspicion salvation got from the devil," she said in a slow detached way.
> "Now what do you mean by that?" Mrs. McIntyre asked, looking at her sharply.

Mrs. Shortley wagged her head but would not say anything else. The fact was she had nothing else to say for this intuition had only at that instant come to her. She had never given much thought to the devil for she felt that religion was essentially for those people who didn't have the brains to avoid evil without it. For people like herself, for people of gumption, it was a social occasion providing the opportunity to sing; but if she had ever given it much thought, she would have considered the devil the head of it and God the hanger-on. (*CS,* 203–4)

This passage consists primarily of psycho-narration (explanation by the narrator of what a character is thinking) and has only one sentence quoting Mrs. Shortley directly. Nevertheless, the passage conveys information about her of a sort quite different from what the narrator leads the reader to expect. The narrator's emphasis is clear from the first sentence of external description; the narrator disapproves of Mrs. Shortley's illusion that she can see what is going on. Mrs. Shortley's quotation seems ridiculous and obviously defensive to the narrator, who sarcastically labels her manner "detached." Then the narrator takes Mrs. Shortley's inability to say anything more as an occasion for some psycho-narration in an authoritarian tone; the narrator claims to understand Mrs. Shortley better than she does herself. A couple of phrases ("didn't have the brains," "people of gumption") suggest the contamination of the narrator's sentences by the character's language, but the narrator allows this contamination in order to point out the absurdity of Mrs. Shortley's thoughts. In detailing her absurdity, however, the narrator also reveals a part of her world view that helps establish her status as the narrator's rival. If she associates Mr. Guizac with the devil, she also believes on the deepest level ("if she had ever given it much thought") that this devil/Displaced Person is the real head of religion. This connection, which the narrator mentions for purposes of ridicule, also is part of the grotesque process through which Mrs. Shortley's stroke becomes a religious experience.

The narrator uses more psycho-narration than narrated monologue with Mrs. Shortley, primarily because psycho-narration makes it easier for the narrator to direct the reader toward conclusions. Narrated monologue, on the other hand, makes it easier for Mrs. Shortley to express her own views. Consider the following passage, which follows Mrs. McIntyre's statement that the Displaced Person saves her money and may deserve a raise:

This was as much as to say that Chancey had never saved her money. Chancey got up at four in the morning to milk her cows, in winter wind and summer heat, and he had been doing it for the last two years. They had been with her the longest she had ever had anybody. The gratitude they got was these hints that she hadn't been saved any money.

"Is Mr. Shortley feeling better today?" Mrs. McIntyre asked.

Mrs. Shortley thought it was about time she was asking that question. Mr. Shortley had been in bed two days with an attack. Mr. Guizac had taken his place in the dairy in addition to doing his own work. "No he ain't," she said. "That doctor said he was suffering from over-exhaustion." (*CS*, 204)

Bits of language typical of Mrs. Shortley but not of the narrator ("Chancey," "her cows," "winter wind and summer heat," "had anybody") indicate that the entire first paragraph of this quotation is narrated monologue, and in this paragraph we hear Mrs. Shortley's voice clearly. The narrator undercuts Mrs. Shortley by inserting the detail that Mr. Guizac had done all of Mr. Shortley's work as well as his own, apparently without overexertion. But the evidence for considering the Shortleys totally corrupt is not fully convincing; Mrs. Shortley manages to communicate to the reader the viability of her world view. She clearly respects her husband and remains loyal to Mrs. McIntyre despite the latter's ungratefulness. We also learn, after this passage, that Mr. Shortley runs a still on the "farthest reaches" of Mrs. McIntyre's place, that on more than one level the Shortleys manage to make for themselves a world different from that allowed them by the authorities.

Most commentators on "The Displaced Person" take the story's opening pages as proof that Mrs. Shortley's view of things is completely erroneous, and it would seem to follow that she cannot rival the narrator. As the Displaced Person and his family arrive on the McIntyre farm, Mrs. Shortley seems ridiculously certain of her own authority. The narrator critically reveals her opinion of herself by saying, "She stood on two tremendous legs, with the grand self-confidence of a mountain, and rose, up narrowing bulges of granite, to two icy blue points of light that pierced forward, surveying everything" (*CS*, 194). An important point to many readers is the fact that she takes no notice of the peacock following her; when Father Flynn points to the bird, she spins around to see what he is pointing at and observes "nothing but a peachicken" (p. 198). To determine the significance of Mrs. Shortley's failure to notice the peacock, one must thoroughly investigate the complex symbolic meanings of this bird. What one discovers is that the peacock is associated with a wide variety of desirable and undesirable qualities, whether one looks to O'Connor's personal opinions on peacocks, to the use of the peacock as a Christian symbol, to the peacock's significance in Greek mythology, or to the explicit references to peacocks in this O'Connor story. The peacock's combination of desirable and undesirable qualities allows the bird to symbolize an oppressive ideal, while at the same time this combination of qualities points to the possibility of a grotesque degradation of the bird's ideality, degradation that can lead to freedom and redemption.

O'Connor's fondness for peacocks is well known; she raised them for years on her farm outside Milledgeville, Georgia. In "The King of the Birds," her essay on peacocks, she concludes by saying, "I intend to stand firm and let the peacocks multiply, for I am sure that, in the end, the last word will be theirs" (*MM*, 21). But she also recognized the bird's undesirable qualities. Describing the peacock when his tail is not spread, she says, "Nothing but his bearing saves this bird from being a laughingstock" (p. 9). And in a letter dated 29 June 1957, she described one of her peacocks as follows: "All that peafowl knows in the way of emotions are two: where do I get the next thing to put in my craw, and where do I keep out of the way of something that wants to kill me until I can find something I want to kill" (*HB*, 228). Josephine Hendin speculates that it is the peacock's negative qualities that O'Connor found attractive:

> Did she admire the ease with which they gobbled up all the flowers in sight, destroying her mother's flower beds and covering the lawn with droppings? Were those majestic birds that broke all the rules what Flannery O'Connor wanted to be? Yet the curse on the bird is its yowl— its ugly voice that makes it most beautiful when silent, a voice that to Flannery O'Connor sounded like "cheers for an invisible parade." Was that invisible parade the procession of misfits, prophets, and lonely and murderous children who unleash their violence so freely in the fiction of Flannery O'Connor?[4]

To O'Connor's Father Flynn, of course, and to many critics, the peacock is symbolic only of Christ. When he sees the bird spread his tail, Father Flynn says, "Christ will come like that!" (*CS*, 226). And there is considerable precedent in Christian iconography for such an association. Peacocks frequently appear in paintings of the Nativity to symbolize the immortality of Christ.[5] But even as a Christian symbol the peacock is more complicated than critics have said, in part because of the source of the symbolism. The use of the peacock to symbolize immortality in Christian art derives from the traditional belief that the peacock's flesh is so hard that it will not rot.[6] St. Augustine, in *The City of God,* for example, brings up peacocks to reinforce his argument that the damned in hell can burn forever; because peacock flesh does not decay, reasons Augustine, we may assume that the bodies of the damned can last eternally.[7]

There is also ample precedent for considering the peacock symbolic of negative moral qualities. E. P. Evans mentions that Christian moralists suspicious of the peacock's beauty have criticized the peacock's feet, gait, and voice, "which it endeavors to conceal under its showy qualities."[8] Francis Klingender discusses a tradition of criticizing the peacock for his poor flight and "flesh" as well, qualities considered to make the peacock comparable to a rich man.[9] George Ferguson refers to the peacock's "habit of strutting and displaying the beauty of its feathers" as the reason for its use as "a symbol of worldly pride and vanity."[10]

In Greek mythology, as well, the peacock mixes desirable and undesirable qualities. John F. Desmond says that the picture of Mrs. Shortley being followed by the peacock "suggest[s] the goddess Hera."[11] The peacock is traditionally associated with Hera,[12] and O'Connor herself refers to this association, although O'Connor also mentions that the peacock "had probably come down in the world" since being Hera's bird (*MM*, 5). Of course, Hera herself is far from an entirely admirable figure. In linking Mrs. Shortley and Hera, the peacock causes us to notice that both are earth mothers with a strong interest in marriage, and that both are "proud" and "jealous" figures with a very low opinion of refugees.[13]

The traditional negative characteristics of the peacock do come up in O'Connor's story. For example, the opening juxtaposition of Mrs. Shortley and the peacock suggests the relevance of the peacock as a symbol of pride. Such suggestions of the peacock's negative characteristics, however, act to complicate rather than deny the peacock's ideality. Mrs. McIntyre's dead husband, the Judge, liked peacocks because of their association with wealth—"they made him feel rich" (*CS*, 218)—but instead of exacerbating the Judge's materialism, the peacocks relieved his desire for money. Mrs. McIntyre says she dislikes peacocks because of the bird's voice—she doesn't like to hear a peacock "scream in the middle of the night" (p. 198)—but she allows the birds to remain on the farm in honor of the Judge.

The strongest single symbolic meaning of the peacock in the story is longevity, an ideal that several characters find oppressive. The characters' attitudes to the bird are more directly connected to their own length of service on the farm than to anything else, including their feelings about Christ. Astor, who knew the Judge, likes the peacocks, and he talks to them within Mrs. McIntyre's hearing to remind her of his seniority. Mrs. McIntyre considers the birds threatening because they have been on the farm longer than she has. Mrs. Shortley, who wants to believe that her family's two years on the farm is a long time, consciously denies the peacocks any significance. For the reader, however, the traditions of peacock symbolism are by no means irrelevant to the story. The story combines the peacock's various desirable and undesirable traits to produce a symbol at once ideal, oppressive, and degraded, so full of meaning as to have no fixed meaning.

Once the peacock's longevity and the associations of divinity are thoroughly investigated, another connection becomes clear. The divine bird with immortal flesh shares its rigid divinity with the granite statue of an angel over the Judge's grave,[14] with this difference: the bird is in its place, but the statue has been displaced, stolen by the Herrins (a family who preceded the Shortleys) when they left the farm. The narrator extends the association even more by telling us that the granite angel reminded the Judge of Mrs. McIntyre. If we combine the narrator's opening description of Mrs. Shortley as a granite mountain with Mr. Shortley's description of her as "God's own angel" (*CS,* 227) or with her vision of herself as a giant displacing angel (p. 200), we have yet another granite angel.

The effect of the narratorial emphasis on these connections seems to be largely satirical, but the comparisons that the narrator calls for also point to another conclusion: on a symbolic level, Mrs. McIntyre and Mrs. Shortley differ from the peacock in that while the bird appears to remain in place, Mrs. McIntyre borders on displacement, and Mrs. Shortley's eventual displacement, like the displacement of the granite angel, is complete. The story's population of granite angels/peacocks points not only to an ideal but to a range of possible degradations of that ideal; the symbolism thus indicates the connection of the grotesque and the ideal. Mrs. Shortley's failure to see the peacock, I would suggest, signals her unconscious plan to displace the ideal abstractions associated with the bird. She does not see the bird itself, but she knows on some level that within herself she contains a grotesque version of the ideals that the bird symbolizes, both traditionally and for Mrs. Shortley personally. Although she has never heard of Hera, there is some significance in the comparison of woman and goddess. Mrs. Shortley does, after all, presume to divine status in the story's opening paragraph, where we see her followed by the peacock: she considers herself capable of "surveying everything" and ignores the sun as if it were merely an "intruder" (*CS,* 194). Thus there is a nonsatiric logic to the narrator's description of Mrs. Shortley and the peacock as religious figures in a "complete procession." Of course, the peacock rather than the woman is the more straightforward representative of ideals in O'Connor's scene, but Mrs. Shortley finally earns the status she presumes to. While the bird is static and ever-present, her unconscious plan involves her in a process that climaxes in her redemptive death.

Mrs. Shortley may seem too stupid to act as a rival to the peacock and to the authoritarian narrator, but as Mikhail Bakhtin says, stupidity is essentially novelistic: "Stupidity (incomprehension) in the novel . . . interacts dialogically with an intelligence (a lofty pseudo intelligence) with which it polemicizes and whose mask it tears away."[15] Ignorance allows fresh investigation of values to keep truth alive, and, however stupid her motivation, Mrs. Shortley's competition with the narrator for authority and her degradation of what the peacock symbolizes lead to redemptive ends. Through the maneuverings of her unconscious, she attains her ideals; at the same time, she abandons her selfhood for the communal "liberty of the children of God." She most resembles the peacock—at once a symbol of the ideal and a symbol freed from fixed meaning—when, rejecting the meaning the narrator attaches to her, she displaces herself.

To understand the process by which Mrs. Shortley brings about her redemption, we must identify the ideal state to which she desires to return. This central ideal, as the peacock suggests, is stability: being in place. Mrs. Shortley associates this stable place-ment with love, unity, and religion. Of course she possesses only a degraded version of each of these values, both because of the corruption of her society and because of her personal degradation. With the arrival of the Displaced Person, however, her tenuous connection to her ideals allows her to use the grotesque positively. Her reaction to the Guizacs' arrival suggests that she sees the Displaced Person as a more useful representative of the ideals asso-ciated with the peacock. Her first impression of the refugees is that she and the Guizacs have much in common: "they looked like other people" and "the woman had on a dress she might have worn herself and the children were dressed like anybody from around" (*CS*, 195). This recognition of similarity becomes complicated as Mrs. Shortley learns more about these people who resemble her and her kin, for the Guizacs suggest at once both ideals and degra-dations. They are at home on the McIntyre farm, yet suggestive of displacement; she calls them the "Gobblehooks," a name indicating an eagerness to be victimized, to "gobble a hook." The Guizacs also suggest love and unity for Mrs. Shortley—although, of course, in peculiar ways; the kiss Mr. Guizac places on Mrs. McIntyre's hand shocks Mrs. Shortley, as does his plan to unite his niece in marriage with the black worker Sulk. The reverse side of the ideal of unifying love becomes apparent in Mrs. Shortley's remembrance of a newsreel showing a mass of dead, naked Poles in a concentration camp. A third pair of ideals and degradations that the Guizacs suggest for Mrs. Shortley has to do with religion: she knows that they are religious, but she considers their religion corrupt.

The meaning of the Guizacs' religion to Mrs. Shortley is crucial. As I said before, she associates the Displaced Person with the devil and considers the devil the head of religion. Her grotesque reversal of religion puts her in the position of taking more seriously than anyone else a literal equation of Mr. Guizac with the figure at the head of religion. The more significant point is that Mrs. Shortley considers the Guizacs' religion corrupt because it has "not been reformed" (*CS*, 205). Thus Mrs. Shortley manages to consider the Guizacs' Catholicism at once degraded and representative of an original ideal. In equating the unchanging with the corrupted, Mrs. Shortley is able to connect her own grotesque corruption to ideals. The only thing in Mrs. Shortley's life over which she has some control is her victimization. Somewhat like Astor, the black worker who advises Sulk that their strength is in their weakness, because "your place too low for anybody to dispute with you for it" (p. 206), Mrs. Shortley finds her primary source of power in her ability to choose her victimization. Once Mrs. Shortley takes the step of equating an ideal—the Guizacs' unreformed religion—with a victimizing force, she can effect her achievement of that ideal. In spite of her conscious aversion to Mr. Guizac, whom she associates with the dead bodies she has seen in the newsreel, she desires what the Displaced Person means to her. She loves the way her husband portrays a paralyzed man swallowing a burning cigarette butt; less consciously she sees in the Displaced Person an even stronger combination of sex and death, for Mr. Guizac kisses hands while Mr. Shortley has no "time to mess around" (p. 195), and she associates the Displaced Person with a roomful of naked dead bodies, not just one man pretending to be a corpse as he lies in bed with his wife. For Mrs. Shortley, the figure at the head of religion is one who promotes sex and death; displacement, which provides the entry into this divine sex/death, becomes her desire. In spite of her conscious belief that she is at war with Mr. Guizac, she fights for her own victimization.

Mrs. Shortley's fantasies prepare for this victimization. In a vision of a "war of words" between Polish and English, she sees "Polish words, dirty and all-knowing and unreformed" making the English words like themselves: "She saw them all piled up in a room, all the dead dirty words, theirs and hers too, piled up like the naked bodies in the newsreel" (*CS*, 209). When she has her vision and announces a prophecy, she produces a similar scene: she predicts that "The children of wicked nations will be butchered" and adds, "Legs where arms should be, foot to face, ear in the palm of hand." Her final prophetic questions—"Who will remain whole? Who will remain whole? Who?" (p. 210)—are often taken to refer to the fate she expects the Guizacs to suffer, but these questions suggest a general victimization, one that will include Mrs. Shortley herself. Most O'Connor critics have a very negative opinion of Mrs. Shortley's visions. Frederick Asals considers her prophecy "ambiguous" and contrasts it to other, more surely "genuine revelations."[16] David Eggenschwiler considers her to be "the most clearly developed case of demonic revelation"[17] in O'Connor's works. In my view, however, these visions prepare for Mrs. Shortley's redemption through self-victimization. It is surely significant that when she produces her prophecy, as Stuart Burns notes, she is "commanded by a gigantic peacock."[18] The commanding figure's "fiery wheels with fierce dark eyes in them" (*CS*, 210) recall the peacock's tail; her inability to tell "if the figure was going forward or backward" recalls the peacock's gait. Her most grotesque vision is clearly connected to a symbol of her ideals.

As Mrs. Shortley spies on Father Flynn and Mrs. McIntyre, she learns that Mrs. McIntyre intends to give Mr. Shortley his notice the next day. Mrs. Shortley's response is to pack and leave as soon as possible—in other words, to displace herself. This action may appear to be one of only two options: the Shortleys can be fired by Mrs. McIntyre, or Mrs. Shortley can displace the family herself. But a third option exists. When she overhears Mrs. McIntyre's plan, Mrs. Shortley has a secret—Mr. Guizac's intention to marry his niece to Sulk—that she knows "would floor Mrs. McIntyre" (*CS*, 208). To avoid displacement, Mrs. Shortley could simply tell Mrs. McIntyre her secret. But Mrs. Shortley's unconscious desire for redemption through displacement pushes this reasonable option aside. She never tells Mrs. McIntyre the secret. This point suggests that Mrs. Shortley jumps to the conclusion that her destiny is like that predicted in her prophecy for the "children of wicked nations" (p. 210); she wants to believe she is destined to join the dead Poles in the newsreel. The fact that she refuses to tell the secret also helps one realize that the narration leads one away from a full recognition of the significance of Mrs. Shortley's actions. Rather than making clear to the reader that she desires her displacement, the narrator obscures the causes of her behavior by withholding from the reader until well into the second section of the story the substance of Mrs. Shortley's secret.

Mrs. Shortley dies of a stroke as the family is leaving Mrs. McIntyre's farm; at that moment she experiences an orgasmic entry into a world of dead, naked Poles. And in the context of the unconscious plan Mrs. Shortley constructs, this experience amounts to redemption. She paradoxically demonstrates her commitment to the ideals she associates with the Displaced Person (most notably, stability) in the only way she can: by making herself Mr. Guizac's victim. And as she renounces her individual superiority to the suffering community, she escapes the oppression to which the separate self is subject (including, on one level, her oppression by the narrator) and achieves the freedom available in the communal. Thus Mrs. Shortley manages to achieve the "great experience" attributed to her only sarcastically by the narrator (*CS,* 214). Of course, there is no indication that she is conscious of her redemption; I would not claim that she learns finally to love Mr. Guizac. In fact, my conclusion that she lays the tracks for her redemptive trip to the oven almost requires—for three reasons— that redemption be experienced only as annihilation. First, redemption must seem to her to be a form of victimization if she is to be able to bring it about. Second, it is only through contrast to her conscious revulsion to annihilation that we can detect the strength of her unconscious desire for redemption. Third, her physical annihilation makes a moment of redemption into her final, constant state.

I do not mean to deny that Mrs. Shortley is victimized at the end of her section of the story. It is also true that she does not communicate to her immediate family the content of her ultimate vision: at death she is, in a sense, more isolated than ever. Furthermore, after she is dead, she is made into a granite angel once again, quoted by Mrs. McIntyre as an authority on Mr. Guizac and called "God's own angel" by Mr. Shortley (*CS,* 223, 227). At least at the moment of her death, however, Mrs. Shortley succeeds in overcoming the constraints placed upon her by Mrs. McIntyre and the narrator; by displacing herself, she achieves redemption.[19]

"A Good Man Is Hard to Find" seems to contain many elements of "The Displaced Person." The narrator of "A Good Man Is Hard to Find" initially speaks with a tone as authoritarian as that of the narrator of "The Displaced Person," and at the end of "A Good Man Is Hard to Find," we find another dead woman about to join a pile of dead bodies. However, the narration of "A Good Man Is

Hard to Find" is less consistent, and the grandmother's spiritual life differs considerably from Mrs. Shortley's. Certain patterns in the narration of "A Good Man Is Hard to Find" lead us to expect that, like Mrs. Shortley, the grandmother is responsible for what happens to her, but the grandmother's redemption—if we can call it that—is of a more traditional sort, and it is the narrator's consciousness that is most clearly redeemed in this story. At the beginning of "A Good Man Is Hard to Find," however, the narrator seems consistently vicious. This narrator delights in detailing the grandmother's nagging and the obnoxious quarrels of the children, John Wesley and June Star. The narrator's negative evaluation of the family is also found in grotesque descriptions, such as that of the children's mother, whose head is a cross between a cabbage and a rabbit, and that of the grandmother's valise as a hippopotamus head.

Another sign of the narrator's viciousness is the repeated suggestion that the story is sure to end in death. The narrator begins the story by showing the grandmother warning her son Bailey about The Misfit; the narrator's placement of such a reference to The Misfit in the first paragraph obviously presages the family's encounter with him. The narrator ends a detailed paragraph on the grandmother's clothes, significantly, with a reference to her thoughts on accidental death; she is dressed so that she would appear a lady to "anyone seeing her dead on the highway" (*CS*, 118). Her exclamation about some roadside graves receives more of the narrator's attention than do most of her other comments during the journey. And the narrator makes a point of locating the family outside of a town too appropriately named "Toombsboro" when the grandmother starts having the flawed reminiscence that precedes the car accident. One might say, in fact, that the narration leads the reader to expect causation in a sequence of events that occurs by chance. It is interesting to note that a fragment of a working draft for "A Good Man Is Hard to Find" has the cat Pitty Sing jump into the front seat of the car and "cause" the accident without any urging from the grandmother.[20] In the story's final version, however, the narration leads one to try to consider the grandmother responsible for what happens. When the grandmother announces that she recognizes her captor, The Misfit says, "It would have been better for all of you, lady, if you hadn't of reckernized me" (*CS*, 127); the grandmother's son, Bailey, responds to this apparent indication that the entire family is going to be shot by saying "something to his mother that shocked even the children." Although the family's execution was probable before the grandmother recognized The Misfit, the narration, like Bailey, leads the reader to consider her responsible for the intimations of death that the narrator has presented, as well as the fatal culmination. Some critics, accepting at face value these implications of the narration, believe that the grandmother is responsible. Several critics agree that it is her recognition of The Misfit that causes him to shoot the family.[21] Frederick Asals says that the grandmother helps bring about the accident through her "rampant selfishness, her sentimentality, gentility, nostalgia, materialism, and uncertain hold on reality."[22] R. V. Cassill calls her "the guide to disaster" and concludes that her "responsibility for the outcome should not be minimized."[23]

However, it has also been argued that the foreshadowings of death in the story are too superficial for the deaths at the story's end to be logically predictable, much less attributable to the grandmother. As Martha Stephens says, it is only in "a trivial sense" that "everything that happens is the grandmother's fault."[24] I agree that the foreshadowings are superficial, but this superficiality is precisely the point. The narrator places more emphasis on how the story is going to end than is justified, so that the narration seems to lead one toward adopting the motto of The Misfit—"No pleasure but meanness" (*CS,* 132)—a motto accepted by all the characters in this story except the children's mother and the grandmother. The superficial foreshadowings and the ambiguity of the grandmother's role in the family's liquidation ultimately make us aware of how little control the grandmother exercises. As we examine the process by which the grandmother's redemption comes about, we can see how little she resembles the self-transforming Mrs. Shortley.

The opening of the story makes clear that the grandmother does not desire a trip into the region where The Misfit is loose, and although the grandmother is "the first one in the car, ready to go" (p. 118) on the trip the next morning, her desire to travel contains no unconscious desire to encounter the threat of The Misfit. She seems to feel that to stay at home is dangerous; she takes the cat along because "he might brush against one of the gas burners and accidentally asphyxiate himself." The foreshadowings of death presented by the narrator never clearly indicate that the grandmother unconsciously desires death. Although she does believe that if she dies on the highway, she should look like a lady to passersby, there is no indication that she actually has this thought at the point in the story when the narrator relates it. Her comment upon some graves beside the highway does not serve to reveal an unconscious desire to die: she does not even take death seriously; instead, she translates the graveyard into an allusion to O'Connor's least favorite work of popular fiction, *Gone with the Wind* (p. 120). If the grandmother were going to bring about her own transformation, one would expect that her talk with Red Sammy Butts about The Misfit and the definition of the good man would contain evidence that she wishes to be victimized by The Misfit. When Red Sammy's wife begins to speculate on the likelihood that The Misfit will attack, however, Red Sammy cuts her off; like the grandmother, Red Sammy is interested in The Misfit only as a basis for mindless complaints and self-congratulation. I might add that the character of Red Sammy Butts and his conversation with the grandmother about Europe are full of potential for the operation of the positive grotesque. Red Sammy is wonderfully Bakhtinian—"THE FAT BOY WITH THE HAPPY LAUGH," according to one of his roadside signs (p. 121)—and the evocation of Europe could operate, as it does in "The Displaced Person," to suggest ideals. But neither of these possibilities is developed.

Like Mrs. Shortley, the grandmother has secrets, but her use of them suggests no unconscious motive. When she lies about a "secret panel" in the house that she wants to visit, there is no reason to believe that she is plotting to undercut herself; the family would not have caught her in a lie even if they had visited the house, for they had no plans to go inside. When she has the "horrible thought" that the house is in Tennessee, not Georgia, there is no indication that she has anticipated the result of such a realization. The cat's leap is not under her control, as it would need to be if we were going to see that she desires and causes the accident. She may have the opportunity to produce murderous rage in Bailey—to bring out his own misfit qualities—after the accident, but she keeps her secret about the location of the mansion and lies that she injured an organ "so that Bailey's wrath would not come down on her all at once" (p. 125).

When the grandmother attracts the attention of the occupants of The Misfit's car, she has no way of knowing who is in the car, and her waving is in response to the mother's expressed hope that "maybe a car will come along" (p. 125). The view that the grandmother attracts The Misfit is also refuted by his statement that he had seen the accident (p. 126). If this were another O'Connor story, her "peculiar feeling" that "his face was as familiar to her as if she had known him all her life" might suggest that she could foresee The Misfit's effect upon her; in this story, however, the reason for her feeling is that she had read a news story about The Misfit the day before. As I have mentioned, some critics have charged the grandmother with bringing about the massacre when she says that she recognizes The Misfit, and The Misfit does imply that he will have to kill them because he has been recognized, but there is no reason to think that the massacre was not inevitable once The Misfit found them. Even as The Misfit says he would "hate to have to" kill, his casual gesture of burial suggests that he feels no hesitation to commit murder: "The Misfit pointed the toe of his shoe into the ground and made a little hole and then covered it up again" (p. 127).

The grandmother calls The Misfit a good man, but there is no sign that she is making him into her redeemer; she is simply trying to save her life. In the words of The Misfit's father, she is one of those who "can live their whole life out without asking about it" (p. 129). Even as her defenses are destroyed, it is difficult to find an indication that she desires the destruction. Her repetition of the name "Jesus" so that "it sounded as if she might be cursing" (p. 131) and her expression of doubt about the actions of Jesus—"Maybe He didn't raise the dead" (p. 132)—could perhaps be seen as a grotesque inversion of religion like Mrs. Shortley's, but the emphasis here is on destruction rather than creation. The grandmother is losing her banal preconceptions much more than she is constructing a fresh world view. Insofar as she remains conscious of a strategy, her intention seems to be to subjugate The Misfit by turning him into a manipulable child, like Bailey. She had suggested that The Misfit wear Bailey's clothes, and while "standing up looking down on him," she had "noticed how thin his shoulder blades were" (p. 129), as if The Misfit were a frail child. Even as her apparent awakening is forced upon her, her actions are to some extent authoritarian. She says to The Misfit, "Why you're one of my babies. You're one of my own children!" (p. 132), but what she recognizes as characteristic of one of her children seems to be his pain; The Misfit's face is "twisted . . . as if he were going to cry." As Josephine Hendin says, it is appropriate that at the moment of the grandmother's supposed breakthrough, all of her children are a pile of dead bodies in the woods,[25] and The Misfit's rejection of the grandmother's gesture is in part a response to her attempt to subjugate him.

It is tempting, nevertheless, to say that when the grandmother breaks through her banality and recognizes a bond between herself and The Misfit, she achieves a redemption of a traditional sort: a conscious acceptance of the action of grace. The problem is that we cannot see inside her mind. Insofar as we know that she possesses an ideal to which she wishes to return, it is the "ideal" of east Tennessee elegance. If she achieves redemption, then, she surely may be counted among the least cooperative of the redeemed. In relation to the grandmother, the common critical generalizations about the action of grace on unwilling souls are basically justified.

If the grandmother is not responsible for bringing about her own murder, one wonders what purpose the narration serves. A number of critics have complained that the story's narration is inappropriate in a variety of ways. For example, William S. Doxey says that "A Good Man Is Hard to Find" ultimately "fails as a short story" because "the point-of-view shifts from the grandmother to the Misfit and the reader is suddenly left . . . without a focus of narration."[26] Martha Stephens argues that "we get a clearer view here than anywhere else of the tonal problem that exists . . . in nearly all of O'Connor's fiction."[27] Even Caroline Gordon and Allen Tate, personal friends of O'Connor, state in the commentary to "A Good Man Is Hard to Find," in their anthology *The House of Fiction,* that O'Connor's handling of point of view is weak:

> Her lapses result, seemingly, from her reluctance, or it may be inability, to solve the first problem which confronts any writer of fiction: on whose authority . . . is this story told? Miss O'Connor, as it were, backs off, takes a running jump and lands in the middle of her usually troubled waters. The lay reader is fascinated from start to finish and only an occasional purist will be distressed when he realizes that she is playing fast and loose with an age-old convention; in her stories the Omniscient Narrator . . . , one who, seeing all and knowing all, has immemorially been presumed to be elevated considerably above the conflict, often speaks like a Georgia "cracker."[28]

Some of O'Connor's statements about her art invite these charges. In a letter dated 13 January 1961, O'Connor wrote, "Point of view never entered my head when I wrote that story ["A Good Man Is Hard to Find"]. I just wrote it. It's all seen from the eye of the omniscient narrator and that's that. I never gave it a thought" (*HB,* 426). And in some remarks given to introduce a reading of this story, O'Connor almost seems to admit that the second half of the story shifts into an overemphasis on The Misfit and the murders; she claims that "in this story you should be on the lookout for such things as the action of grace in the Grandmother's soul, and not for the dead bodies" (*MM,* 113). Perhaps I should point out that both of these statements are rhetorical. In the first instance (contained in a letter to Louise Abbot), O'Connor was apparently talking her way out of writing something about point of view in "A Good Man Is Hard to Find," and in the second instance she was responding to the overemphasis that she felt some readers had placed on the deaths in the story. Nevertheless, these statements by O'Connor are misleading. What I want to suggest is that the story's strange point of view is in fact at the heart of the story, and that O'Connor was a more skillful technician than her comments indicate.

The remarks in which O'Connor downplays the dead bodies also provide a starting point for an examination of O'Connor's handling of point of view. O'Connor tells her audience that "like the Greeks you should know what is going to happen in this story so that any element of suspense in it will be transferred from its surface to its interior" (*MM*, 108–9). And she goes on to say that "this is the story of a family of six which, on its way driving to Florida, gets wiped out by an escaped convict who calls himself the Misfit" (*MM*, 109). O'Connor's disclosure focuses more of the audience's attention on the narration and the narrator, and less on the tale's events. One finds that the apparent inconsistency in point of view is the result of changes in the narrator. Claire Katz Kahane says, "O'Connor as narrator plays the role of scourge,"[29] and Kahane concludes that O'Connor's fiction "dramatizes a psychic determinism more profound even than Freud's and constructs a literary form that allows no escape from the infantile determinations of personality."[30] In the second half of "A Good Man Is Hard to Find," however, Kahane's theory is unsatisfactory. The narrator's meanness diminishes as The Misfit arrives to destroy the family literally. What is left of that meanness is directed primarily at Bailey, the most repressed and orderly member of the family, and the character that the narrator of the first half of the story most resembles and is most nearly sympathetic to. In the second half, the narrator approaches objectivity and focuses on the potentially redemptive conversation between the grandmother and The Misfit rather than on the murders. We witness the redemption of the narrator's consciousness more clearly than we are able to witness the grandmother's. When this shift in the narrator's attitude occurs, the story seems to become disorderly and to escape the narrator's control. But in the loss of control, the narrator resembles the grandmother and The Misfit, who also lose control of carefully planned plots. The grandmother's realization—that her memory has failed her about the mansion she leads the family toward—occasions her literal "letting the cat out of the bag," an act that not only ruins her plans but also leads to Bailey's wrecking the car. The Misfit apparently begins his conversation with her merely to kill the half hour or so that it will take for his partners to kill the family, but he allows the conversation to affect him much more than he had expected it to. One might even say that the conversation is potentially redemptive *because* it gets out of anyone's control, and that the narrator's story, like The Misfit, gets "aloose from the . . . Pen" (*CS,* 117). The narrator, like the grand-mother and The Misfit, then, is thrown off balance by the material of the story. The ultimate effect of the narrator's imbalance is to connect meaningfully the grandmother's experience to the experiences of Bailey and The Misfit. Whereas she may achieve an insight as she reaches out to The Misfit as her own, Bailey dies without such an insight, and The Misfit not only rejects his own moment of insight but even refuses to say he believes that the grandmother became a good person at the moment of her death: " 'She *would of* [my emphasis] been a good woman,' The Misfit said, 'if it had been somebody there to shoot her every minute of her life' " (p. 133). Believing, apparently, that goodness cannot be produced by a mo-mentary acceptance of grace (see chapter 6), The Misfit uses his gun in an attempt to establish order, put himself in control, and, in a sense, end the story.

But the narrator manages to make clear the limits of The Misfit's view by refusing to accept The Misfit's ending. The narrator con-tinues the story long enough to quote The Misfit saying, "It's no real pleasure in life" (p. 133), a line that shows that the grand-mother, however stubborn she was about avoiding her momentary insight, did affect The Misfit. The narrator becomes silent only after having been transformed from a figure with much of Bailey's repressed anger and The Misfit's destructiveness into a redeemed consciousness. The narrator finally seems more aware than either Bailey or The Misfit that the grandmother can be good despite a lifetime of banality. Perhaps the "good man" in the story's title is the narrator; perhaps it is because the narrator has no body that the good man is so hard to find.

The redemption of O'Connor's narrator toward the end of "A Good Man Is Hard to Find" leads me to speculate here, finally, on why O'Connor wrote so many stories dramatizing the sort of redemption Mrs. Shortley achieves, and only a handful of generally minor stories (those discussed in chapter 5) dramatizing a more traditional sort of redemption. One answer is that O'Connor found Mrs. Shortley's redemption more satisfying as art, because the grandmother's redemption cannot be fully revealed. "A Good Man Is Hard to Find," however, is the story O'Connor most often read aloud, so it seems peculiar that she rarely wrote comparable stories. The answer to this problem, I would suggest, is that when O'Con-nor read this story to audiences, she became the narrator. She could reexperience Mrs. Shortley's sort of redemption by writing another story, but when O'Connor wanted to experience the traditional sort of redemption, as experienced by the narrator and perhaps the grandmother, all she had to do was read aloud "A Good Man Is Hard to Find."

1. For example, see Robert Fitzgerald, "The Countryside and the True Country," p. 78.

2. The original version is in *Sewanee Review* 62 (1954): 634–54.

3. In a letter dated 15 November 1954, O'Connor said that the original, short version of "The Displaced Person" could be substituted for the long version in *A Good Man Is Hard to Find* (*HB*, 72).

4. Hendin, *World of O'Connor*, p. 15. O'Connor compares the peacock's cry to "a cheer for an invisible parade" in "The King of the Birds" (*MM*, 15).

5. Gertrude Grace Sill, *A Handbook of Symbols in Christian Art* (New York: Collier, 1975), p. 121; and George Ferguson, *Signs and Symbols in Christian Art* (New York: Oxford University Press, 1954), p. 22.

6. Sill, *Handbook of Symbols*, p. 24; and Ferguson, *Signs and Symbols*, p. 22.

7. Saint Augustine, *The City of God*, trans. Marcus Dods (New York: Modern Library, 1950), pp. 766–67.

8. Evans, *Animal Symbolism in Ecclesiastical Architecture* (London, 1896; reprint, Detroit: Gale, 1969), pp. 311–12.

9. Klingender, *Animals in Art and Thought to the End of the Middle Ages,* ed. Evelyn Antal and John Harthan (Cambridge: MIT Press, 1971), p. 371.

10. Ferguson, *Signs and Symbols*, p. 23.

11. Desmond, "O'Connor, James and the International Theme," p. 11.

12. George Howe and G. A. Harrer, *A Handbook of Classical Mythology* (New York: Crofts, 1929), p. 121.

13. Ibid., pp. 121–22. Hera favored the Greeks in the Trojan War and continued to torment "refugees" such as Aeneas.

14. In her *Sacred and Legendary Art*, 2 vols. (1896; reprint, New York: AMS, 1970), 1:56, 78, 113, Mrs. Anna Brownell Murphy Jameson discusses pictures of angels with wings having peacock feathers. In *Birds with Human Souls: A Guide to Bird Symbolism* (Knoxville: University of Tennessee Press, 1978), Beryl Rowland notes that in Chaucer's time "angels' wings made of peacocks' feathers were so commonplace that Chaucer was able to reverse the image and refer to the 'pekok with his aungels fetheres bryghte' without explanation" (p. 129). The appropriateness of associating the peacock with a statue on a grave is further indicated by Evans in *Animal Symbolism in Ecclesiastical Architecture:* "The peacock, being sacred to Juno, became a symbol of the apotheosis of Roman empresses, as Jupiter's eagle was of Roman emperors. For this reason these birds were carved on the tombs of the apotheosized, and on funeral lamps. From pagan monuments of the dead they passed to Christian sepulchres, on which they signified the Christian's conception of apotheosis, the ascension of the sanctified soul and its union with God" (pp. 310–11).

15. Bakhtin, "Discourse in the Novel," p. 403.

16. Asals, *Flannery O'Connor*, p. 208.

17. Eggenschwiler, *Christian Humanism of O'Connor*, p. 95.

18. Burns, "Freaks in a Circus Tent," p. 20.

19. Recalling the original meaning of the word *heroic* (one "sacrificed to Hera"), one might call Mrs. Shortley heroic. See Robert Graves, *The Greek Myths*, 2 vols. (Baltimore: Penguin, 1955), 1:52. My connection of displacement and redemption differs from the view of Peter S. Hawkins, in *The Language of Grace,* that when "a sign becomes free-floating," it becomes "meaningless" and fallen (pp. 23–24).

20. File 154, O'Connor Collection.

21. Bryant, "Reading the Map," p. 304; and Grimshaw, *O'Connor Companion,* p. 39.

22. Asals, *Flannery O'Connor*, p. 150.
23. Cassill, *Norton Anthology of Short Fiction: Instructor's Handbook*, p. 175.
24. Stephens, *Question of O'Connor*, p. 27.
25. Hendin, *World of O'Connor*, p. 149.
26. Doxey, "A Dissenting Opinion," p. 199.
27. Stephens, *Question of O'Connor*, p. 18.
28. Gordon and Tate, *The House of Fiction*, p. 384.
29. Katz [Kahane], "O'Connor's Rage of Vision," p. 56.
30. Ibid., p. 63.

2

DANCERS IN THE FURNACE

Mrs. Turpin, Asbury, Mrs. Cope, Mrs. May

The utter impossibility of any one's soul feeling itself inferior
to another; the intense, overwhelming dissatisfaction and
rebellion at the thought;—these, with the omniprevalent
aspirations at perfection, are but the spiritual, coincident with
the material, struggles towards the original Unity—are, to
my mind at least, a species of proof far surpassing what Man
terms demonstration, that no one soul *is* inferior to another—that nothing is, or can be, superior to any one soul—
that each soul is, in part, its own God—its own Creator.

—Poe,
Eureka

MRS. SHORTLEY, of "The Displaced Person," as presented in the first
chapter, may seem unique among O'Connor's characters, but in an
important sense she is typical of the characters who unconsciously
use the grotesque and in that way achieve redemption. In this
chapter I shall discuss four major stories (three of them O. Henry
award winners) to show that Mrs. Shortley's experience occurs
repeatedly. Before I proceed I should mention two points. The first
involves the issue of the consciousness of characters. In chapter 1, I
said that while Mrs. Shortley remains unconscious of her path
toward redemption, the grandmother has to be conscious of change
to be redeemed. In the first two stories to be discussed in this
chapter, "Revelation" and "The Enduring Chill," the protagonists
seem conscious of their redemption. I hope to make clear that no
self-redeeming character is fully conscious of redemption.

The second point involves a shift of emphasis between the first chapter and the readings that follow, a shift concerning the issue of narration. O'Connor's use of the narrator in "A Good Man Is Hard to Find" is unique; nowhere else in O'Connor does a narrator change so significantly. I have emphasized the narrator's treatment of Mrs. Shortley in order to contrast her experience to the grandmother's, and also in order to describe what I consider O'Connor's most common use of her narrator. In the second chapter and the chapters that follow, I shall have less to say about narration—not because it becomes less important, but because it serves the same purposes in most of the works. In story after story (with the exception, to some extent, of the works to be discussed in chapters 4 and 5), the satirical tone of O'Connor's narrators serves two important functions. It embodies a degraded form of the religiosity that O'Connor's characters frequently manage to redeem, and it reminds us of the necessity for the characters to use the desperate indirections of the grotesque process if they are to achieve redemption. Because the grotesque strategies used by characters vary more than the significance of the narration does, I will henceforth discuss the grotesque more than narration.

Mrs. Ruby Turpin, of "Revelation," and Asbury Fox, of "The Enduring Chill," are, like Mrs. Shortley, the objects of their narrators' satire, despite the fact that they are both members of a higher class than Mrs. Shortley's. Mrs. Turpin is one of O'Connor's banal, self-satisfied farm wives, and Asbury is perhaps the most ridiculous of O'Connor's intellectuals. Like Mrs. Shortley, they both have visions, but whereas critics have often taken Mrs. Shortley's visions to be mere reflections of her illusions, the same critics have had less trouble attributing valid content to Mrs. Turpin's and Asbury's visions.

However, the precise significance of Mrs. Turpin's vision of hordes on a fiery bridge is not altogether a matter of critical agreement. And O'Connor's letters show her to have been inconsistent in her opinion of "Revelation" while she was writing it. It was the ending of the story that most troubled her, and the sequence of versions shows O'Connor trying to make clear that Ruby is not entirely corrupt. In a letter dated 25 December 1963, O'Connor mentioned that a friend who had read a draft of "Revelation" had called Mrs. Turpin "evil" and had suggested that O'Connor omit the final vision, which the friend considered to be a confirmation of Mrs. Turpin's evilness. O'Connor's reaction was, "I am not going to leave it out. I am going to deepen it so that there'll be no mistaking Ruby is not just an evil Glad Annie" (*HB*, 554). As she finished revising the story, O'Connor made the final vision less obviously of Mrs. Turpin's making. One late draft, for example, contains the statement that the Turpins, "marching behind the others" toward heaven "with great dignity," were "driving them, in fact, ahead of themselves, still responsible as they had always been for good order and common sense and respectable behavior."[1] In the published text, the Turpins are still at the end of the procession, but there is no mention of them "driving" the others on, and they are "accountable" rather than "still responsible." Another significant difference between the draft and the published text is the addition in the final version of the fact that Mrs. Turpin sees that her "virtues" are "being burned away" (*CS*, 508). In both these revisions there is less emphasis on Mrs. Turpin's smug perspective, more emphasis on what shocks her.

The final version makes the vision more clearly redemptive, and one apparent implication of the revisions is that Mrs. Turpin's revelation is supernatural in origin. This implication is misleading, however; there is still much in Mrs. Turpin's vision to suggest that she produces it, and the primary effect of O'Connor's revisions is to make Mrs. Turpin's unconscious more clearly responsible for her vision of entry into a heavenly community. This view may seem peculiar when one considers Mrs. Turpin's bigotry and banality, but one's impression of that bigotry and banality is the result of the narrator's emphasis in describing Mrs. Turpin. The narrator emphasizes the ridiculous aspects of Mrs. Turpin rather than making fully apparent the tracks she has laid to carry herself to the oven in which individuality is renounced and the ideal of heavenly community achieved.

The primary objection to the view that Mrs. Turpin's change originates from within is probably that the reader seems to witness the beginning of Mrs. Turpin's transformation. When a girl in a doctor's waiting room, a girl named Mary Grace, throws a book at Mrs. Turpin and tells her, "Go back to hell where you came from, you old wart hog" (p. 500), we seem to see Mrs. Turpin being forced toward transformation entirely against her will. Even though O'Connor's names are sometimes ironic (such as June Star, Joy Hopewell, Bernice Bishop), Mary Grace's name suggests to some critics that she specifically represents the theological concept of grace. Patrick J. Ireland, for example, calls Mary Grace "a messenger from God."[2] And the vast majority of critics have agreed that Mrs. Turpin's revelation is forced upon her by the ugly girl.

Even John R. May, who considers Mrs. Turpin the best example of an O'Connor character whose life is interpreted and transformed by words of revelation, can attribute to her only the ability to have "allowed herself to be cut down to size by the word."[3]

In order to see how Mrs. Turpin uses the grotesque to bring about her own transformation, we must examine her psyche before Mary Grace attacks her. Such an examination shows Mrs. Turpin to desire her own demotion in the scale of being and to have practiced causing it. One of Mrs. Turpin's nighttime fantasies—even as it reflects her banality, bigotry, and self-righteousness—comes to a conclusion in which she is demoted:

> Sometimes Mrs. Turpin occupied herself at night naming the classes of people. On the bottom of the heap were most colored people, not the kind she would have been if she had been one, but most of them; then next to them—not above, just away from—were the white-trash; then above them were the home-owners, and above them the home-and-land owners, to which she and Claud belonged. Above she and Claud were people with a lot of money and much bigger houses and much more land. But here the complexity of it would begin to bear in on her, for some of the people with a lot [of] money were common and ought to be below she and Claud and some of the people who had good blood had lost their money and had to rent and then there were colored people who owned their homes and land as well. There was a colored dentist in town who had two red Lincolns and a swimming pool and a farm with registered white-face cattle on it. Usually by the time she had fallen asleep all the classes of people were moiling and roiling around in her head, and she would dream they were all crammed in together in a box car, being ridden off to be put in a gas oven. (*CS*, 491–92)[4]

Although a number of critics have assumed that Mrs. Turpin fully intends for this fantasy to establish a stable hierarchy and that reality intrudes upon her, the stability of Mrs. Turpin's other ridiculous fantasy denies such an explanation. In the other fantasy, Jesus tells her that she must be "a nigger or white-trash," and Mrs. Turpin brings the absurd fantasy to a neat conclusion: "Finally she would have said, 'All right, make me a nigger then—but that don't mean a trashy one.' And he would have made her a neat clean respectable Negro woman, herself but black" (p. 491). Fantasies about class and race have a way of making reality conform, not vice versa, and when Mrs. Turpin imagines herself on the way to the oven, the most reasonable conclusion is that her banal hierarchy has collapsed because she desires the collapse. Her oven fantasy transforms her grotesque prejudices about class and race into a force for redemption.

It is interesting that even before Mrs. Turpin reaches the point in her fantasy when the collapse of the hierarchy occurs, she refers to the people she is categorizing as a "heap," a word that implies that the collapse into a communal mass is inherent in the grotesque habit of categorizing people. Consequently, when Mrs. Turpin finds herself in the doctor's office and, carefully noting the quality of everyone's shoes, begins to build the hierarchy again, she must know on some level that the results of such hierarchical ordering is the communal oven. And her thoughts and actions in the waiting room do indeed reveal an unconscious desire to disrupt the hierarchy she has created, so that she may be redeemed into the community. One violation of the class hierarchy in Mrs. Turpin's system of belief is her agreement with a gospel hymn on the radio in the doctor's office. When she hears the line "When I looked up and He looked down," her mind supplies the last line: "And wona these days I know I'll we-eara crown" (p. 490). Here Mrs. Turpin envisions for herself an eventual displacement from her position in her imagined hierarchy. In this instance Mrs. Turpin imagines that a disruption of the hierarchy would move her up, but in her handling of Mary Grace, Mrs. Turpin works to move herself down. When she first notices Mary Grace reading a book and occasionally scowling at her, she thinks that Mary Grace "appeared annoyed that anyone should speak while she tried to read" (ibid.). The next thing Mrs. Turpin says—"That's a beautiful clock" (p. 492)—seems intended merely to break the silence, and Mary Grace, we are told, lets Mrs. Turpin know about her disgust: "The ugly girl . . . cast an eye upward at the clock, smirked, then looked directly at Mrs. Turpin and smirked again." The narration obscures the fact that when she figures out that Mary Grace will be infuriated by a gratuitous comment, that is what Mrs. Turpin produces. The narrator's reports of Mrs. Turpin's fantasies about hierarchies are placed between the statement that empty talk irritates Mary Grace and Mrs. Turpin's next vapid remark.

As the conversation strays on and Mary Grace grows angrier, Mrs. Turpin projects her own destructiveness onto the girl. One sign of such projection is the description of Mary Grace's eyes as "lit all of a sudden with a peculiar light, an unnatural light like night road signs give" (p. 492). These words are from Mrs. Turpin's perspective, since they follow a sentence expressing a thought that only Mrs. Turpin can have: "[Mary Grace] looked straight in front of her, directly through Mrs. Turpin and on through the yellow curtain and the plate glass window which made the wall behind her." The words are the narrator's, but the thought is Mrs. Turpin's, for she "turned her head to see if there was anything going on outside that she should see" (p. 493). Consequently, the comparison of the light in Mary Grace's eyes to the reflected light of road signs suggests that what Mrs. Turpin sees in Mary Grace is a reflection of Mrs. Turpin's own desires. A related projection of Mrs. Turpin's thoughts onto Mary Grace occurs as the girl makes an ugly face. Mrs. Turpin feels "certain that the girl had made it at her," and Mrs. Turpin imagines that the girl has "known and disliked" her "all her life—all of Mrs. Turpin's life, it seemed too, not just all the girl's life" (p. 495).

When Mary Grace becomes destructive, Mrs. Turpin is absolutely convinced that the girl should be listened to; apparently destruction and truth are closely tied in Mrs. Turpin's mind. Even after Mary Grace throws the book at her, Mrs. Turpin makes an extra effort to ask the disturbed, partially sedated girl for a message. And when she receives that absurd message, she decides it is true, so true that she cannot tell her husband, Claud, what happened, because she fears he will agree that she is a hog from hell. There is good reason to doubt that Mrs. Turpin's awed response to Mary Grace's attack is the necessary one. The white-trash woman insults Mrs. Turpin almost as nastily as Mary Grace does, but Mrs. Turpin has no trouble dismissing the white-trash woman's insult because Mrs. Turpin is able to consider the source.

The conversation Mrs. Turpin has with the white-trash woman is worth examining, however, for it reveals part of Mrs. Turpin's strategy for undercutting the hierarchy she has set up. As Mrs. Turpin describes the operation of the Turpin farm, she mentions that the Turpins have hogs and that she is tired of "buttering up niggers" to get them to work (p. 494). The white-trash woman's response is to place herself above Mrs. Turpin: " 'Two thangs I ain't going to do: love no niggers or scoot down no hog with no hose.' And she let out a bark of contempt." Mrs. Turpin and Mary Grace's mother agree, however, that "you had to *have* certain things before you could *know* certain things." Thus they agree, in one sense, that social elevation depends upon relationships with humans on the lowest social level and even with nonhumans. Another of Mrs. Turpin's potentially profound clichés is "You have to have a little of everything" (p. 493). In one sense, this saying implies that Mrs. Turpin has a little of every quality that places people in their various positions on the social ladder. Even as she defends herself against the white-trash woman's opinions, Mrs. Turpin senses disruptions of the hierarchy. In response to the complaint about hogs, Mrs. Turpin quickly points out, of course, that her hogs are far from the "nasty stinking things" the white-trash woman considers them.

The Turpins' hogs' feet "never touch the ground" (ibid.). Mrs. Turpin also sees that the angelic associations of a hog whose feet never touch the ground are a displacement of the natural hierarchy; she calls the white-trash child a "poor nasty little thing" and notes that he is dirtier than the Turpins' hogs.

The ease with which Mrs. Turpin rejects the white-trash woman's criticism suggests that she should have no trouble dismissing Mary Grace's attack. Mary Grace belongs to a higher class than the white-trash woman, but Mrs. Turpin demotes the ugly girl by revising the fantastic offer from Jesus into "All right, you can be white-trash or a nigger or ugly" (p. 492). Mrs. Turpin's fascination with Mary Grace results from Mrs. Turpin's ability to find in Mary Grace the disruption of hierarchy that she desires. When she receives her curse from Mary Grace, she becomes completely serious, and she spends the rest of the story bringing up to consciousness the full expression of the revelation she has prepared for herself. Her conscious protests confirm her real convictions: " 'I am not,' she said tearfully, 'a wart hog. From hell.' But the denial had no force" (p. 502). Mrs. Turpin is so convinced that she is a wart hog that it is not until she has returned home that it occurs to her to recall that others also deserve condemnation: "She had been singled out for the message, though there was trash in the room to whom it might justly have been applied. The full force of this fact struck her only now" (ibid.).

When she needs additional confirmation of the truth of Mary Grace's accusation, she gets the black workers on the farm to reject the girl's message in a way that will make Mrs. Turpin certain of its validity. As she gives the black workers water, Mrs. Turpin knows that they will flatter and defend her excessively and maddeningly: "Mrs. Turpin knew exactly how much Negro flattery was worth and it added to her rage" (p. 505). When she tells the workers what Mary Grace did, she knows that they will respond with praise for herself, which Mrs. Turpin herself will reject: " 'She pretty too,' the other two said. 'Stout as she can be and sweet. Jesus satisfied with her!' " Mrs. Turpin condemns the workers for their defense and thus indirectly condemns herself: "Idiots! Mrs. Turpin growled to herself. You could never say anything intelligent to a nigger. You could talk at them but not with them." After talking to the black workers, Mrs. Turpin is ready to go to the pigpen, looking like "a woman going single-handed, weaponless, into battle" (ibid.); she is ready at last to defeat her conscious mind.

To counter my notion that Mrs. Turpin is the source for her revelation, one might point out that she complains about the revelation she anticipates. As long as the hierarchy still exists, according to Mrs. Turpin, there is no value in demoting the elevated and elevating the lowly. But such a complaint itself implies that Mrs. Turpin is deeply aware of the meaning of the revelation she gives herself. David Eggenschwiler has said that when she goes to the pigpen, she has to "confront a Jesus who is more than a reassuring echo of her self-righteousness."[5] She gets much more than trivial reassurance, it is true, but her answer does indeed come from an echo; when Mrs. Turpin asks God, "Who do you think you are?" (*CS,* 507), her question "returned to her clearly like an answer from beyond the wood" (p. 508). That Mrs. Turpin unconsciously controls her awakening is reinforced by the fact that when she begins to ask her questions about Mary Grace's accusation, Mrs. Turpin reinterprets it. She does not merely ask how she is like a hog, but asks, "How am I a hog and me both? How am I saved and from hell too?" (p. 506). Mary Grace's charge suggests the grotesque process, but it needs the adjustment supplied by Mrs. Turpin. Mrs. Turpin is like a hog from hell, and she is going back where she came from, but her real origin, Mrs. Turpin senses, is heaven, and her residence in hell is a stopover on her way back to heaven.

The final vision of a "vast horde . . . rumbling toward heaven" (p. 508) has caused a surprising amount of critical controversy. Critics seem to have forgotten at times that the final vision filters through Mrs. Turpin's consciousness. Frederick Asals, for example, takes the reference to the burning away of virtues to mean that "all that the visionary procession . . . clearly carries into eternity with it is the purifying action of the fire itself."[6] But what Mrs. Turpin consciously defines as virtuous in herself—being "accountable . . . for good order and common sense and respectable behavior" (*CS,* 508)—is hardly the only virtue. It is also surprising how many critics who interpret the final vision positively—as valid, offering redemption—have questioned whether Mrs. Turpin benefits from her final vision. Perhaps the critics' tendency to look for gloom at the end is a reaction to the fact that the opening pages of the story have as much laughter in them as anything O'Connor wrote. But the jokes told in the waiting room are deadly serious business. For one thing, the jokes that Mrs. Turpin directs at herself serve to reinforce her image of herself as properly self-scrutinizing and self-conscious. When she squeezes into the chair that the narrator describes as "tight as a corset," Mrs. Turpin says, "I wish I could reduce"; and when Mary Grace's mother says, "Oh, *you* aren't fat," Mrs. Turpin's response is, "Ooooo I am too" (p. 489). Most of the other pleasantries also reinforce prejudices. Jokes about blacks demean blacks, and "sweetness" directed at low-class whites establishes superiority in those who are sweet to them. But this is not to imply that laughter is merely reactionary. Although O'Connor's laughter in this story makes forms rigid,[7] this effect can also help bring about destruction. Mrs. Turpin's inflated pride in her good disposition is finally justified in a sense of which she is not aware, for her laughter helps to set up her displacement. Her conscious horror at the revelation she prepares for herself indicates at once the strength and wisdom of the unconscious.

Ruby Turpin may seem fully conscious of her redemption. She does, after all, hear "the voices of the souls climbing upward into the starry field and shouting hallelujah" (*CS*, 509) even after her vision fades. Like Mrs. Shortley, however, Mrs. Turpin remains unconscious of the sense in which her redemption lies in her freedom from the narrator's analysis of her individuality. Like Mrs. Shortley's stroke, the knowledge Mrs. Turpin achieves is as "abysmal" as it is "life-giving" (p. 508). Mrs. Turpin surely will fall away from her moment of redemption as consciousness again asserts itself. That final "hallelujah" could even be taken as an overly positive, conscious reduction of Mrs. Turpin's redemption.

Highly conscious characters have a particularly difficult time achieving redemption in O'Connor's stories. Asbury Fox, of "The Enduring Chill," is the O'Connor intellectual who most clearly completes a grotesque self-redemption.[8] Critics of this story agree almost universally that Asbury learns his lesson as the Holy Ghost descends upon him at the end of the story, but they still often see problems in the ending. A few critics dislike the waterstain/bird on Asbury's bedroom ceiling as a symbol for the Holy Ghost. Some think that the meaning of the ending is too thoroughly stated and that the action of grace is too easily perceived. Most of the dissatisfaction seems to be based on the assumption that Asbury is merely the "lazy ignorant conceited youth" (*CS*, 377) Father Finn says he is and that Asbury's redemption is forced upon him entirely against his will. This assumption seems to be the reason for Caroline Gordon's selection of "The Enduring Chill" as her example of a weak O'Connor story: "The flaw in 'The Enduring Chill' seems to me a failure of tone: the language does not match the high seriousness of the subject matter."[9] In other words, Gordon objects to the satirical tone in a story about conversion.

The way to resolve this problem is to recognize the extent to which Asbury uses satire on himself and overcomes the narrator's satire. Unconsciously desiring home and religion, Asbury can bring himself toward both these ideals only by grotesquely defining his return home and his dealings with religion as attacks upon his mother or as symptoms of his disease. After putting himself on a train and arriving home, Asbury orchestrates a series of ridiculous scenes—he is a better artist than he realizes—in which he destroys his conscious understanding of his behavior and prepares for his final vision. Ultimately, Asbury is like the farm women who dream of ovens, although the only reference to a trip toward annihilation is the sarcastic comment by Asbury's sister when the Foxes arrive home: "The artist arrives at the gas chamber" (*CS*, 363).

In the opening paragraph, Asbury's thoughts reveal his unconscious knowledge that he is recovering the values of his past. Asbury's surprise when he learns that he looks ill implies that his illness is not the only reason for his return. He tells himself that the reason he wants to die is to teach his mother a lesson, but this rationalization hides from him his true motives. The narrator even tells us that when his train arrives in Timberboro, "Asbury felt that he was about to witness a majestic transformation, that the flat of roofs might at any moment turn into the mounting turrets of some exotic temple for a god he didn't know" (p. 357). Asbury fights this momentary vision as soon as he has it, but such a strategy is necessary for him to maintain his ignorance of what he is doing. Virtually every critic of this story comments upon this passage as a foreshadowing of the ending, but the extent to which Asbury controls his revelation is not articulated in the story and thus not realized by the critics. Asbury's lack of recognition is not merely an obstacle to his transformation; it is a necessary precondition to it. Asbury calls for the Holy Ghost throughout the story, but he must not recognize that he is doing so until he can no longer resist redemption.

What Asbury does recognize is that he wants to torment his mother. He goes home telling himself that she should receive shocks from his death and from a Kafkaesque letter, which reads in part as follows:

> "I came here to escape the slave's atmosphere of home," he had written, "to find freedom, to liberate my imagination, to take it like a hawk from its cage and set it 'whirling off into the widening gyre' (Yeats) and what did I find? It was incapable of flight. It was some bird you had domesticated, sitting huffy in its pen, refusing to come out!" The next words were underscored twice. "I have no imagination. I have no talent. I can't create. I have nothing but the desire for these things. Why didn't you kill that too? Woman, why did you pinion me?" (*CS*, 364)

Asbury's argument with his mother over his illness shows that the issue of Asbury's survival is a war of wills—one Asbury knows he will lose—rather than a matter of medicine. Mrs. Fox insists, "People just don't die like they used to," and informs Asbury that she will keep him alive through the force of her will: " 'Do you think for one minute,' she said angrily, 'that I intend to sit here and let you die?' " (p. 372). Asbury's response is to feel his "first distinct stroke of doubt"; on some level he knows he will survive. The Yeats quotation is particularly important, for as Asbury compares himself to the bird in the Yeats poem, he surely knows that this particular bird's freedom is undesirable: like the lost falcon in Yeats, Asbury would be better off finding his way home.

Asbury's insistence on his coming death hides other motives for his plan to make this visit "permanent" (p. 365). His decision that he is dying coincides with the exhaustion of his money. His rationalizations about avoiding suicide show that he really wants to live. By contrasting himself to a friend named Goetz, Asbury reveals that he intends to live. Goetz sees everything as illusion on the basis of an acquaintance with Eastern religion; Asbury tells himself that he cannot "see it all as illusion" (p. 359), an assertion that suggests the special status in Asbury's mind of the temple illusion he had at the story's beginning. His disagreement with Goetz is reinforced by Asbury's agreement with a Jesuit priest who, at a New York party Asbury attended, spoke of the Holy Ghost. Asbury tells himself he likes the priest (significantly named "Vogle," or *bird*) because he is worldly and "would have understood the unique tragedy of his death" (p. 360), but the priest also promises salvation.

Asbury's attraction to his farm home and its virtues is suggested also by his fantasies about cows. In a dream about his burial, Asbury imagines that after he is buried, he feels "a presence bending over him and a gentle warmth on his cold face" (p. 374). He tells himself that "this was Art come to wake him and he sat up and opened his eyes," but for a moment, still within his dream, Asbury recognizes his real desire: "All around him the cows were spread out grazing in the moonlight and one large white one, violently spotted, was softly licking his head as if it were a block of salt." Asbury's dream points to the cause of his illness—drinking unpasteurized milk—but surely Asbury cannot be aware of this connection. The primary reason Asbury would dream of being a cow's block of salt is that he desires some connection to the physical life of the farm community.[10] He even has a version of this vision during his return to the family farm. A glimpse of the coming breakthrough is provided by his shared stare with a cow; the "small walleyed Guernsey was watching him steadily as if she sensed some bond between them" (*CS*, 362).

The most important symbol of home for Asbury, however, is one he can see from his sickbed. Shortly after he recalls the passage in the letter to his mother where he calls himself a pinioned bird, he stares at the water stains above his bed, which have always reminded him of "a fierce bird with spread wings. It had an icicle crosswise in its beak and there were smaller icicles depending from its wings and tail" (p. 365). The illusion he associates with it has always been that it was "about to descend mysteriously and set the icicle on his head" (p. 366). Clearly he relates the two birds, to some extent identifying himself as the Yeatsian bird with the terrifying bird over his bed. As Frederick Asals says, "Although Asbury's mind attempts to deny it, this [terrifying bird] is a bird he deeply desires to know."[11]

To submit to the ideals symbolized by the bird, Asbury has to destroy his conscious motives for coming home. In his relations with everyone in his community, therefore, he constantly brings about the most awkward of situations and consequently forces himself to reject the false notions he is unconsciously ready to drop. A major segment of his strategy involves clergymen, especially priests. Asbury's laughter at Doctor Block's treatments and at the mention of "Doctor" Bush, the retired minister, is almost entirely negative. But when Asbury thinks of inviting a Jesuit over, he "could not understand why he had not thought of this sooner" (*CS,* 371). One reason, of course, is that he cannot fully admit why he wants a priest. What he tells himself is that a Jesuit is the perfect visitor because "nothing would irritate his mother so much." Momentarily, Catholicism becomes a grotesque degradation of his mother's Protestantism, and Asbury is able to confront a spokesman for religion because he tells himself that his motives are antireligious.

Asbury gets from the Jesuit's visit precisely what he unconsciously wants. Although the half-blind, half-deaf "Father Finn— from Purrgatory" (p. 375) seems different from the intellectual Jesuit Asbury met in New York, Finn is actually a better embodiment of what Asbury desires. What attracted Asbury to the New York Jesuit was his superiority: "Asbury identified his own feelings immediately in the taciturn superior expression" (p. 360) of Ignatius Vogle, S.J. If Father Finn is anything, he is the possessor of a superior attitude. Finn asks Asbury question after question about his prayers, his purity, the catechism, and so on, and dismisses his attempts to change the subject to James Joyce or the "myth of the dying god" (p. 375). In this conversation, which ends when Mrs. Fox decides that the priest is too rough, Asbury achieves the desired humiliation and subjugation by a superior figure. Although the exchange between the Jesuit and Asbury is generally considered to show how complete is Asbury's delusion, the priest's comments on the Holy Ghost indicate that Asbury *must* be responsible for what happens to him. The priest says, "How do you expect to get what you don't ask for? God does not send the Holy Ghost to those who don't ask for Him. Ask Him to send the Holy Ghost" (p. 376). Asbury's assertion, that "The Holy Ghost is the last thing I'm looking for!" is literally correct; his discovery of the Holy Ghost is to occur at the end of his long, backward search.

Asbury's use of the black workers Randall and Morgan is another step in his strategy of self-destruction. The last time he was home, Asbury smoked cigarettes in the dairy barn with them and tried to get them to join him in drinking the warm, unpasteurized milk that has given Asbury undulant fever. But Asbury knows his attempts at communion have failed:

> A few afternoons later when he was standing outside the milk house about to go in, he heard Morgan ask, "Howcome you let him drink that milk every day?"
> "What he do is him," Randall said. "What I do is me."
> "Howcome he talks so ugly about his ma?"
> "She ain't whup him enough when he was little," Randall said.
> The insufferableness of life at home had overcome him and he had returned to New York two days early. (P. 370)

Asbury's remembrance of his previous attempts at communion indicates that he knows they cannot succeed, although in order to make additional attempts, he must tell himself that there were successful moments. His desire for "some last meaningful experience" (p. 378) is well calculated to produce disaster. He reminds himself of the moment of fellowship with the blacks, although he also surely knows how empty that moment was. The narrator's description of Asbury "preparing himself for the encounter as a religious man might prepare himself for the last sacrament" (p. 379) is much more accurate than the ironic tone implies. He plays the role of the "dying god" on a ridiculous level so that he may achieve the redeemed godliness that comes with the destruction of the self. The final encounter with Randall and Morgan is, of course, a farce. The workers refuse to say that Asbury looks sick, they refuse to accept Asbury's charade that he considers them his equal, and each takes a package of cigarettes when Asbury clumsily tries to arrange a final communal smoke. When they leave, Asbury thinks that "there would be no significant experience before he died" (p. 380), but he is now primed for his breakthrough.

When Doctor Block's car drives up, Asbury has "a sudden terrible foreboding that the fate awaiting him was going to be more shattering than any he could have reckoned on" (p. 381). The final description of the bird's descent, after Asbury learns that he has a nonlethal disease, is a culmination toward which Asbury has been working all his life. He feels that "the last film of illusion was torn as if by a whirlwind from his eyes," replaced, of course, by another illusion: "He saw that for the rest of his days, frail, racked, but enduring, he would live in the face of a purifying terror" (p. 382). Asbury chooses to see himself as one forced into revelation; he labels his "last . . . protest" as a "feeble" and "impossible" one (ibid.), imagining himself the victim of Block, whose gaze entered Asbury "like a steel pin" and held down his resistance "until the life was out of it" (p. 381). Although Asbury is conscious of his revelation, his experience is also redemptive in a sense he never realizes. As he destroys all that separates him from the community, he frees himself from the narrator's negative portrait of him. Like the black workers who refuse to accept the roles assigned them by Asbury-as-sham-god, Asbury escapes the role assigned him by the authoritarian narrator, and it is in his moment of free selflessness that Asbury becomes godlike.[12]

In "A Circle in the Fire" the enlightenment of the protagonist, Mrs. Cope, is considerably less evident than in "Revelation" or "The Enduring Chill." The outward manifestations of Mrs. Cope's redemption are slight: Mrs. Cope's awakening, as the woods around her farm burn, produces only a miserable look on her face. The comparatively ambiguous ending of this story calls for even more attention to the protagonist's preparation for her momentary awareness. John F. Desmond expresses the typical critical uncertainty about "A Circle in the Fire" when he says that the story dramatizes only "a truncated myth: Mrs. Cope's epiphany at the end only reveals her true place in the fallen world. There is no direct evocation of Christian Redemption."[13] And some critics doubt whether Mrs. Cope achieves any insight. Like O'Connor's other farm wives, Mrs. Cope is the object of the narrator's satire. When one examines the extreme terms in which Mrs. Cope expresses her thankfulness to God for her prosperity, however, one discovers that her words contain their own grotesque reversal. Like Mrs. Shortley and Mrs. Turpin, Mrs. Cope fantasizes about people in boxcars, but surprisingly, considering her fear of fire, Mrs. Cope associates the boxcars with mere displacement (she imagines Europeans being sent to Siberia)[14] rather than with cremating ovens. John R. May says that Mrs. Cope "prefers to cope with genuine misfortune by keeping it at the safe distance of 'poor Europeans' in Siberian boxcars,"[15] but she desires such misfortune; she has, as David Eggenschwiler says, a "promising insecurity," which prepares for the "providential humbling that she has not known she desires."[16]

One of the most interesting aspects of "A Circle in the Fire" is the way in which the farm wife and the trash wife become very much alike. (Other examples are Mrs. McIntyre and Mrs. Shortley, in "The Displaced Person"; Mrs. May and Mrs. Greenleaf, in "Green-leaf"; and Mrs. Hopewell and Mrs. Freeman, in "Good Country People.") Several critics have noted the strong similarity of Mrs. Cope to Mrs. Pritchard, who raises the issue of the grotesque in the story's first paragraph. She is obsessed and delighted with the story of a distant relative in an iron lung who gave birth to a child. Both mother and child died, but Mrs. Pritchard seems primarily interested in the question of how the woman became pregnant while in an iron lung. Mrs. Cope may seem to evade such grotesquerie; actually she defines her personal set of values by reacting to it. For example, when Mrs. Pritchard complains, "All I got is four abscess teeth," Mrs. Cope's answer defines the absence of additional pain as reason for cheerfulness: "Well, be thankful you don't have five" (*CS,* 177). Mrs. Cope also is thankful that certain things do not happen at all: "We might all be destroyed by a hurricane. I can always find something to be thankful for" (ibid.). Of course, Mrs. Cope does seem to believe that her world contains metaphysical threats: the nut grass she pulls is like "an evil sent directly by the devil to destroy the place" (p. 175); the wind suggests an all-con-suming fire in Mrs. Cope's woods; and the black workers are "as destructive and impersonal as the nut grass" (p. 177). But Mrs. Cope always turns the bad into good. The similarity of Mrs. Cope and Mrs. Pritchard is clearest when they agree that the woman in the iron lung "had plenty to be thankful for": "She could be thankful she wasn't dead" (p. 178). (And according to both Mrs. Cope and Mrs. Pritchard, there is plenty to be thankful for when the woman *is* dead.) Mrs. Cope can feel grateful about "misfor-tune" as easily as she can feel grateful for good fortune. Her strategy for delighting in destruction and death and Mrs. Pritchard's strategy are sides of one coin.

Mrs. Cope and Mrs. Pritchard thus cooperate to invest every-thing with positive and negative energy. Everything is a sign of God's providence, for which Mrs. Cope is grateful, and everything is a sign of coming disaster. Mrs. Cope senses so many threats that she feels sure of her own destruction as soon as several problems "come at once" (p. 177), and as everything takes on negative energy, everything becomes a destructive problem. The ultimate extension of Mrs. Cope's values is to desire bad fortune as well as good. That Mrs. Cope desires disaster is indicated even as she speaks of her good fortune: " 'Think of all we have. Lord,' she said and sighed, 'we have everything,' and she looked around at her rich pastures and hills heavy with timber and shook her head as if it might all be a burden she was trying to shake off her back" (ibid.).

In her unconscious desire for destruction, Mrs. Cope joins everyone else on the farm. Even her child, Sally Virginia, allies herself with the destructive forces for the sake of "meanness" (p. 176); she occasionally scares her mother by suggesting that the woods are on fire. The boys from Atlanta who burn the farm, then, are merely implementing the desire of everyone else in "A Circle in the Fire." Certainly the boys desire death; for Powell, death could provide a chance to return to the Cope farm, as W. T. Harper tells Mrs. Cope (p. 180). And in Powell's mind, the Cope farm itself suggests destruction; while playing on the grounds of the development where he lived in Atlanta, Powell had said that there "was a horse down there name Gene and if I had him here I'd bust this concrete to hell riding him!" (p. 182). Despite protestations to the contrary, Mrs. Cope is convinced that the boys are to bring her long-desired destruction. The narrator's description of Mrs. Cope's manner of speaking to Powell—"as if she were talking politely to a gangster" (p. 183)—suggests that she classifies them with her other transcendental threats. The boys commit a variety of destructive acts without being stopped by Mrs. Cope. The grotesquely religious quality of the boys' behavior is suggested when the boys lie to Mrs. Cope about whether they have been riding her horses: "They all said 'No mam!' at once in loud enthusiastic voices like the Amens are said in country churches" (ibid.). Although the boys never speak honestly in Mrs. Cope's presence, she learns of the religious dimension to their destructiveness; Mrs. Pritchard tells her that Mr. Pritchard heard the smallest boy respond to charges of dropping cigarettes in her woods by saying, "Man, Gawd owns them woods and her too" (p. 186).

At the end, Sally Virginia sees the boys bathing and playing in the cow trough in the back pasture. She notices Powell looking through eyeglasses "splashed with water," and for one significant moment, she sees through Powell's eyes: "The trees must have looked like green waterfalls through his wet glasses" (pp. 191–92). Hidden in the woods, she watches the boys run naked around the pasture, and then she listens and watches as the boys dress and decide to burn the woods. Running back to the house as the woods begin to burn, Sally Virginia feels the same misery that she sees on her mother's face: "It was the face of the new misery she felt, but on her mother it looked old and it looked as if it might have belonged to anybody, a Negro or a European or to Powell himself" (p. 193). And in the story's final, controversial sentence, Sally Virginia hears "a few wild high shrieks of joy as if the prophets were dancing in the fiery furnace, in the circle the angel had cleared for them." Most critics consider this ending overly positive; but within the context of the desire for destruction shared by the residents of the Cope farm, the boys are indeed a positive force. The shared misery is in a sense what everyone has wanted; the ending even suggests that the city boys are capable of sharing Mrs. Cope's point of view. Although their nudity and their description as prophets dancing in fire make them look like Mrs. Shortley's Poles come alive in the oven, the boys have also considered subjugating the farm by putting a parking lot on it. Mrs. Cope's strict control, of course, has been producing a sort of subjugation of her farm for years; the boys' resemblance to Mrs. Cope clarifies the fact that even a strict imposition of order helps bring about an enlivening destruction.

Mrs. Cope is unconscious of using the grotesque positively, but she invests her entire environment with grotesque significance. And it is precisely in such grotesque maneuvers that characters achieve their momentary, redemptive freedom from the constrictive, passive role assigned them by the narrator. In their community of misery these characters achieve a freedom of which they remain unconscious. From this perspective, the shocking last line of "A Circle in the Fire" also makes more aesthetic sense. In their transformation into prophets, the three boys are freed from the merely destructive role Mrs. Cope consciously assigns them.

"Greenleaf," which does not contain either railroad or oven imagery, provides one of O'Connor's fullest examples of self-redemption. Surprisingly enough, it has been singled out, at times, as a story in which the protagonist shows no desire to be transformed. Frederick Asals, for example, considers "Greenleaf" to be "the single O'Connor work . . . in which the protagonist . . . seems to harbor no longing, however suppressed, for the divine."[17] In coming to this conclusion, critics follow the lead of the narrator, who is consistently critical of Mrs. May. The narrator presents Mrs. May as complaining, self-righteous, thoroughly conventional, capable of being redeemed only by force. The narrator further complicates our understanding of Mrs. May's experience by applying a layer of imagery with mythic significance of which the characters are unaware: the story's first sentence describes the bull outside Mrs.

May's window as a "patient god come down to woo her" (*CS*, 311). Such mythic imagery is usually said to reinforce O'Connor's Christian message, but a question about the mythological references is raised by Carol Shloss, who asks what specifically Mrs. May realizes as she is gored by the bull at the story's end. Shloss finds no satisfactory answer, because, she says, the bull's mythic qualities are too complicated and Mrs. May's knowledge of the mythic symbolism too ambiguous to produce a clear answer.[18] Shloss maintains, and I agree, that in order to know what Mrs. May realizes as she dies, we must study her psychology without reference to the narrator's interpretations. I believe that Mrs. May's fatalistic complaints and the statements about her sense of taboo reveal her strategy for transformation.

After the narrator opens "Greenleaf" by describing the bull and shows Mrs. May shooing the bull away, the narrator reports that in her dreams she had interpreted the bull as the force that is to destroy her, her farm, everything except her employees, the Greenleafs:

> She had been conscious in her sleep of a steady rhythmic chewing as if something were eating one wall of the house. She had been aware that whatever it was had been eating as long as she had had the place and had eaten everything from the beginning of her fence line up to the house and now was eating the house and calmly with the same steady rhythm would continue through the house, eating her and the boys, and then on, eating everything but the Greenleafs, on and on, eating everything until nothing was left but the Greenleafs on a little island all their own in the middle of what had been her place. (*CS*, 311–12)

The narrator interprets the bull as a "country suitor" (p. 312), and the narration implies that Mrs. May considers the bull a sexual threat only to her heifers. However, Mrs. May's expectation that she is to be destroyed actually contributes to her eventual acceptance of the bull as a lover. By examining the grotesque symbolism of the bull for Mrs. May, we can discover how she translates the goring by the bull into a religious experience.

When Mrs. May learns from her son Scofield that the bull belongs to the Greenleaf boys, O.T. and E.T., the news merely confirms her previous fantasy about the bull, that somehow its elementally destructive force is in league with the Greenleafs. Most of Mrs. May's feelings about the bull have to do with her feelings about the Greenleafs, and most of her feelings about the Greenleaf family are responses to Mrs. Greenleaf, who is probably O'Connor's most grotesquely religious character. Mrs. Greenleaf lives filthily, has five snuff-dipping daughters, and engages in prayer healing:

Every day she cut all the morbid stories out of the newspaper—the accounts of women who had been raped and criminals who had escaped and children who had been burned and of train wrecks and plane crashes and the divorces of movie stars. She took these to the woods and dug a hole and buried them and then she fell on the ground over them and mumbled and groaned for an hour or so moving her huge arms back and forth under her and out again and finally just lying down flat and, Mrs. May suspected, going to sleep in the dirt. (Pp. 315–16)

Mrs. Greenleaf's grotesquerie when Mrs. May first witnesses her prayer healing produces almost a stereotype of the positive grotesque: " 'Oh Jesus, stab me in the heart!' Mrs. Greenleaf shrieked. 'Jesus, stab me in the heart!' and she fell back in the dirt, a huge human mound, her legs and arms spread out as if she were trying to wrap them around the earth" (p. 317). Some critics question the value of Mrs. Greenleaf's religion, one critic doing so precisely because it is a "purely physical" religion.[19] Mrs. Greenleaf is certainly too grotesque for Mrs. May. In order for Mrs. May to transform herself, she must find an alternative route, but her response to Mrs. Greenleaf points the way. One of the strongest critiques of a character in O'Connor's works is the narrator's treatment of Mrs. May's reaction when she sees and hears Mrs. Greenleaf on her hands and knees groaning the name "Jesus": "She thought the word, Jesus, should be kept inside the church building like other words inside the bedroom. She was a good Christian woman with a large respect for religion, though she did not, of course, believe any of it was true" (*CS,* 316). The harsh criticism of Mrs. May in this passage also indicates that two taboo subjects, religion and sex, are related for Mrs. May. The grotesque religious experience that Mrs. May seems to work to bring about throughout the story is her figurative insemination by the Greenleaf bull. Certainly the threat that Mrs. May consciously senses from the bull is primarily genetic or sexual; she fears that the bull will "ruin the breeding schedule" (p. 314) by breeding all of her cows.

Mrs. May associates the bull's threat with both Mr. Greenleaf and the Greenleaf sons. Mrs. May's labeling of the Greenleafs as "scrub-human" (p. 317) shows her association of them all with the biologically inferior scrub bull. And Mrs. May consistently acts—and has acted for some time—to make the Greenleaf family what they are. She tells herself that it is her employment of Mr. Greenleaf when no one else would have him that accounts for his success. The narrator says that "she had always doubted she could do better" (p. 313) than to hire Mr. Greenleaf; her doubt suggests that to some extent she desires a bad worker of Mr. Greenleaf's sort. Mrs. May also feels that "Mr. and Mrs. Greenleaf had aged hardly at all" (p. 319) during their time on the May farm, and Mrs. May feels that she is the reason for their vitality: "They lived like the lilies of the field, off the fat that she struggled to put into the land." Furthermore, Mrs. May seems at times to be completely unable to control Mr. Greenleaf. He allows the Greenleaf bull to wander freely about the May farm for days, in violation of her orders, and he consistently exasperates Mrs. May with his avoidance of duty. Mrs. May compliments herself, however, with the thought that she can handle Mr. Greenleaf; such a thought indicates that Mrs. May tacitly allows his irritating behavior.

Mrs. May's responsibility for the Greenleaf sons is more complicated. She complains that the Greenleaf boys have had too many good times on her farm, but she also insists that O.T. and E.T. should have been her sons and that Mrs. Greenleaf should have had the May boys as sons. Mrs. May's attitude toward the Greenleafs is further complicated by her belief that World War II allowed them to rise on the social ladder. She goes so far as to say, "If the war had made anyone, . . . it had made the Greenleaf boys" (p. 318). Mrs. May's apparent belief that her actions have reinforced the effects of World War II allows one to relate her actions to the references to the war in the rest of O'Connor's works. The war usually reminds O'Connor characters of the oven that burns away differences between people; consequently, her feeling that her actions reinforce those of the war would suggest again that she works to bring herself and the Greenleafs to the same social level. And John F. Desmond suggests that O'Connor, in describing the Greenleaf boys' progress after their exposure to European culture, expresses an "affirmative" view of history.[20] Insofar as Mrs. May's actions have reinforced the influence of Europe, we may consider her to be unconsciously cooperating with the subversive forces O'Connor characters typically associate with Europe.

Despite all her protests that she wishes to be rid of the bull, Mrs. May never quite takes the action that would force its removal. She tells Mr. Greenleaf that she might charge O.T. and E.T. for the time their bull has been on her land, because "then it wouldn't happen again" (*CS,* 322). But by failing to demand payment, she implies that she accepts the bull's presence. When she looks for the Greenleaf sons to complain, even her response to the silence of the Greenleaf children demonstrates her willingness to be the Greenleafs' equal. Faced with the children's refusal to tell her where O.T. and E.T. are, Mrs. May feels "as if she were on trial for her life, facing a jury of Greenleafs" (p. 324).

Mrs. May constructs a set of fatalistic expectations—much like Mrs. Cope's—which make it inevitable that Mrs. May will eventually have some transforming experience. In describing the management of the farm, she says, "Everything is against you," and then elaborates: "The weather is against you and the dirt is against you and the help is against you. They're all in league against you" (p. 321). Later, after summarizing her problems with the bull, she says, "I'm the victim. I've always been the victim" (p. 327). Her need to regard herself as victimized explains the full meaning of her insistence that she will die when she is "good and ready" (p. 321). In a sense, that is what she does. The same determination is behind her warning to her sons that they will "find out what *Reality* is when it's too late!" (p. 320). Such a statement points to the O'Connor character's typical strategy: to back into a course of action until it is impossible to withdraw; and Mrs. May intends to face reality only when she cannot back out. When she forces Mr. Greenleaf to get his gun and drives him out to shoot the bull, she is determined to experience disaster. She thinks that Mr. Greenleaf would "like to shoot me instead of the bull" (p. 330). She also imagines that Mr. Greenleaf will refuse to kill the bull until forced to, and, later, that Mr. Greenleaf might be gored. Even then, she would experience the desired disaster, for if Mr. Greenleaf were gored, she would be sued: "She thought of it almost with pleasure as if she had hit on the perfect ending for a story she was telling her friends" (p. 333). She dismisses the fantasy because "Mr. Greenleaf had a gun with him and she had insurance," but in this context, Mrs. May's fantasy reveals even more about her desires.

After Mr. Greenleaf goes after the bull, she rests her head on the hood of her car and closes her eyes. She wonders "why she should be so tired when it was only mid-morning" (p. 332), but since it is in dreams that she has felt herself the bull's victim, her action is appropriate. Awakening, she honks her horn to call Mr. Greenleaf (and, perhaps, the bull). She sees the bull come from the woods, alerts Mr. Greenleaf, and then

> looked back and saw that the bull, his head lowered, was racing toward her. She remained perfectly still, not in fright, but in a freezing unbelief. She stared at the violent black streak bounding toward her as if she had no sense of distance, as if she could not decide at once what his intention was, and the bull had buried his head in her lap, like a wild tormented lover, before her expression changed. One of his horns sank until it pierced her heart and the other curved around her side and held her in an unbreakable grip. She continued to stare straight ahead but the entire scene in front of her had changed—the tree line was a dark wound in a world that was nothing but sky—and she had the look of a person

whose sight has been suddenly restored but who finds the light unbearable. (P. 333)

Described as one who allows the bull to gore her because of her
"freezing unbelief" and as one who finds her insight "unbearable,"
Mrs. May seems to some critics as one blind, as one incapable of
understanding the revelation presented to her. The narrator's comparison of the bull to a "tormented lover" seems to some critics
unconvincing; to others it signifies that the bull is a messenger from
God.[21] In my opinion, however, the ending finds Mrs. May in
transition, from a state in which she must hide from herself the
significance she attaches to things, into a momentary redemption.
If she has considered the bull a sexual being related to all the forces
by which she wants to be destroyed, her "freezing unbelief" and her
inability to "decide at once what his intention was" are signs of her
sexual reluctance on the conscious level. Her maneuvers
throughout the story to transform herself make sense of the narrator's final statement that the dying Mrs. May "seemed . . . to be
bent over whispering some last discovery into the animal's ear"
(*CS,* 334). As with the other self-redeeming protagonists, however,
there is a level of her redemption which only the reader sees;
although the story ends with a puzzle—what does she whisper?—
the reader appreciates, more than Mrs. May can, her rejection of the
role assigned her by the narrator. In allowing the Greenleaf bull his
freedom, she achieves her own.

1. File 189, O'Connor Collection; my quotation is from May's *The Pruning Word,*
p. 165.
2. Ireland, "Place of O'Connor," p. 59.
3. May, *The Pruning Word,* p. 115; see also pp. 113–14.
4. The inserted word "of," omitted from *The Complete Stories,* appears in *Everything That Rises Must Converge,* p. 217.
5. Eggenschwiler, *Christian Humanism of O'Connor,* p. 44.
6. Asals, *Flannery O'Connor,* p. 225.
7. A more clearly destructive and positive form of laughter appears in "A Temple
of the Holy Ghost." See chapter 3.
8. Other intellectuals do achieve or approach a grotesque religious experience
(Calhoun, in "The Partridge Festival"; Hulga, in "Good Country People"; Thomas,
in "The Comforts of Home"), but critics have been less inclined to see their
experience as positively religious.
9. Gordon, "Rebels and Revolutionaries," p. 51.
10. Asbury's dream of himself as a block suggests a sort of kinship to Doctor
Block, as Jefferson Humphries implies in *The Otherness Within,* p. 133. The dream
may also suggest that Asbury is a pillar of salt or the salt of the earth.
11. Asals, *Flannery O'Connor,* p. 224.
12. Asbury's control of his momentary insight is suggested by O'Connor's revi-

sion of "The Enduring Chill" as part of her never-completed third novel, *Why Do the Heathen Rage?* Stephen Driggers reports, in "Imaginative Discovery in the O'Connor Typescripts," pp. 113–14, that O'Connor's revision has the young invalid jump out of bed and run from the room to reject his supposed moment of revelation.

13. Desmond, "O'Connor, James and the International Theme," p. 8.

14. O'Connor apparently associated a trip to Siberia with a trip to the ovens. In "Image and Imagination," p. 127, Harvey Klevar reprints an article from the 21 July 1949 issue of the Milledgeville *Union-Recorder;* Klevar says that this article is the source for "The Displaced Person." The article also shows that the displaced persons who escaped the oven also escaped deportation to Siberia: "Prior to their incarnation [*sic*] in the D.P. camp, Mr. Jeryczuk worked for the Austrian Railway Company. In 1942 they were in Poland, where all the Polish young people were sent to Siberia. They fled to Austria to escape this fate, and were married there." In a letter dated 25 December 1951, O'Connor wrote that a "refugee family" was expected on the O'Connor farm that night. She mentions several details that appear in "The Displaced Person": curtains from "chicken-feed sacks," the likelihood that the refugees will go to Chicago, and the skepticism of the "dairyman's wife" that "they'll know what colors even is" (*HB*, 30).

15. May, *The Pruning Word*, p. 80.

16. Eggenschwiler, *Christian Humanism of O'Connor*, pp. 37, 39.

17. Asals, *Flannery O'Connor*, p. 223.

18. See Shloss, *O'Connor's Dark Comedies*, pp. 65–72.

19. Ryan, "Three Realms of O'Connor's 'Greenleaf,' " p. 43.

20. Desmond, "O'Connor, James and the International Theme," p. 15.

21. Louise Westling argues, in *Sacred Groves and Ravaged Gardens*, pp. 161–71, that "Greenleaf" and "A Circle in the Fire" illustrate O'Connor's inability to reconcile her Christian condemnation of the protagonists with her allusions to the traditional associations of gardens with female power; Westling implies that the bull in "Greenleaf" ought to be Mrs. May's servant rather than her enemy. I believe that my reading, which considers Mrs. May in control of the bull's meaning, helps to answer Westling's interesting objections.

3

THE CYCLE
OF THE GROTESQUE
"A Temple of the Holy Ghost"
and "The Partridge Festival"

Beyond the grotesque lies . . . the grotesque.
—Geoffrey Galt Harpham,
On the Grotesque

THE ENDINGS of the stories discussed so far may seem fully resolved.
Mrs. Shortley dies at her moment of revelation in "The Displaced
Person," as does Mrs. May in "Greenleaf." And the other protagonists—Mrs. Turpin, Asbury, and Mrs. Cope—seem to have
learned a lesson once and for all. But the grotesque process counters
such completion; redemption is momentary, and the surviving
protagonists are left at a point of departure. The two stories to be
discussed in this chapter emphasize the ongoing interplay between
the grotesque and the ideal. The situations in "A Temple of the Holy
Ghost" and "The Partridge Festival" are comparable to that in
"Greenleaf," where Mrs. Greenleaf practices a grotesque religion
into which Mrs. May finally initiates herself despite her disgust for
Mrs. Greenleaf. The hermaphrodite in "A Temple of the Holy
Ghost" and the mass murderer in "The Partridge Festival" are
degraded physically, but the protagonists' attitudes toward these
degraded figures are complicated. The child protagonist of "A
Temple of the Holy Ghost" and Calhoun of "The Partridge Festival" both idealize the peculiar figure; the child sees the hermaphrodite playing the role of a priest, and Calhoun sees the mass
murderer as heroic. The grotesque process in these stories is somewhat more complicated, as a result, and the stories do not produce
the usual impression of resolution; the moments of redemption for
the child and Calhoun are clearly moments only. The stories do,

however, provide insights into forces that counter resolution in all of O'Connor's works.

"A Temple of the Holy Ghost" is often called O'Connor's most overtly Catholic story. Most critics correctly describe the initiation of the story's protagonist—an ugly, fat, twelve-year-old girl—in religious and sexual terms. But they also say that the child learns to be pious, humble, and repressed: that she learns to give up her grotesque meanness.[1] One reason for these conclusions is the narrator's encouragement to adopt such an attitude, even when it produces a false resolution to the grotesque. Examining the peculiar workings of the protagonist's psyche, one discovers that she makes grotesque meanness central to maturity. As she escapes the weak role ascribed to her by the narrator, she achieves the momentary freedom of membership in a community of "temples."

It is easy to see why the narrator's perspective has been widely accepted. The apparently omniscient narrator often understands the child better than she consciously understands herself. Early in the story, for example, the narrator shares the child's disapproval of the two fourteen-year-old girls who come from the convent school to visit, but the narrator also disapproves of the child's laughter at her visitors, because the child's motives are not pure. The child envies the two girls' adoption of sexual roles—they put on lipstick and wear loud clothes and high heels—and the child's laughter is partly defensive, even as it expresses more aggression than the laughter in "Revelation." As escorts are sought to take the visiting girls to the fair, the narrator's critique of the child's motives continues. As the child suggests possible escorts, her laughter makes her cry, hit the table, fall on the floor, and roll about. The child's behavior consistently betrays her desire. When the visitors from the convent eat dinner outside with the local boys chosen to take them to the fair, the child refuses to eat with them. But when the narrator describes the dinner scene from the child's perspective, the desire that accompanies the child's disgust is clear: "The lanterns gilded the leaves of the trees orange on the level where they hung and above them was black-green and below them were different dim muted colors that made the girls sitting at the table look prettier than they were" (*CS*, 242).

After the visitors return from the fair and tell their story of the hermaphrodite, the child makes the hermaphrodite the basis for a dream that gains the narrator's full approval. In the dream, the child idealizes the freak-show audience and the hermaphrodite. Men in the audience are "more solemn than they were in church"; the women look "stern and polite, . . . standing as if they were waiting for the first note of the piano to begin the hymn." And the hermaphrodite becomes a priest, or preacher, who piously says, "I am a temple of the Holy Ghost" (p. 246). The child's vision of the hermaphrodite as priest is a strategy endorsed to some extent by the Catholic Church. The "*Tantum Ergo,*" a benediction hymn sung by the visitors from the convent to their horrified Church of God escorts, says in part, "*Et antiquum documentum / Novo cedat ritui*" (translated in the *Saint Andrew Daily Missal* as "Types and shadows have their ending, / Newer rites of grace prevail"). The hermaphrodite's speech is, in a sense, a new ritual that necessarily succeeds old ones. Various critics have concluded that the child's idealization of the hermaphrodite constitutes a large part of the story's message. The narrator's increasingly serious tone also implies that the child learns humility and piety in the dream, and the child does have the hermaphrodite say, "If anybody desecrates the temple of God, God will bring him to ruin and if you laugh, He may strike you thisaway" (*CS*, 246). Generally critics point to the hermaphrodite's meekness and piety to explain the hermaphrodite's representation of an ideal.

However, this critical attitude encouraged by the narration fails to take into account the extent to which it is good to be "struck" by God.[2] One suggestion of this possibility is the hermaphrodite's blue dress, clothing traditionally associated with the Virgin, who, like the hermaphrodite, could say, "God made me thisaway," or "This is the way He wanted me to be and I ain't disputing His way" (*CS*, 245). By examining the psyche of the child while avoiding a jump to the narrator's conclusions, one discovers that the child learns to value the meanness that causes one to be struck by God and to become like the freak. The ideal she wishes to achieve—becoming a mature, saintly temple—is to be reached through the "ugliness" that produces physical punishment. One point to notice about the child's psyche is that she has a distorted understanding of the hermaphrodite's condition, and she herself makes the hermaphrodite grotesque even as she idealizes the hermaphrodite into a priest. Even before she hears that the freak is "a man and woman both" (ibid.), she assumes that the hermaphrodite has two heads, and she never understands what the hermaphrodite lifted its blue dress to show. It is appropriate that the child should imagine that the hermaphrodite's special quality involves the head, for she feels that the head is the part of the body controlling all important functions, including sex.[3] She knows that at the convent her visitors' minds are kept off sex because the nuns "keep a grip on their necks" (*CS*, 236), and she describes a rabbit having rabbits by saying, "It spit them out of its mouth" (p. 246). The head is so important to her that in her fantasies of martyrdom, only beheading can kill her.

Because the child is preoccupied with the head, her notion of what it means to be struck by God necessarily involves that part of the body. At one point the cook warns that God's punishment is directed at the head: "God could strike you deaf dumb and blind" (p. 242). When the child thinks about the martyrs, she recalls their "stiff stretched composed faces" as they wait "to have their tongues cut out" (pp. 242–43). The best indication of the child's notion of what it means to be struck by God appears in her fantasies on the hermaphrodite, the one character who clearly has been struck by God. The child can imagine the hermaphrodite's voice and can visualize the faces of the audience, but she cannot visualize the hermaphrodite's head. Apparently, the child thinks that if the hermaphrodite does not have two heads, it must have no head at all.

Looking at the child's various misunderstandings of the hermaphrodite from another perspective, however, we see that she uses them to construct a strategy for her own redemption. Like the other self-redeemers discussed so far, the child is oppressed—in her case, most noticeably oppressed by physical immaturity. The ideals of maturity and saintly martyrdom seem nearly unreachable to her. However, she does control her ugly looks and ugly words—both functions of the head. Within the context of her problem, her vision of the hermaphrodite provides her the opportunity to transform her negative grotesquerie into positive grotesquerie. By considering grotesquerie of face and word to result in being struck by God, she brings the extent of her grotesquerie fully under her own control. And by considering the hermaphrodite an ideal figure, a temple of the Holy Ghost, she makes her own grotesquerie a pathway to her ideals. In the child's mind, consequently, the hermaphrodite's imagined headlessness is both threatening *and* desirable, simultaneously a punishment and a sign of the martyrdom that admits one to paradise. Whereas in her early fantasies of martyrdom the child imagines herself going to heaven only because an impossible piety gets her beheaded, the child's grotesque misunderstanding of the hermaphrodite makes it easier for her to bring about a figurative beheading and redemption. The narrator seems to imply that the threat of being struck by God is enough to teach the child to be "good." However, the child believes that beheading and the meanness that merits beheading are desirable, and desirable *despite* her feeling that the loss of the head means obliteration: the loss of intellect and sexuality, of mind and body. The child herself is slow to realize fully the value of her grotesque, sexual, laughing meanness, grasping it only at the story's end, *after* the dream sequence that the narrator seems to consider the crucial part of the story.

At the end, the child tries to make the experiences earlier in the story into the occasion for her entrance into the sort of maturity in which one is "good," but another kind of maturity takes its place. When she accompanies her visitors back to the convent and is escorted to the chapel for benediction, the child is in a mean mood; she thinks, "You put your foot in their door and they got you praying" (*CS*, 247). As the "*Tantum Ergo*" is sung, the child tries to make herself a solemn, pious, nice daughter: "Her ugly thoughts stopped and she began to realize that she was in the presence of God. Hep me not to be so mean, she began mechanically. Hep me not to give her so much sass. Hep me not to talk like I do." As always during prayer, however, the child's mind becomes "empty," and when the priest raises the monstrance with the Host in it, the child recalls the hermaphrodite: "She was thinking of the tent at the fair that had the freak in it. The freak was saying, 'I don't dispute hit. This is the way He wanted me to be' "(p. 248). Insofar as the reader is to assume that the hermaphrodite's words apply to the child's situation, the message she receives is that what she had considered freakish in herself—her meanness, laughter, ugly talk—is the way God wants her to be. She may be punished for meanness, but the punishment is also a reward.

The child actually feels the value of freakishness better than does the freak, who remains solemn; she makes herself into a grotesque improvement upon the hermaphrodite. It is appropriate, then, that when the child is on her way home in the back seat of a man's automobile—where, as the story has reminded us emphatically, it is important to remember that one's body is a temple of the Holy Ghost—the child's thoughts again become mean. Looking at her driver, she observes "three folds of fat in the back of his neck" and thinks his ears are "pointed almost like a pig's" (p. 248).[4] Another indication that the story affirms meanness—and, in fact, the first clue that we should pay particular attention to the child's use of the grotesque—is in the story's point of view in the opening paragraph. The story's opening words, "All weekend," are of course written from a point in time *after* the events of the entire story. And although the child is not the narrator, the ridiculing tone of the opening paragraph clearly reflects the attitude of the child. For this laughing, mean attitude to be sustained by the child after the weekend's events, her spiritual awakening must not preclude meanness as a trait of her maturity.

The story's ending might lead one to conclude that the child's identification with the hermaphrodite ultimately dissolves; when she learns that some preachers from town have had the police shut down the fair, the child sees the sun as "an elevated Host drenched in blood" (*CS*, 248). Because she has previously associated the Host with the hermaphrodite, it is reasonable to assume that this vision of the sun indicates that the child's thoughts are on the hermaphrodite. And when the child imagines the sinking sun leaving "a line in the sky like a red clay road hanging over the trees," one might conclude that the hermaphrodite's path is a road the child will not take. She is, after all, on her way back to safety at home. But from another perspective, the child is closer to the hermaphrodite than ever at the story's end, for, like the hermaphrodite, she begins to feel what it is like to be struck by God. As she is leaving the convent, the child feels herself "swooped down on" by a nun who "nearly smothered her in the black habit, mashing the side of her face into the crucifix" (ibid.). Although the child does not take the hermaphrodite's path immediately, the symbolic action of the nun's painful embrace gives her a strong sense of what lies in store for her.[5] That the child's path may be more successful than the hermaphrodite's is suggested by the fact that the meek, pious hermaphrodite has failed to achieve society's tolerance, a failure that calls into question both meekness as a means and being tolerated as a goal. On her way home, the child hears that the fair has closed; the town's preachers "inspected it and got the police to shut it on down" (*CS*, 248).[6] Like many of O'Connor's protagonists, the child learns that willful rebellion like hers, rather than submissive piety, leads to paradise.

The story's conclusion is especially noteworthy because the protagonist seems to achieve a momentary, redemptive freedom without clearly achieving an ideal. We can be more certain that the child achieves a moment of redemption from the limited, passive role assigned her by the narrator, than we can be that she achieves maturity (arguably a nonexistent quality in O'Connor's works). If we are to conclude that the child achieves an understanding of an ideal, I think we have to look back to the child's understanding of the hermaphrodite as both two-headed and headless. In the child's identification with the hermaphrodite, we may feel that she equates obliteration with the doubleness (and the ideal) of marriage.

In many ways, "The Partridge Festival" seems totally unlike "A Temple of the Holy Ghost." The protagonist, Calhoun, one of O'Connor's pseudointellectuals, returns to his ancestral home of Partridge to write an exposé of the town's treatment of a man named Singleton, who had shot five prominent citizens and one bystander at the start of the azalea festival founded by Calhoun's great-grandfather. Critics of the story find in it little more than the unmasking of Calhoun. Leon Driskill says that "The Partridge Festival" is a "story which bleakly lays out the facts of human frailty without illumination of hope" and which "suggests the impossibility of overcoming one's natural propensity."[7] O'Connor herself did not rate the story highly. In a letter dated 21 May 1964 to Robert Giroux, O'Connor called "The Partridge Festival" a "very sorry story" (*HB*, 579), one that she did not want to include in her second story collection.

One of the most interesting things about "The Partridge Festival"—and what seems to separate it from "A Temple of the Holy Ghost"—is that even though it is a late story and even though its characters go through the sort of psychic transformation typical of O'Connor's characters, there is little explicit reference to religion. The near absence of religious reference in this story suggests either that the transformation O'Connor characters experience is *not* essentially religious, or—the alternative I prefer—that the religiosity of the characters' experience need not be translated into religious terminology to be understood. What makes "The Partridge Festival" comparable to one of O'Connor's most explicitly Catholic stories is the complex interplay between the grotesque and the ideal. A festival, according to Bakhtin an institutionalized use of the grotesque, is here idealized and trivialized, or at least it is in the mind of Calhoun, who "expected to write something that would vindicate the madman" (*CS*, 424). The fact that the festival was founded by the protagonist's great-grandfather might seem to make it more difficult for him to enter into the genuinely festive spirit, but actually this fact makes it easier. Calhoun's resentments about his community and ancestors allow him to supply some of the destructive impulse necessary for a true carnival. Consequently, Calhoun, more clearly than most characters in O'Connor who follow similar patterns, works to achieve a place in a community through his very *attack* upon that community. Calhoun's commercial activity is a clear indication that Calhoun longs to be part of a community; he tells himself that his earnings as a salesman allow him to be an individualistic, genuine "rebel-artist-mystic" nine

months of the year, but he knows he does the selling only because
he likes it.

Calhoun's strategy for bringing about his reentry into his community is to appear to do the opposite; by taking the festival as the
essence of Partridge, he turns his attacks into affirmations. In trying
to grotesquely invert the values of Partridge, Calhoun becomes,
like his great-grandfather, a founder of its celebration. To bring
himself back full circle to his great-grandfather's values, Calhoun
identifies with the man he consciously believes to be his great-
grandfather's opposite—Singleton. Rather than consciously recog-
nizing his resemblance to the "round-faced, bald, altogether unre-
markable-looking" (p. 422) great-grandfather and his ilk, Calhoun
tells himself that he resembles the murderer: "Though his eyes were
not mismatched, the shape of his face was broad like Singleton's;
but the real likeness between them was interior" (p. 423). Calhoun
insists upon his resemblance to Singleton so that he will eventually
be forced to acknowledge their real relationship. Unconsciously,
Calhoun acknowledges the resemblance between himself and his
great-grandfather, and consequently, between himself and all of
Singleton's victims. And while he says he wants to identify with
Singleton, he also thinks of himself and Singleton as near opposites,
for Calhoun resembles both Singleton and the great-grandfather:
"His doubleness, his shadow, was cast before him more darkly than
usual in the light of Singleton's purity" (p. 424).

There are signs throughout the story that Calhoun senses unconsciously that he is transforming himself. When Calhoun called his
Aunt Bessie to tell her that he was coming to Partridge, he told
himself that he was coming "because Singleton had captured his
imagination," but he tells his aunt that "he was coming to enjoy the
festival" (p. 421). The ambiguity of the phrase "coming to enjoy"
expresses Calhoun's longing to learn to be a part of the festival even
though he tells himself that the statement is hypocritical. As Calhoun and a woman he meets, Mary Elizabeth, discuss Singleton
and attack Partridge, they actually call into question the corruption
of the festival and the town. In a sense, Singleton's shooting of the
five dignitaries is perfectly in line with the purposes of festival. The
bringing down of powerful figures had already been represented
within the festival by Singleton's imprisonment for not buying a
festival badge, and Singleton's revenge is a more elaborate version
of the same element of festival. Moreover, Calhoun's view of
Singleton as a heroic figure actually makes the mass murderer
better suited to the role of scapegoat. The fact that the festival's

founder would not have seen the shooting as reason to end the festival strikes Calhoun as corrupt, but according to the standards of festival—at once celebratory and destructive—the great-grand-father's attitude would have been reasonable. Consequently, the "languid reverence" (p. 426) with which the people of Partridge observe the spilled blood on the courthouse porch is appropriate for one phase of the festival cycle.

Calhoun's similarity to Singleton is a similarity he shares with the people of Partridge. The little girl Calhoun meets says that Singleton is a "bad bad bad man," but she quickly adds that if people were cruel to her, she too would "shoot them" (p. 429). Calhoun assumes that the punishment of Singleton requires that the town feel superior to him, but this child instinctively realizes that Singleton is in everyone. Even the aesthetic standards Calhoun professes reinforce the spirit of carnival. "Life does not abide in abstractions" (p. 436), Calhoun says; this principle explains the need for festival. Mary Elizabeth's disgusted assertion that "they prostitute azaleas!" (p. 434) also points to an element of festival: any ideal, even that of a flower, is undercut by the spirit of festival. And as Calhoun gets to know Mary Elizabeth, with whom he has much in common, it becomes clear that rebellion itself does not isolate one completely from society. The malice that the couple express toward each other demonstrates their conviction that they share hypocrisy, and each attacks the other knowing on some level that both will be unmasked.

As Calhoun and Mary Elizabeth prepare to go see the murderer, there are several indications that Calhoun expects the actual Singleton he finds at Quincy State Hospital. Calhoun suspects that "it would be better to see Singleton at a later date when he would perhaps have responded to treatment" (p. 437). And when he tries to reconstruct his ideal image of Singleton, Calhoun cannot bring himself to hold to the picture: "Calhoun tried to concentrate on Singleton. Feature by feature, he brought the face together in his mind and each time he had it almost constructed, it fell apart and he was left with nothing" (pp. 438–39). Insofar as he expects the visit to challenge his salesman self, he fears the visit. But Calhoun also dreams that when he visits Singleton, it will be to sell him a refrigerator.

Singleton, of course, turns out to be an insane animal who tries to expose himself to his horrified visitors. When Calhoun and Mary Elizabeth are back in their car, they see Singleton's face in each other. They are surprised, not because Singleton is unlike them, but because he is too much like them. And, almost immediately, Calhoun extends his resemblance to Singleton to include a resemblance to his merchant great-grandfather. The ending of "The Partridge Festival" has produced a variety of interpretations. Kathleen Feeley, for example, calls the moment at which Calhoun and Mary Elizabeth sense their kinship to Singleton a "false epiphany,"[8] to be followed by their true one. Carter Martin considers the story "ambiguous to a fault,"[9] in part because drafts of the story suggest more positive endings than the "stultifying and ambiguous capitulation to mediocrity" that the published version seems to provide.[10] George D. Murphy and Caroline L. Cherry, who say that Singleton "represents the unconscious," feel that Calhoun, having "romanticized both the unconscious and the process of individuation," is able only to settle for "the safety that the constricted values of the unintegrated, consciousness-oriented personality provide."[11]

But what Calhoun realizes at the end of the story is that he is both the dull founder of a community project *and* the animalistic destroyer essential to the festival, and that the role of destroyer is always to be followed by the role of community leader. If there were no link between the master salesman/great-grandfather and Singleton in the festival process, Calhoun's revelation would indeed seem inconsistent. In his acknowledgement of resemblance to these two individuals linked in ritual, however, Calhoun rejoins a larger festive community. And the great-aunt's harping on the need for Calhoun to find himself a girl is climaxed by the feeling, shared by Calhoun and Mary Elizabeth, that the visit with Singleton produces a "predestined convergence" likely to lead to "marriage or instantaneous deaths" (*CS*, 442). In the context of Calhoun's and Mary Elizabeth's final revelation, their relationship seems destined to result in the height of conventionality. As in "A Temple of the Holy Ghost," marriage indirectly becomes one of the story's ideals; we can at least conclude that the dread felt by Calhoun and Mary Elizabeth for what they see coming ensures that the next festival will take place. While Calhoun may thus seem to be a representative of twentieth-century separation from folk wisdom, the story of his unmasking is also in some ways a demonstration of the ability of Calhoun and his ilk to reconnect themselves to the vital currents of communal wisdom. Even as he rejoins the mundane community of Partridge, he achieves a redemptive freedom from the restricted role of ineffectual rebel assigned him by the narrator. And at the story's end, Calhoun seems to realize that he has in himself the spirit of the ancestor "whose gift of life had pushed straight forward to the future to raise festival after festival" (p. 444).

Like "A Temple of the Holy Ghost," "The Partridge Festival" points to the future rather than resolving itself neatly, but the process these stories reflect is essential to O'Connor's works. The juxtaposition of these stories makes an excellent case for the religious quality of all of O'Connor's works, no matter how secular they seem and no matter how peculiar the redemptions may be. The child's experience in "A Temple of the Holy Ghost" is obviously religious, although her redemption seems unusual. The similarity between Calhoun's experience and the child's suggests that everything in O'Connor is religious, including the positively grotesque process. The importance of the cyclical nature of the grotesque—constantly reengaging and reforming oppressive ideals, especially religious ones—should not be understated. If the grotesque merely led back to ideals without changing them, and without producing communal freedom, the grotesque could be considered merely a part of the ideals' strategy for perpetuating themselves. It is part of the paradox of each of these stories—and, to some extent, of all of O'Connor's works—that the force which drives characters to use the grotesque seems to come simultaneously from within the characters themselves and from within the community. The child transforms herself but also seems to react to a Catholic tradition of the new ritual; Calhoun tricks himself into conventionality but also seems to be following his ancestors' pattern. It may seem that the child and Calhoun are caught up in forces over which they have no control, but I would insist that the individual's contribution to the use of the grotesque is essential to its positive potential. If the individual makes no contribution, the grotesque remains negative, reactionary, distracting.

This problem resembles the one raised by Peter Barnes's play *Laughter!* which opens with the Author on stage to attack comedy: "A sense of humor's no remedy for evil. Isn't that why the Devil's always smiling? The stupid're never truly laughed out of their stupidities, fools remain fools, the corrupt, violent and depraved remain corrupt, violent and depraved. Laughter's the ally of tyrants."[12] The Author goes on to claim that "laughter's too feeble a weapon against the barbarities of life. A balm for battles lost, standard equipment for the losing side; the powerful have no need of it." And as if to reinforce this attack on comedy, the play's epilogue presents two Jewish comics in concentration-camp clothing, feebly telling jokes as they die:

> Bieberstein: I could be wrong but I think this act is dying.
> Bimko: The way to beat hydro-cyanide gas is by holding your breath

for five minutes. It's just a question of mind over matter. They don't mind and we don't matter.

They fall to their knees.

Bieberstein: Those foul, polluted German bastardized . . .

Bimko: Hymie, Hymie, please; what you want to do—cause trouble?

They collapse on the floor, gasping.[13]

It is easy to romanticize the grotesque, as many critics and writers—especially southern writers—have done, to forget that despite its playfulness, the grotesque is a complex strategy, easily trivialized. "A Temple of the Holy Ghost" and "The Partridge Festival" make clear that the purpose of the grotesque is never fully accomplished; for a moment of redemption to last, the redeemed character must die, as many O'Connor characters do. And because the achievement of ideals in both these stories is ambiguous, the importance of the relationship between protagonist and narrator becomes more apparent. Certainly the child and Calhoun manage to free themselves from the narrator's constraints, so that in the rivalry between narrator and character we find our clearest evidence of redemption. The stories discussed in the next chapter, two of them among O'Connor's most popular, almost obscure the complex interplay between narration and the grotesque.

1. May, in *The Pruning Word,* says that the hermaphrodite's message "transforms a hateful child into a maturing adolescent" (p. 74). Allen, in "Memories of a Southern Catholic Girlhood," says that "the child unconsciously realizes that her ugly behavior defiles the Spirit of Love that dwells in her, a Temple of the Holy Ghost" (pp. 88–89).

2. Hendin, in *World of O'Connor,* says that the tradition behind the "freak's mass" produces "a gothic veneration of ugliness and deformity as signs of grace, and of the fortunate nature of the fall," but she also says that the grotesque religion of the child's dream "has lost its sense of heaven" (p. 84).

3. Consequently, the child's concentration on the hermaphrodite's head does not, as Louise Westling says, in "O'Connor's Mothers and Daughters," p. 521, merely transform a sexual issue into a religious one. Kahane, in "Gothic Mirrors and Feminine Identity," makes a statement something like Westling's: the hermaphrodite's "freakishness is a sign of grace precisely because it is never visually defined" (p. 61). The child's uncertainty about the hermaphrodite's body fosters the child's fantasies, but they do not as a result exclude the grotesquely physical.

4. Martin, in *The True Country,* p. 112, says that this line shows the limit of the child's transformation. And A. R. Coulthard, in "From Sermon to Parable," says that this line "casts some final doubt on whether the young protagonist's conversion has really taken" (p. 58).

5. My argument that the story strongly implies the continuation of the grotesque process provides an answer to Louise Westling's argument that O'Connor allows her protagonist the comfortable illusion that she can ignore the future. See *Sacred Groves and Ravaged Gardens,* pp. 142–43.

6. It may seem that this story presents a critique of Protestantism as cut off from the positive qualities of the grotesque, for Protestants apparently shut down the fair, and the Protestant Wilkins boys are horrified by the Catholic song about a new ritual. On the basis of such details, apparently, Suzanne Allen says, "Because of the individualism of their evangelical belief, [such characters] cannot accept their part in the physical world . . ." ("Memories of a Southern Catholic Girlhood," p. 84). The Wilkinses themselves suggest a link between religion and physicality, however, when they sing hymns as love songs, and the Wilkinses supply the car that is essential to the Catholic girls' increased awareness of the physical grotesque.

7. Driskill, " 'Parker's Back' vs. 'The Partridge Festival,' " pp. 483, 487.

8. Feeley, *Flannery O'Connor*, p. 49.

9. Martin, "Genesis of O'Connor's 'The Partridge Festival,' " p. 47.

10. The drafts are discussed ibid., pp. 51–52. The quotation is from p. 51.

11. Murphy and Cherry, "O'Connor and Integration of Personality," p. 90.

12. Barnes, *Laughter!* (London: Heinemann, 1978), p. 2.

13. Ibid., p. 70.

4

MEN GENTLY SCOLDED

Parker, Mr. Head, Tanner

Be a sinner and sin boldly.

—Martin Luther,
1 August 1521 letter to Philip Melanchthon

THE SIGNIFICANCE of O'Connor's authoritarian narration becomes most apparent in those stories where the narrator is less critical of the protagonist. In "Parker's Back," "The Artificial Nigger," and "Judgement Day," we have protagonists who redeem themselves, but in each instance the narrator is comparatively mild. "Parker's Back" and "The Artificial Nigger" are nevertheless among O'Connor's most popular stories. The shift in "Parker's Back" away from O'Connor's usual relationship between narration and the grotesque raises interesting questions about her art. The narration of "The Artificial Nigger" produces ambiguity. Only in "Judgement Day" is the narration seriously limiting.

In these stories, the narrator seems to understand the protagonist thoroughly and to analyze the protagonist's psyche accurately. As the narrator's pronouncements take over, several problems arise. The reader loses the inclination to pay close attention to a protagonist's unconscious maneuvers. When the narrator accurately describes, analyzes, and approves of a character's unconscious maneuverings, the reader wonders why those maneuvers have to be unconscious. Differences between the character and the narrator then produce not meaning, as is the case in most of O'Connor's works, but mere ambiguity. In none of the stories discussed in this chapter do the characters free themselves entirely from the role ascribed by the narrator. I realize I may be accused of taking these stories to task for nonconformity to my critical construct; consequently I shall attempt to explain the extent to which they are simply O'Connor's attempts to write in response to particular motives and according to different artistic rules.

The comic elements and religious message of "Parker's Back" have led many critics to name this story O'Connor's best. The reason for such estimates, I believe, is that "Parker's Back" is explicit about the protagonist's unconscious use of the positive grotesque; the narrator apparently agrees that Parker's unconscious redeems him. But the story may lose something because of the narrator's sympathy for and understanding of Parker; we are drawn away from the psyche of the character and toward the narrator's neat analyses. When Parker has the tractor accident that sends him to have his back tattooed, for example, we are not encouraged to interpret Parker's unconscious strategy in contrast to a narrator's strictly orthodox explanation. The narrator's assertions, such as that "if he had known how to cross himself he would have done it" (*CS*, 520), fill in the particulars of Parker's psyche. And as the narrator's voice shows itself to be authoritative, Parker and the grotesque are both in danger of becoming trivial. If the narrator makes clear the story's ideals, the grotesque tattoos on Parker degrade and enliven ideals only for him; for the reader, closer of course to the narrator, Parker's maneuvers become mere entertainment. Several critics have noted Parker's similarity to Enoch Emery in *Wise Blood,* but the narration of the Enoch sections in the novel is quite different from the narration of Parker's story.

Not all critics have admired "Parker's Back." Carol Shloss calls it "contrived, its message offered at the expense of credibility."[1] And David Eggenschwiler nearly adopts my perspective when he says that Parker "is probably Miss O'Connor's most obvious case of subliminated will to believe. In fact, the story suffers from being too pat, too explicit throughout in its symbols and authorial comments."[2] O'Connor herself said in a letter dated 21 January 1961 that "getting the right tone" for "Parker's Back" was giving her "a lot of trouble" (*HB*, 427). But these dismissals of the story are overly harsh; "Parker's Back" works according to rules different from those of other stories, and O'Connor's own doubts may be discounted. After all, she had doubts about almost everything she wrote. "Parker's Back" deserves our attention here because Parker's self-redemption is so explicit, and because, to some extent, O'Connor manages to transfer the narrator's usual function to a character—Parker's wife, Sarah Ruth Cates.

Parker refuses to approach religion directly: when his mother tried to drag him to a revival, he ran away from home and joined the navy (*CS*, 513). The formula for Parker's grotesque transformation and his return to religion is easy to pinpoint. The start of Parker's feeling for tattoos came when he saw a tattooed man at the fair; he became obsessed with tattoos, and the narrator tells us that he was changed without his knowledge. What impressed Parker about the man at the fair was that "the arabesque of men and beasts and flowers on his skin appeared to have a subtle motion of its own" (ibid.). In other words, Parker is fascinated by his vision of the communion of all physical existence. Tattoos clearly suggest the positive physical grotesque.

Parker forces himself into a psychic transformation through his marriage to Sarah Ruth Cates, whose strict religious standards represent for Parker the ideals he unconsciously desires. Parker establishes contact with religious ideals through his physical attraction for the woman he associates with those ideals, and his constant protests about the marriage allow him to avoid admitting his attraction. The decision to have a tattoo of the suffering face of Christ put on his back, then, is part of Parker's unconscious strategy for using his devotion to his wife to bring himself to Christ. Parker's conscious motivation in getting the tattoo of Christ on his back is to please his wife: "He visualized having a tattoo put there that Sarah Ruth would not be able to resist—a religious subject" (p. 519). Although Sarah Ruth denies such a connection, of course, Parker is still operating on the connection between religion and sex he used when he first said to her, "I'd be saved enough if you was to kiss me" (p. 518).

Parker overcomes his reluctance to have a tattoo on his back, the only place left for one, by seeing a sign. Parker interprets an accident—he runs a tractor into a tree—as a religious experience from which there is no turning back: he thought that "there had been a great change in his life, a leap forward into a worse unknown, and that there was nothing he could do about it. It was for all intents accomplished" (p. 521). Then when he chooses the pattern for his tattoo, he considers his choice to be out of his hands. Leafing through the book of tattoos, Parker hears a voice telling him to "GO BACK" to a particular face of Christ; this is the one that he orders the tattooist to put on him. What attracts Parker to the Byzantine Christ with its "all-demanding eyes" (p. 522) is its resemblance to Sarah Ruth, who also has penetrating eyes. When Parker returns home, the results are surprising but inevitable. For a moment, as he pronounces his full secret name (Obadiah Elihue Parker) to Sarah Ruth at the door, Parker's tattoo is successful in revealing the secret self Parker has been making himself into: "All at once he felt the light pouring through him, turning his spider web soul into a perfect arabesque of colors, a garden of trees and birds and beasts" (p. 528). This momentary vision fulfills the promise of the positive grotesque; as Melissa Hines points out, Parker's grotesquerie goes all the way back to the origins of the grotesque "in architectural decoration."[3] But when Parker shows the tattoo to Sarah Ruth, she is no less demanding than before:

> "God? God don't look like that!"
> "What do you know how he looks?" Parker moaned. "You ain't seen him."
> "He don't *look*," Sarah Ruth said. "He's a spirit. No man shall see his face."
> "Aw listen," Parker groaned, "this is just a picture of him."
> "Idolatry!" Sarah Ruth screamed. "Idolatry! Enflaming yourself with idols under every green tree! I can put up with lies and vanity but I don't want no idolator in this house!" and she grabbed up the broom and began to thrash him across the shoulders with it. (*CS,* 529)

From one perspective, it is easy to fit this ending into the pattern found in other stories. As soon as Parker approaches the ideal, he must be shocked back into a renewal of the grotesque cycle; as we saw in the last chapter, the grotesque is never satisfied. But it is appropriate that as Parker is symbolically reborn at the end—our last view of Parker shows him "leaning against the tree, crying like a baby" (p. 530)—he has also become a grotesque Christ like the one on his back. However mild the story's narration, the final image of "large welts . . . formed on the face of the tattooed Christ" (p. 529) makes clear the basic connection between religion and the grotesque.

The real complexity of "Parker's Back" comes from the similarity of Sarah Ruth Cates to the typical O'Connor narrator. Sarah Ruth is one of the most authoritarian figures in O'Connor's works, exceeded, if at all, only by Hazel Motes's mother. Although Parker is attracted to her religion, the kind of religion she represents for him is ambiguous. On one hand, in her similarity to Christ, she represents an ideal; on the other hand, she also professes a degraded set of religious strictures. She is "forever sniffing up sin" (p. 510) and even considers churches "idolatrous" (p. 518). Parker needs both of Sarah Ruth's symbolic roles. She implies ideal religion even as she torments Parker with her degraded standards, and thus she both represents Parker's goal and—somewhat like the typical O'Connor narrator—indicates the need for the indirection of the grotesque in reaching that goal.

In light of Sarah Ruth's complexity, Parker's experience also seems more complex. In most O'Connor stories, the protagonist

achieves communal freedom by escaping the restricted role assigned by the narrator. In "Parker's Back," however, Parker seems
to achieve his first real sense of individuality simultaneously with
his introduction to communal life; it is as he names himself fully at
the doorway that he has his vision of himself as "a garden of trees
and birds and beasts" (p. 528). In a sense, the story questions the
usual sequence from the individual to the communal. The ending
further complicates matters. Although Parker's beating at the end
may appear to deny the success of his tattoo, in actuality the tattoo
produces the desired effects. Sarah Ruth is made angry, and the
beating reveals Parker's entrance into the suffering community. It is
hard to believe Parker does not on some level desire his beating, for
he had seen Sarah Ruth at their first meeting as an "angel" (p. 512)
even though she beat him with a broom then as well. What is
surprising about the ending is that we get our most moving illustration of Parker's need for the grotesque—his inability to live up to
Sarah Ruth's standards—after he has apparently succeeded in reaching his ideals. He seems, appropriately, to have the time sequence
backward. The ultimate positive effect of Sarah Ruth's complexity,
I think, is to open up "Parker's Back" so that it illustrates at least
three contradictory theories about the relationship between redemption and history. To some extent, Parker's redemption involves going backward to a paradise of birds, beasts, flowers, and
men, but Parker also seems to achieve redemption through the
cyclical process of the grotesque, and his redemption also implies
evolutionary progress. The story thus comments upon the rest of
O'Connor's work; many readers will agree that Sarah Ruth's complexity more than compensates for whatever simplification there is
to Parker's characterization.

Like "Parker's Back," "The Artificial Nigger" has gotten its share
of votes as one of O'Connor's best stories, and Sally Fitzgerald
reports that O'Connor "often" said the story was "the best thing
she would ever write" (*HB*, xviii). The most interesting praise for
the story comes from Carol Shloss, a critic generally skeptical of
religious readings; Shloss considers "The Artificial Nigger" to be
"one of [O'Connor's] most engaging stories," apparently because
of "O'Connor's willingness to assume the full privilege of omniscient author."[4] However, Shloss's argument points to a problem in
"The Artificial Nigger." As Shloss says, the narrator is basically
authoritative—there is nothing in the head of Mr. Head that the
narrator does not know—but the narrator consistently describes the
experiences of Mr. Head and his grandson, Nelson, in terms which

are much too elevated for either of them to understand. There is more of a gap between the narrator and Mr. Head than there is between the narrator of "Parker's Back" and O. E. Parker, but in "The Artificial Nigger" it is difficult to figure out what to make of this gap. The narrator's pronouncements generally reinforce and extend what seems to be going on in Mr. Head's psyche. Consequently, those places where Mr. Head and the narrator have different views of what is going on tend to undercut the reader's opinion of Mr. Head: whereas most of O'Connor's protagonists achieve freedom by turning away from the narrator's strictures, Mr. Head's departures from the narrator's ideals lead him into error.

Nevertheless the narration makes it clear that the protagonist, Mr. Head, uses a trip to Atlanta to transform himself. Although O'Connor's drafts of the story sometimes treat Nelson as the more important character,[5] Mr. Head is actually the protagonist of the published version. It is Mr. Head who has had some previous experience with the city and who unconsciously considers the city to be the home of transcendental realities. In order to force himself to take the trip, Mr. Head tells himself that it "was to be a lesson that the boy would never forget. He was to find out from it that he had no cause for pride merely because he had been born in a city. He was to find out that the city was not a great place" (*CS*, 251). And in order to make sure that Mr. Head forces himself to see a large portion of the city, he tells himself that Nelson needs "to see everything there is to see in a city so that he would be content to stay at home for the rest of his life." One of the ideals Mr. Head unconsciously desires to subvert is his own authority. He and Nelson constantly bicker over Mr. Head's parental authority, and as long as they stay in the country, Mr. Head's authority is secure. When Nelson questions whether Mr. Head knows his way around the city after fifteen years away from it, Mr. Head asks Nelson if he has ever seen Mr. Head lost. Nelson answers, "It's nowhere around here to get lost at" (p. 250), and it is precisely this possibility for getting lost that makes the city Mr. Head's desired destination. As Mr. Head and Nelson make their train trip, Mr. Head shows and explains as many things as possible to Nelson in order to reinforce his authority, including Nelson's "first nigger" (p. 255). The black man Nelson sees is immediately made part of the power struggle between Nelson and Mr. Head, and Nelson's "fierce raw fresh hate" (p. 256) for the black man is a result of the black man's place in this struggle.

When Mr. Head and Nelson arrive in the city and leave the domed train terminal, Mr. Head's severe lack of confidence—expressed through the narrator's diction—betrays his unconscious desire to become lost: "He *thought* that *if* he *could* keep the dome *always* in sight, he *would* be able [my emphases] to get back in the afternoon to catch the train again" (p. 258). Because he has brought along Nelson, Mr. Head obliges himself to keep moving, constantly increasing the likelihood of getting lost. What Mr. Head expects to experience once he is lost becomes apparent when he tells Nelson about the "sewer system, how the entire city was underlined with it, how it contained all the drainage and was full of rats and how a man could slide into it and be sucked along down endless pitchblack tunnels" (p. 259). These tunnels and their blackness take on more significance as the story proceeds. Nelson relates the sewers "with the entrance to hell and understood for the first time how the world was put together in its lower parts" (ibid.). As soon as Nelson notices that Mr. Head has taken him in a circle, Mr. Head picks a path that gets them lost, and we become aware of another, more problematic meaning of the pitch-black tunnels. Shortly after he takes the new path, the sexual implications of the city become apparent: "Mr. Head, glancing through one window, saw a woman lying on an iron bed, looking out, with a sheet pulled over her. Her knowing expression shook him" (p. 260). Later Nelson has a similar and more explicit experience; when they are thoroughly lost in a black section of town, he asks a black woman for directions and is overwhelmed by her: "He wanted to look down and down into her eyes while she held him tighter and tighter. He had never had such a feeling before. He felt as if he were reeling down through a pitch-black tunnel" (p. 262).

The more Mr. Head asserts his authority, the more certain is his overthrow and his fall into the tunnels. When Nelson takes a nap, Mr. Head hides behind a garbage can so that when Nelson awakes, he will think he has been abandoned; Mr. Head tells himself that "it is sometimes necessary to teach a child a lesson he won't forget, particularly when the child is always reasserting his position with some new impudence" (p. 264). It is worth noting that as Nelson sleeps, he is "half conscious of vague noises and black forms moving up from some dark part of him into the light." The connection between blackness and the unconscious in this line is reinforced by O'Connor when she refers, in a letter dated 4 May 1955, to "black forms moving up from [Nelson's] unconscious" (*HB,* 78). Mr. Head's strategy succeeds in bringing about what he desires when Nelson awakes. Nelson runs down the street, collides with a woman, and injures her ankle, and Mr. Head's authority receives the ultimate challenge: the injured woman calls out, "You've bro-

ken my ankle and your daddy'll pay for it! Every nickel! Police!
Police!" (*CS*, 264). As Mr. Head approaches the scene of the accident, we are told that "he had never in his life been accosted by a
policeman" (p. 265). And when he imagines "the approach of the
policeman from behind," Mr. Head subverts his authority over
Nelson: " 'This is not my boy,' he said. 'I never seen him before.' "
The fact of the matter is that "there was no policeman in sight," but
Mr. Head has achieved his downfall, and as Nelson makes evident
his refusal to forgive him, Mr. Head feels himself making the
descent that he had prepared: "The old man felt that if he saw a
sewer entrance he would drop down into it and let himself be
carried away" (p. 267).

But the symbolism of blackness promises both descent and renewal. As Mr. Head feels himself "wandering into a black strange
place," Nelson feels the power of blackness preparing him to forgive Mr. Head: "But every now and then his mouth would twitch
and this was when he felt, from some remote place inside himself, a
black mysterious form reach up as if it would melt his frozen vision
in one hot grasp" (p. 267). Mr. Head projects the next stage of his
spiritual renewal onto a bald man in knickers walking his bulldogs.
Mr. Head at once asks for directions to the train and to forgiveness:
"Oh Gawd I'm lost! Oh hep me Gawd I'm lost!" Although he gets
directions to the train, Mr. Head must receive Nelson's forgiveness,
and the occasion (although perhaps not the cause) for the forgiveness is a grotesque lawn statue of a black male of indeterminate
age. O'Connor wrote in a letter dated 4 May 1955 that "what I had
in mind to suggest with the artificial nigger was the redemptive
quality of the Negro's suffering for us all" (*HB*, 78), but the statue
has provoked a wide variety of interpretations.

On the basis of the connections I have pointed out, one would
expect that the statue brings together conclusively for Mr. Head
and Nelson the battle for authority and the symbolism of blackness. They gaze at the statue "as if they were faced with some great
mystery, some monument to another's victory that brought them
together in their common defeat" (*CS*, 269). Just as Mr. Head and
Nelson have been defeated by each other and by the city, the statue
suggests the defeat of blacks by the city and by whites. Mr. Head
blurts out as he attempts to "explain once and for all the mystery of
existence" for Nelson, "They ain't got enough real ones here. They
got to have an artificial one." The pronoun "they" refers here to the
city that oppresses both the blacks and Mr. Head. The statue also
brings the symbolism of blackness to something of a conclusion,
for, whatever our uncertainty about the ending (which I shall

discuss shortly), the statue suggests the community of the unconscious and the power of the grotesquerie that can accompany degradation and defeat. Although the statue "was meant [by its maker] to look happy," its grotesquerie expresses a different message, much as the grotesquerie of the usual O'Connor protagonist does: "The chipped eye and the angle he was cocked at gave him a wild look of misery instead" (p. 268). The white men share with the statue not only a "common defeat," but also a common strategy for overcoming that defeat.

It should be noticed that the statue does not resolve everything. The sexual theme that Mr. Head and Nelson associate with blackness is forgotten. This omission suggests that Mr. Head's final understanding of his experience can only be partial, although Mr. Head feels as he gets off the train back home that he understands life completely:

> Mr. Head stood very still and felt the action of mercy touch him again but this time he knew that there were no words in the world that could name it. He understood that it grew out of agony, which is not denied to any man and which is given in strange ways to children. He understood it was all a man could carry into death to give his Maker and he suddenly burned with shame that he had so little of it to take with him. He stood appalled, judging himself with the thoroughness of God, while the action of mercy covered his pride like a flame and consumed it. He had never thought himself a great sinner before but he saw now that his true depravity had been hidden from him lest it cause him despair. He realized that he was forgiven for sins from the beginning of time, when he had conceived in his own heart the sin of Adam, until the present, when he had denied poor Nelson. He saw that no sin was too monstrous for him to claim as his own, and since God loved in proportion as He forgave, he felt ready at that instant to enter Paradise. (Pp. 269–70)

Ronald Schleifer says, "We never question the fact that the realization described—its language and its theology—is simply beyond the frontier language and evangelical Christianity of Mr. Head."[6] But actually the gap between the narrator's pronouncement and the character's understanding has caused considerable debate. Gilbert H. Muller praises the ending, saying that it "produces an astonishing effect which combines a disengagement from the climax with a prolongation of the moral consequences."[7] The basis for such praise seems often to be that the narrator's voice, assumed to be totally accurate, takes care of any apparent problems. Louis D. Rubin, Jr., goes so far as to say that it is "essential" that "the authorial voice . . . offers a final, summarizing commentary in which the human meaning and significance of what has happened are pronounced."[8] However, other critics have considered the narration a problem. Louise Y. Gossett says that the ending "slips into exegesis rather than narration."[9] And A. R. Coulthard considers the conversion of Mr. Head to be "so overstated . . . that one is tempted to speculate that it is intended to be bogus."[10] Although Coulthard does not consider Mr. Head's conversion bogus, several critics have taken that step. Paul W. Nisly considers Mr. Head "locked in the complete isolation of . . . pride and self-love."[11] It is worth noting that O'Connor's drafts for "The Artificial Nigger" make the ending more ambiguous, and that, as Frederick Asals points out, in the drafts Mr. Head's conclusions about his experience are "clearly erroneous."[12]

I belabor the critical controversy over the penultimate paragraph of "The Artificial Nigger" because I believe the controversy results from the story's uncharacteristic narration. We become most aware of the gap between the narrator's language and Mr. Head's understanding in the penultimate paragraph, but the gap has existed all along. Our consciousness of the gap grows in this paragraph because the narrator presumes to close the gap, to equate the narrator's formulations with Mr. Head's thoughts, and it becomes extremely difficult to know how much of the narrator's authority to attribute to Mr. Head. Prior to the ending, the narrator's comparison of events and characters in the story to more elevated parallels has not caused serious problems. Early in the story, for example, the narrator says that Mr. Head "might have been Vergil summoned in the middle of the night to go to Dante" (*CS*, 250). Such elevated comparisons are easily understood as the narrator's satirical exaggeration of Mr. Head's too-high opinion of himself. But as the similarities between Mr. Head's experiences and Dante's *Inferno* pile up, one wonders what to make of the parallel. Critics have constructed readings on the basis of parallels between Mr. Head's and Nelson's trip and the journey of Dante into hell, but in general, such parallels merely point out the narrator's view, which is overstated. At the end, when the narrator's view and Mr. Head's view seem to combine, the reader is likely to stumble. Mr. Head knows nothing of the parallels to the *Inferno* that might justify a high estimation of his experience, and the narrator ignores the overly ideal quality of Mr. Head's final state.

Using the grotesque as a standard, I propose two observations. In this story, which has probably the most explicitly spelled out religious experience in O'Connor's works, a religious experience which the narrator considers complete and secure, the characters retreat most forcefully from their insights. Their religious experience is apparently genuine, but having penetrated to the heart of communal mystery in the city, the men rush back to their country town, to its false security, and to their individual identity. Nelson's final words—"I'm glad I've went once, but I'll never go back again!" (p. 270)—indicate that the two have no intention of allowing their ideals to be tested ever again. Having never freed themselves from the narrator, they seem to be in danger of settling for a constricted religious sense. From a second point of view, however, such a closure of the grotesque process is impossible. Nelson's assertion that he intends to stay at home forever resembles Mr. Head's assertions early in the story that he dislikes the city. Nelson's ideals will surely be tested again. Only at the end are we likely to realize that such an unstated, unconscious inclination to continue the grotesque process is preferable to the narrator's pronouncements.

Despite Ralph C. Wood's argument that "Judgement Day" opened "new possibilities"[13] for O'Connor that she did not live to explore, "Judgement Day" seems to me to mark the less-than-successful end of O'Connor's struggle to rework the material with which she began her career. For several reasons, O'Connor's first published story, "The Geranium," concerns a protagonist with whom the author sympathizes, and although she made many changes as she revised the story, she never overcame her sympathy for her protagonist. The revision of "The Geranium" into "Judgement Day" is important because critics often use these two stories to generalize about O'Connor's increasing skill and religiosity during her career; several critics, such as Alice Walker and Claire Kahane, have used them to examine O'Connor's views on race relations.[14] Because of the problems with narration, however, it is unfortunate that "The Geranium" and "Judgement Day" have evoked such generalizations.

Examining Tanner's process of self-transformation in "Judgement Day," we find that his conscious and unconscious understandings of it are compatible. He decides that by returning to his black friend, Coleman, in Georgia, he will achieve all that is worth achieving, and Tanner gives his return a religious dimension. He imagines that upon his return he will pretend to be dead, but his fantasy also suggests a faith in his resurrection; he dreams of jumping out of a coffin and announcing Judgment Day to Coleman and Hooten, the train stationmaster. But Tanner's vision of his return need not come in a dream; whereas O'Connor characters' dreams usually express unconscious desires, Tanner need not hide anything from his conscious mind, not even death; imagining his return, Tanner thinks, "Once he got in the freight car, he would lie down and rest. During the night the train would start South, and the next day or the morning after, dead or alive, he would be home. Dead or alive." He adds, "It was being there that mattered; the dead or alive did not" (*CS,* 532). Needless to say, "Judgement Day" contains no oven at the end of the train trip.

In "Judgement Day," then, the protagonist's consciousness, his unconscious, and the narrator's view of things are all compatible. This is not to say that the narrator does not provide grotesque descriptions of Tanner. And certainly the plot of Tanner's story indicates that he uses the grotesque positively. But the grotesque has no necessary function in this story. Tanner's conscious commitment to his ideals is clear; they produce no dread in him for the grotesque to overcome. And even if Tanner does die without achieving his dream literally, such a failure does not matter, because Tanner has no spiritual problems. Another way of stating the problem in the narration of "Judgement Day" is to say that O'Connor was too close to both her protagonist and her narrator. Although critics frequently equate O'Connor with her narrator, "Judgement Day" illustrates the problems that result when such an identification indeed exists. In the early versions of the story, the O'Connor narrator seems to share much of the author's sympathy for her protagonist. "The Geranium," the original version of the story, expresses some of O'Connor's homesickness while she was living in Iowa, and the narration of "The Geranium" presents the extremely regionalistic protagonist as a character thoroughly deserving of sympathy. Dudley, an old white southerner, is stuck in New York City, where he dreams of returning to his old southern home and his friends there. Although O'Connor gives Dudley personality flaws and makes her northern black character appear friendly, the story comes close to sentimental longing for the South. As a consequence of the narrator's sympathy for the protagonist, Dudley's grotesquerie is of the sentimental sort more characteristic of Carson McCullers. O'Connor even considered ending "The Geranium" pathetically, with Dudley's suicide.[15]

The difficulty of revising the story correlates to O'Connor's strong identification with her main character. She directs more satire at the main character in later versions, but the essential identification of narrator with character remains. "Getting Home," a late version of her northern story, suggests O'Connor's awareness of this problem. Here, O'Connor attempts to make the daughter more important, and the old man does not even appear for the first several pages of the story.[16] "An Exile in the East," an earlier revision of "The Geranium," reflects even less progress in O'Connor's continuing struggle with her protagonist's regionalism, despite major plot changes. While "The Geranium" implies that the relationship between Dudley and his southern black friend Rabie is a good one because it follows a southern pattern, "An Exile in the East"[17] is an attempt to *demonstrate* the superiority of a southern form of racial understanding, so that the story approaches propaganda. Whereas in "The Geranium" Dudley and Rabie had lived separately, in "Exile" the two friends, renamed Tanner and Coleman, respectively, had lived together happily for years before Tanner moved to the North. To find O'Connor overcoming her sympathy for her protagonist's narrow regionalism, we must look to "Judgement Day," which presents a weaker connection between southern society and the Tanner/Coleman relationship. In this final revision of O'Connor's northern story, the religious theme finally becomes primary, but O'Connor's narrator still identifies with the protagonist. For an O'Connor character, Tanner is a fairly uninteresting figure, taken up where other protagonists are let go; if O'Connor had continued to focus attention exclusively on Hazel Motes in the last chapter of *Wise Blood,* she might have produced the sentimentality we have in "Judgement Day."

1. Shloss, *O'Connor's Dark Comedies,* p. 113.
2. Eggenschwiler, *Christian Humanism of O'Connor,* p. 74.
3. Hines, "Grotesque Conversions and Critical Piety," p. 26.
4. Shloss, *O'Connor's Dark Comedies,* pp. 118, 123.
5. One draft in the O'Connor Collection, File 158, presents from Nelson's perspective the scene in which he cannot find Mr. Head and runs into a woman.
6. Schleifer, "Rural Gothic," p. 483.
7. Muller, "City of Woe," p. 212.
8. Rubin, "O'Connor's Company of Southerners," p. 69.
9. Gossett, *Violence in Recent Southern Fiction,* p. 96.
10. Coulthard, "From Sermon to Parable," p. 62.
11. Nisly, "Prison of the Self," p. 54.
12. Asals, *Flannery O'Connor,* p. 80; May reprints the ending of a draft of "The Artificial Nigger" in *The Pruning Word,* pp. 160–61.
13. Wood, "From Fashionable Tolerance to Unfashionable Redemption," p. 10.
14. Walker, "Beyond the Peacock"; Kahane, "Artificial Niggers."
15. John May reprints in *The Pruning Word,* pp. 23–24, a typescript variant for the ending from File 12, O'Connor Collection. Stephen Driggers, in "Imaginative Discovery in the O'Connor Typescripts," pp. 1–28, surveys the sequence of stories leading to "Judgement Day." Significant parallels exist between "The Geranium" and parts of McCullers's *The Heart Is a Lonely Hunter,* but O'Connor said the story was inspired by Caroline Gordon's "Old Red" (*HB,* 200).
16. This typescript of "Getting Home" is in File 194, O'Connor Collection.
17. "An Exile in the East," *South Carolina Review* 11 (1978): 12–21.

5

THE GRANDMOTHER'S RELATIVES

"But," cried her heart, casting aside the charm and beginning to ache, "I can't let him go! There must be some way!"
"I won't think of it now," she said again, aloud, trying to
push her misery to the back of her mind, trying to find some
bulwark against the rising tide of pain. "I'll—why, I'll go
home to Tara tomorrow," and her spirits lifted faintly.

—Mitchell,
Gone with the Wind

IN ADDITION TO THE GRANDMOTHER in the early "A Good Man Is
Hard to Find," protagonists in four stories achieve enlightenment
in a manner other than by unconsciously using the grotesque
process. Three of these stories ("A Late Encounter with the Enemy," "A Stroke of Good Fortune," and "The River") are from
O'Connor's first published collection, and one ("Everything That
Rises Must Converge") is a late story. In all four stories the narrator's perspective is never seriously challenged; the narrator's suggestions of negative grotesquerie never give way to positively grotesque maneuvers by the characters. O'Connor wrote few stories of
this sort, one suspects, because such a story is likely to be exclusively satirical, as is the case with "A Late Encounter with the
Enemy" and "A Stroke of Good Fortune." O'Connor's accomplish-
ment in sustaining interest in the grandmother of "A Good Man Is
Hard to Find" impresses us more in comparison to O'Connor's
modest success with the protagonists of these two satirical stories.
"The River" is unique, and important, in O'Connor's corpus,
dealing as it does with a protagonist so innocent of religious concepts as to be in no need of the grotesque as a strategy for redemption. Harry/Bevel Ashfield's experience links the two major versions of redemption this study investigates. In "Everything That
Rises Must Converge," enlightenment is forced upon a character
whose unconscious maneuverings have failed. Julian's experience

suggests a distinction between self-redemption and a more traditional redemption.

Like the grandmother of "A Good Man Is Hard to Find," George Poker Sash of "A Late Encounter with the Enemy" is a negatively grotesque old person with a bad memory, whose only enlightenment comes at death. As he enters the building where his granddaughter, Sally Poker Sash, is about to graduate from college, he feels "a little hole beginning to widen in the top of his head" (*CS,* 141). And as the ceremony proceeds, the hole grows and "General" Sash is overwhelmed, and finally killed, by memories:

> He saw his wife's narrow face looking at him critically through her round gold-rimmed glasses; he saw one of his squinting bald-headed sons; and his mother ran toward him with an anxious look; then a succession of places—Chickamauga, Shiloh, Marthasville—rushed at him as if the past were the only future now and he had to endure it. Then suddenly he saw that the black procession was almost on him. He recognized it, for it had been dogging all his days. He made such a desperate effort to see over it and find out what comes after the past that his hand clenched the sword until the blade touched bone. (P. 143)

The General exemplifies the death of the abstract, clichéd ideal. He had lived the last years of his life doing nothing but embodying the Confederacy at various functions. But as the ideal dies, there is nothing to take its place. It is precisely the absence of freedom, of anything "after the past," that seems to cause his death. What makes the General interesting is that he has no respect for the tired ideals of southern history and family tradition that he represents: "He had forgotten history and he didn't intend to remember it again" (p. 142). To some extent, then, the General allies himself with the satirical narrator's voice, but we cannot say confidently that the General desires redemption. The only thing he knows that he likes in life is his memory of an appearance at a movie première, apparently the première of *Gone with the Wind,* and the General's fondness for the event involves a value system more banal even than that of the Old South—the values of Hollywood: "Every person at it had paid ten dollars to get in and had to wear his tuxseeder. I was in this uniform. A beautiful gul presented me with it that afternoon in a hotel room" (p. 136). In the context of such desires, his death carries little implication of an opening up into communal freedom or a reformation of his ideals. Whatever enlightenment is forced upon him seems merely destructive.

For the General's granddaughter, however, the General *does* represent ideals, and she plans to use General Sash at her graduation to support her view of herself: "She meant to hold her head very high as if she were saying, 'See him! See him! My kin, all you upstarts! Glorious upright old man standing for the old traditions! Dignity! Honor! Courage! See him!' " (p. 135). The General's death can be nothing but a horror for her. In a nightmare about the General, she says, "See him!" and turns around to find him wearing nothing but a hat; the dream suggests her awareness that the General's symbolism is crumbling, but she in no way desires or tries to bring about his death. If she has a revelation, it will be like the General's and the grandmother's.

"A Stroke of Good Fortune" concerns a situation with considerable potential for the comically positive grotesque: a revelation of a pregnancy. But the story comes off as a rather bitter satire. Ruby Hill senses nothing positive in her pregnancy, and the narration encourages us to disapprove of her attitude; the most famous critical remark about "A Stroke of Good Fortune" is Stanley Edgar Hyman's labeling of the story as "a leaden tract against complacency and contraception."[1] The narrator of "A Stroke of Good Fortune" opens the story by comparing Ruby's head to a vegetable, a comparison which increases in significance in its connection with Ruby's disgust over her brother's fondness for collard greens. The narration implies that Ruby is first and foremost a biological entity. From one point of view, then, the grotesque comparison at the opening of the story is to be taken quite literally: Ruby is a vegetable, growing, and it is merely perverse of her to want to be anything else.

Part of what is interesting in this story is the heavy use of narrated monologue; "A Stroke of Good Fortune" reflects O'Connor's early use of this style (the story comes from a discarded section of *Wise Blood).* The narrated monologue allows Ruby to communicate her views directly to the audience; theoretically, therefore, it should be possible to accept Ruby's perspective on things in spite of the narrator. Ruby does not seriously rival the narrator, however; she does little more than make herself ridiculous.[2] The passage in which Ruby admits she is getting fat provides a good illustration:

> It was natural when you took on some weight to take it on in the middle and Bill Hill didn't mind her being fat, he was just more happy and didn't know why. . . . He would never slip up. She rubbed her hand across her skirt and felt the tightness of it but hadn't she felt that before? She had. It was the skirt—she had on the tight one that she didn't wear often, she had . . . she didn't have on the tight skirt. She had on the loose one. But it wasn't very loose. But that didn't make any difference, she was just fat. (*CS,* 105)

Ruby's thoughts here simply constitute denial, and there is little to suggest that her perceptions ever rival the narrator's. However, a few critics have taken Ruby Hill's narrated monologue as a feminist statement. Louise Westling, for example, says that "whether or not she intended to do so, Flannery O'Connor has made a vivid protest against sentimental stereotypes of motherhood."[3] Ruby attracts some sympathy from readers because she remembers the dread-fulness of her mother's childbearing:

> She remembered when her mother had had Rufus. She was the only one of the children who couldn't stand it and she walked all the way in to Melsy, in the hot sun ten miles, to the picture show to get clear of the screaming, and had sat through two westerns and a horror picture and a serial and then had walked all the way back and found it was just beginning, and she had had to listen all night. All that misery for Rufus! And him turned out now to have no more charge than a dish rag. She saw him waiting out nowhere before he was born, just waiting, waiting to make his mother, only thirty-four, into an old woman. (*CS*, 97)

Unlike a character who rivals the narrator, however, Ruby does not in any way propose for herself a positive alternative to the misery of childbearing or grotesquely see the misery as a link to an ideal; she merely wishes that her illness could be heart trouble. Westling insists that "no solution to Ruby's problem is offered,"[4] but when the grotesque becomes positive, death itself ceases to be a problem. What Ruby considers "good fortune," as predicted for her by a fortune teller, is a move from the city to the suburbs. The reader is reluctantly forced, consequently, to agree with the narrator's ridicule of Ruby, most of which involves painfully obvious hints that she is pregnant. Ruby sits on a toy pistol belonging to six-year-old Hartley Gilfeet, whose first name suggests the real cause of Ruby's "heart trouble," whose last name suggests a fetus, and whose father is the phallically named Rodman. And even the pistol is phallic; as soon as she sits on it, Ruby thinks, "Nine inches of treacherous tin!" (*CS*, 98). Hartley is associated with the fortune-teller's prediction for Ruby by his nickname, "Little Mister Good Fortune." As Hartley roars up the stairs shooting his pistol, Ruby suffers a stroke of realization that her good fortune is a baby, and the narrator uses echoes to press home the point.

> "Good Fortune," she said in a hollow voice that echoed along all the levels of the cavern, "Baby."
> "Good Fortune, Baby," the three echoes leered.
> Then she recognized the feeling again, a little roll. It was as if it were not in her stomach. It was as if it were out nowhere in nothing, out nowhere, resting and waiting, with plenty of time. (P. 107)

Ruby finally senses that she is part of the community of physical bodies, but this realization is forced upon her against her will.

In both "A Late Encounter with the Enemy" and "A Stroke of Good Fortune" there are hints of the positive grotesque—in the General's desire to see beyond the past, in Ruby's pregnancy—but neither story strongly confronts the reader with the notion of self-redemption. "The River," in contrast, dramatizes redemption without the character's use of the grotesque, and yet the protagonist seems to cooperate fully with his redemption. The key to the story's uniqueness is that Harry Ashfield, the young boy who is the protagonist, is completely unaware of religion when the story begins. That Harry's home is a religious vacuum becomes apparent when Harry is with his babysitter, Mrs. Connin:

> You found out more when you left where you lived. He had found out already this morning that he had been made by a carpenter named Jesus Christ. Before he had thought it had been a doctor named Sladewall, a fat man with a yellow mustache who gave him shots and thought his name was Herbert, but this must have been a joke. They joked a lot where he lived. If he had thought about it before, he would have thought Jesus Christ was a word like "oh" or "damn" or "God," or maybe somebody who had cheated them out of something sometime. When he had asked Mrs. Connin who the man in the sheet in the picture over her bed was, she had looked at him a while with her mouth open. Then she had said, "That's Jesus," and she had kept on looking at him. (*CS*, 163)[5]

Harry does not have to use the unconscious to trick himself into taking religion seriously. It is surely important that the narrator says that Harry changes his name to Bevel—the name of an evangelist Harry encounters—on the spur of the moment, that "he had never thought at any time before of changing it" (p. 159). In other stories, such a statement would point to a split between conscious understanding and unconscious maneuvering, but the conscious and unconscious levels of mind so nearly coincide here that the statement can be taken literally.

One interesting aspect of "The River" is that the joking of Harry's parents is not supposed to gain the reader's approval. Since the value of the grotesque so often lies in its reversals and playfulness, it may seem odd that play is not valuable here. One apparent explanation is, again, that Harry is unaware of religious ideals. This ignorance is apparent in the passage concerning Harry/Bevel's baptism. Asked if he has ever been baptized, Harry rolls his eyes "in a comical way" and jokingly says, "My name is Bevv-vuuuuul" (p. 167). When the preacher maintains his serious look, Harry sees a difference between the river and his home: "Where he lived everything was a joke. From the preacher's face, he knew immediately that nothing the preacher said or did was a joke" (pp. 167–68). When Harry and Mrs. Connin return to his house, his parents, already tired from one party, are nonetheless about to start another. When his parents and their friends find the religious book that Harry has stolen from Mrs. Connin, they make fun of it. Without religious ideals, the Ashfields' humor merely piles the unserious atop the unserious, so that they surround themselves with meaninglessness. Rather than using the grotesque to send themselves to an oven, they are, as their name suggests, already burned out. The ideals upon which the positive grotesque could depend have been desecrated without reidealization, so that Harry has never become aware of the ideals his parents joke about. Harry's parents illustrate the danger discussed at the end of chapter 3: their use of the grotesque merely trivializes.

The notion of religion that Harry attains is constructed on the basis of the ideals he learns during the course of the story. Rather than setting up a contrast between the character's conscious and unconscious systems of belief, the story sets up a contrast between conventional forms of religion and the child's personal understanding of those forms. And even that contrast is not strong. Harry's personal religion is based on a literal interpretation of what he hears and sees rather than a grotesque version of an ideal; he travels to the river and drowns himself at the end because he believes that that is what redemption is all about. The only difference between the narrating consciousness and the main character is one of knowledge. Although the narrator consistently points to Harry's ignorance and misunderstanding, the narrator also seems to be clearly on Harry's side throughout. The characteristically vicious conflict between narrator and character is absent, and the absence of this tension weakens the story.

The Reverend Bevel Summers provides a rationale for not considering Harry/Bevel's drowning a religious experience: "If you just come to see can you leave your pain in the river, you ain't come for Jesus. You can't leave your pain in the river" (p. 165). But the minister pushes his distinction between the watery river in which he stands and the river of Jesus' blood to such an extreme that the distinction collapses: "There ain't but one river and that's the River of Life, made out of Jesus' Blood." While insisting that the river of blood is the only river that matters, the preacher implies that the river before them—the one in which Harry/Bevel later drowns—is the same as that River of Life. Miles Orvell says, "The story fails to convince us that the little boy has done anything but unfortunately confuse a literal meaning and a symbolic meaning,"[6] but one of the points of this story is that sometimes the literal and symbolic coincide: Harry's redemption makes the two one. And Harry has no conscious aversion to redemption: although he has only a partial understanding of religion, his experience is straightforward and consciously desired to a degree found almost nowhere else in O'Connor's works.

To find a character in "The River" who participates in the positive grotesque, we must look to Mr. Paradise, a man who heckles the preacher at each river meeting because the cancer over Mr. Paradise's ear has not been healed. Mr. Paradise's heckling and his display of the purple cancer on his temple are his ways of participating in the ritual and working to force himself grotesquely toward redemption. The minister's insistence that one must "Believe Jesus or the devil!" and "Testify to one or the other!" (p. 166) is in fact fulfilled by Mr. Paradise. Late in the story we are informed that Mr. Paradise constantly sits on the river bank staring at the river with an "unbaited fishline in the water" (p. 173), a practice which shows that in his own perverse way, he considers the river a source of redemption. Thus, while he may be in a sense demonic, he is not "the incarnation of the devil."[7] He probably considers Harry, whom he has seen baptized, to be a representative of the religion that Mr. Paradise makes grotesque. Mr. Paradise sets out after Harry with a peppermint stick at the end of the story, apparently intending to molest him. When Harry sees Mr. Paradise coming toward him, he thinks he sees "a giant pig bounding after him, shaking a red and white club and shouting" (*CS*, 174), and the sight makes it easier for Harry to drown himself.

Mr. Paradise tries to save the boy but eventually gives up. The narrator's focus on Mr. Paradise, "staring with his dull eyes as far down the river line as he could see" (p. 174), implies that Harry's experience is quite different from what Mr. Paradise is trying to bring about for himself. But from another point of view, Harry/ Bevel's experience links the two versions of redemptive experience investigated in this study. In some ways the sort of redemption Harry achieves is a traditional one: he is completely conscious that he desires redemption, and his consciousness is entirely in favor of his own redemption. On the other hand, Harry shares with the majority of O'Connor protagonists a redemption that he has brought about himself. When Harry enters the river, we are told, "he intended not to fool with preachers any more but to Baptize himself and to keep on going this time until he found the Kingdom of Christ in the river" (p. 173). The traditionally redemptive qualities of Harry/Bevel's self-determination suggest that the grotesque self-redemption of most O'Connor characters is indeed linked to traditionally religious redemption.[8]

"Everything That Rises Must Converge," the most famous of the stories discussed in this chapter, also raises issues about the connection between grotesque redemption and traditional redemption. It also presents a counterpoint to "The River." The protagonist, Julian, presents a special and problematical version of the psychological patterns explored in this study. He uses the grotesque, but, unlike the vast majority of O'Connor characters, he knows that he does so; and it is only after he finally achieves what he has consciously thought is his goal—his mother's destruction—that he is ready to be entered into "the world of guilt and sorrow" (*CS,* 420) in which he might begin to use the grotesque positively.

The conflict that commonly occurs in an O'Connor story between the narrator's emphases and the character's actions is reduced here. Julian is presented as an egotistical, manipulative pseudo-intellectual, and there is little in Julian's character to call this presentation into question.[9] Julian makes himself grotesque, but he does so consciously, in order to attack his mother, and the narration correctly analyzes the subtleties of Julian's mind. Wanting to degrade himself, he takes off his tie at the bus stop, and when his mother tells him, "You look like a—thug," Julian replies, "Then I must be one" (p. 409). Most of Julian's actions to associate himself with blacks are versions of this gesture, motivated by a desire to seem grotesque to his mother. Despite his opinion that he is more realistic than his mother, Julian is obsessed with elitist pretensions. The narrator pins down Julian on the subject of the family mansion, which he pretends to hate, by saying that Julian "never . . . thought of it without longing. He had seen it once when he was a child before it had been sold. The double stairways had rotted and been torn down. Negroes were living in it. But it remained in his mind as his mother had known it. It appeared in his dreams regularly" (p. 408). Even Julian is conscious that he rather than his mother "could have appreciated it" if the family still owned it. Julian's dealings with blacks demonstrate the same elitism. He enjoys seeing "injustice in daily operation" because "it confirmed his view that with a few exceptions there was no one worth knowing within a radius of three hundred miles" (p. 412). And despite his fantasies of making friends with blacks, of participating in a demonstration with blacks, even of marrying a black, Julian is annoyed when a black woman decides to sit beside him on the bus—that is, until "he saw his mother's face change as the woman settled herself next to him and he realized with satisfaction that this was more objectionable to her than it was to him" (p. 415).

When Julian spreads out a newspaper to hide himself from the others, the narrator takes the opportunity to analyze Julian's view of himself, while using only a few of Julian's own words:

> Julian was withdrawing into the inner compartment of his mind where he spent most of his time. This was a kind of mental bubble in which he established himself when he could not bear to be a part of what was going on around him. From it he could see out and judge but in it he was safe from any kind of penetration from without. It was the only place where he felt free of the general idiocy of his fellows. His mother had never entered it but from it he could see her with absolute clarity. (P. 411)

Julian actually imagines or causes his "victimization" by his mother; he encourages his mother to do things that irritate him. "Yes, you should have bought it" (p. 405), he says about the "hideous hat," which like everything else that she enjoys, "was small and depressed him." Because she wears the hat "like a banner of her imaginary dignity," Julian finds it easier to work up "an evil urge to break her spirit" (p. 409). He even thinks that "he could have stood his lot better if she had been selfish, if she had been an old hag who drank and screamed at him" (p. 407). Julian's total familiarity with his mother's patterns of conversation calls up the rail metaphor and suggests that he encourages her to make racist statements. When his mother brings up the subject of slaves, Julian thinks that she "rolled onto" the topic "every few days like a train on an open track" (p. 408). As the narrator extends the metaphor ("He knew every stop, every junction, every swamp along the way, and knew the exact point at which her conclusion would roll majestically into the station"), Julian seems unaware that he encourages his mother's speech. Julian reminds his mother that "there are no more slaves," surely anticipating the effect of such a reminder. It is noteworthy, however, that the railroad metaphor is applied to Julian's mother, rather than to Julian himself; the mother resembles the typical O'Connor protagonist more than Julian does. Rather than sending himself to the oven, Julian merely asks a black man for a match when he has no cigarettes and when he is on a bus where smoking is prohibited. And despite his fantasies about radical action, Julian is a remarkably passive character.[10]

Although Julian considers his mother the representative of old, tired ideals, she has made herself grotesque to help Julian; their reduced circumstances are in part a result of the cost of Julian's education, and her "teeth had gone unfilled so that his could be straightened" (*CS*, 411). She accepts reduced circumstances better than Julian does. She had "hardly known the difference" (p. 409) when they moved into less-than-elegant neighborhoods. She is able to enter the bus "as if she were going into a drawing room" (p. 410). And she even takes a positive attitude to their hard times and her sacrifices for Julian: "Since, said she, it was fun to struggle, why complain? And when you had won, as she had won, what fun to look back on the hard times!" (p. 411). In the end, Julian's mother offers a penny to a black boy and receives a blow to the head from the boy's mother. In another O'Connor story, this climax would conclude her unconscious plan for self-transformation. But since Julian is the protagonist, our attention focuses upon his forced enlightenment; he has more in common with Sally Poker Sash in "A Late Encounter with the Enemy" than he could admit. When his unconscious maneuverings have been exhausted, Julian's enlightenment comes from outside. Thus Julian's experience presents an interesting variation on Harry Ashfield's. Julian uses the grotesque in a manner that seems to make it useless to him, and his redemption, if it occurs, must come from outside; Harry cooperates so thoroughly with the forces that redeem him that he seems finally to redeem himself, without the grotesque. With these characters O'Connor tests the boundaries of the positive grotesque. Julian seems fully committed to a flawed version of the grotesque, while Harry achieves redemption with less grotesquerie than any of O'Connor's other characters. In the black mother's threatening handbag and Mr. Paradise's peppermint stick, we have images, respectively, of the lightning bolt of grace that can save one whose grotesque vision has failed, and of the positive grotesque not needed.

The characters to be discussed in the next chapter share with Julian a grotesque outlook that is unsuccessful. Unlike these other, similar characters, however, Julian never escapes the narrator's analysis. The redemption that produces communal freedom is never Julian's. The strongly satirical thrust of his story has, in fact, provoked perhaps the most eloquent attack on O'Connor's art ever written. In a review of *Everything That Rises Must Converge,* Irving Howe says,

> Reading the title story, one quickly begins to see the end toward which it moves and indeed must move. The climax is then realized effectively enough—except for the serious flaw that it is a climax that has already been anticipated a number of pages earlier, where it seems already

present, visible and complete, in the preparatory action. . . . There is
pleasure to be had in watching Miss O'Connor work it all out, but no
surprise, for there has been no significant turning upon the premises
from which the action has emerged. The story is entirely harmonious
with the writer's intent, characterized by what might be called the clarity
of limitation. Miss O'Connor is in control of the narrative line from
beginning to end, and by the standards of many critics, that is the
consummation of her art.

But is it? When I think of stories by contemporary writers which live
in my mind . . . I find myself moved by something more than control.
In such stories there comes a moment when the unexpected happens, a
perception, an insight, a confrontation which may not be in accord with
the writer's original intention and may not be strictly required by the
logic of the action, but which nevertheless caps the entire story. This
moment of revelation gains part of its power from a sharp and sudden
brush against the writer's apparent plan of meaning; it calls into question
all "structural analysis"; the writer seems to be shaken by the demands of
his own imagination, so that the material of the story "acts back" upon
him.

This final release beyond craft and control, and sometimes, to be
honest, beyond clarity, is what I find missing in most of Miss O'Connor's stories.[11]

I am inclined to agree with Howe about this particular story, but the
reason this story is predictable, too controlled, is that its protagonist fails to use the grotesque positively. However interesting
Julian's character flaws may be, the fact that the narrator's view of
the story's events is consistently authoritative limits the story. The
unconscious use of the grotesque by O'Connor's protagonists in
opposition to her narrators' usual authoritarianism is what makes
Howe's criticism invalid for the bulk of O'Connor's work. Even
where the operation of the unconscious is problematic (as in the
works discussed in the next chapter), O'Connor's works generally
escape the predictability Howe condemns.

Perhaps it is because "Everything That Rises Must Converge" is
not a typical O'Connor story that O'Connor was able to give it a
title so suggestive of her thematic interests. The title, inspired by
Teilhard de Chardin, suggests the convergence of white and black,
of oppressive parent and rebellious child. If, as John F. Desmond
says, the word "convergence" refers to "the universal drive toward
spiritual union among men, through love,"[12] the title of O'Connor's posthumous collection suggests the sort of unconscious inclination toward redemption explored in this study. It is appropriate
that such a title would be attached to a story in which such an
inclination on the part of the protagonist is absent, in which it
seems that everything must sink and separate.

1. Hyman, *Flannery O'Connor,* p. 19.
2. Kathleen Feeley in *Flannery O'Connor,* pp. 76–77, refers to the weakness of the narrated monologue by saying, "Unfortunately, after the first paragraph, the author speaks in Ruby's authentically dull voice, which can only further stultify the view of life which the story projects."
3. Westling, "O'Connor's Mothers and Daughters," p. 516.
4. Westling, *Sacred Groves and Ravaged Gardens,* p. 149.
5. Miles Orvell, in *Invisible Parade,* p. 175, refers to this section of the story and complains that "there are . . . occasions when the reader may not share a laugh precisely because of the viewpoint O'Connor assumes and the judgment she implies." I would rather say that the humor of this passage requires merely a belief that an absence of ideals is ridiculous.
6. Ibid., p. 35.
7. Muller, *Nightmares and Visions,* p. 59. To find a devil in O'Connor's works, I think we have to find a character who functions as the devil for another character and has no other purpose. While Mr. Paradise functions as a devil for Harry/Bevel, he has a psychic life of his own and yearns for redemption. The closest thing to a purely devilish character in O'Connor's works is Tarwater's rapist in *The Violent Bear It Away.*
8. Norton, in "The Lame Shall Enter First," also suggests a link between grotesque redemption and traditional redemption. See chapter 8.
9. Some critics have attempted to take a somewhat positive attitude toward Julian. Josephine Hendin, in *World of O'Connor,* pp. 102–8, considers Julian's weaknesses entirely his mother's fault. And Robert Coles claims, in *O'Connor's South,* "I heard nothing from civil rights workers during the early 1960s that Julian, in one way or another, doesn't say or come close to saying" (p. 40).
10. Robert Denham, in "World of Guilt and Sorrow," notes that after his brief conversation with the black man, Julian does not speak until he is about to exit the bus (p. 48).
11. Howe, "O'Connor's Stories," pp. 16–17.
12. Desmond, "Lessons of History," p. 40. When asked for the best book of the last thirty years, O'Connor named Teilhard de Chardin's *The Phenomenon of Man,* calling it "a scientific expression of what the poet attempts to do: penetrate matter until spirit is revealed in it." See *The American Scholar* 30 (1961): 618; or *The Presence of Grace and Other Book Reviews,* comp. Leo J. Zuber, ed. Carter W. Martin (Athens: University of Georgia Press, 1983), pp. 129–30.

6

DERAILMENTS
Mrs. McIntyre, The Misfit,
Mr. Shiftlet, Hulga/Joy

> We are discovering that something is developing in the world
> by means of us, perhaps at our expense. And what is more
> serious still is that we have become aware that, in the great
> game that is being played, we are the players as well as being
> the cards and the stakes. Nothing can go on if we leave the
> table. Neither can any power force us to remain.
> —Teilhard de Chardin,
> *The Phenomenon of Man*

IN THE FIRST CHAPTER I contrasted Mrs. Shortley and the grandmother as characters who achieve enlightenment by nearly opposite
means. Each of these characters contrasts with another character in
her own story as well, a character whose awakening does not come
about: Mrs. McIntyre, in "The Displaced Person," and The Misfit,
in "A Good Man Is Hard to Find." It may seem strange to compare
one of O'Connor's most conventional farm wives to the most
famous of her evil searchers for the divine. But both Mrs. McIntyre
and The Misfit consider themselves to be involved in a confrontation with Jesus, whom they regard as responsible for the world's
imbalance, and the confrontation ends in each instance—after a
significant delay—with a departure from the path toward redemption that the character has set. Analysis of their use of the grotesque
will introduce discussions of the skewed operation of the grotesque
in two other stories: "The Life You Save May Be Your Own" and
"Good Country People." The four major characters to be treated in
this chapter generally manage to free themselves from the constricted role assigned to them by the narration, but all of them

finally refuse to recapture the ideal toward which they lead themselves. They never give up the illusion of individuality.

Despite the extreme complexity of her story, Mrs. McIntyre has inspired little critical controversy. As I mentioned earlier, O'Connor said (in a letter dated 25 November 1955) that she was trying to show that Mrs. McIntyre is "set . . . on the road to a new kind of suffering, not Purgatory as St. Catherine would conceive it (realization) but Purgatory at least as a beginning of suffering" (*HB*, 118). There is some question about whether she receives grace at the end of her story after consenting to the killing of Mr. Guizac, the Displaced Person, but she is generally considered a simple, easily understood character. The view that she is a simple character relates to the common notion that the McIntyre farm is static and secure until the Displaced Person arrives. The notion that Mr. Guizac causes the story's events has led to a distorting emphasis on Guizac in the criticism. He is important, but only as the other characters react to him; he arrives on the farm in a state of selflessness somewhat similar to the state that the majority of O'Connor characters move toward. The McIntyre farm is far from stable when the Displaced Person arrives; to a large extent, the subject of the story is the difference between Mrs. Shortley's and Mrs. McIntyre's strategies for redemption, strategies they have worked on for some time. It may be true, as Ihab Hassan says, that generally O'Connor believes that "evil springs wherever the spirit refuses mediation in forms of communal existence or incarnation in gestures of love," that "the pure gothic impulse, isolation or pride, is invariably demonic."[1] But in "The Displaced Person," Mrs. Shortley's isolated, prideful vision brings about her redemption, and Mrs. McIntyre's failure to complete her redemption is in part the result of her ties to Mr. Shortley and the blacks.

Mrs. McIntyre's plan for transforming herself depends upon ideals she associates with her first husband, called the Judge, who left her the farm but who also desired the destruction of the farm and of the social system that supports it. Thus the Judge seems to represent both ideals and grotesque degradations of ideals. When Mrs. McIntyre met him, he apparently represented only the "ideal" of wealth; it was for his money that she married him. But there was more to the relationship. Her marriage to the Judge constituted her "happiest and most prosperous" years, in part because, regardless of the old man's wealth, "she had liked him" (*CS*, 218). The narrator satirizes the Judge, but one gets the impression that Mrs. McIntyre may have been attracted to the old man's physical grotesquerie: "He was a dirty snuff-dipping Court House figure, famous all over the county for being rich, who wore hightop shoes, a string tie, a gray suit with a black stripe in it, and a yellowed panama hat, winter and summer. His teeth and hair were tobacco-colored and his face a clay pink pitted and tracked with mysterious prehistoric-looking marks as if he had been unearthed among fossils."

When he died, it turned out that the Judge was bankrupt, a fact that has deprived him of little of his ideal stature in Mrs. McIntyre's mind. What actually attracted her to him is not destroyed; Mrs. McIntyre even keeps his peacocks "out of a superstitious fear of annoying the Judge in his grave" (p. 218). Although she consciously respects the Judge only because of the business sense she attributed to him, her attachment to him is much more emotional and subversive than she herself knows. Even as she tells herself that she does everything possible to keep the farm going, her acceptance of the Judge's wisdom reveals some of her unconscious motives. The Judge's clichés provide the standards by which Mrs. McIntyre runs the farm, but these clichés consistently suggest their antitheses, usually because of the manner in which the Judge used them. For example, she quotes one of the Judge's sayings, "Money is the root of all evil," to show that she does not like to give up her money to hire "worthless people," but as she and Astor recall the Judge's views, it becomes apparent that the Judge wished he did not need to have any money at all:

> "Money is the root of all evil," she said. "The Judge said so every day. He said he deplored money. He said the reason you niggers were so uppity was because there was so much money in circulation."
>
> The old Negro had known the Judge. "Judge say he long for the day when he be too poor to pay a nigger to work," he said. "Say when that day come, the world be back on its feet." (P. 215)

Earlier, Mrs. Shortley recites another of the Judge's clichés in order to show the value of having black workers, and Mrs. McIntyre agrees, but the cliché itself seems to express the Judge's doubt that there is any value in the master/servant relationship between black and white: "You can always tell a nigger what to do and stand by until he does it" (p. 208). Another cliché that Mrs. McIntyre recalls—"The Judge had said always hire you a half-witted nigger because they don't have sense enough to stop working" (p. 219)— reinforces the notion that the Judge knew that whites exploit black workers. And the most popular of the Judge's clichés among the inhabitants of the McIntyre farm, although not undercut by a description of the Judge's use of it, is thoroughly undercut by the present users of it. The slogan "The devil you know is better than the devil you don't" is repeated so often—usually to justify the ways things are done on the farm—that nearly everything is in danger of being labelled devilish.

Miles Orvell notes that "the picture of the Judge . . . seems, ironically, to go beyond Mrs. McIntyre's understanding of him."[2] But unconsciously she understands much of what drove the Judge, and it is his values that she tries to recapture. Such an unconscious plan apparently provides the motivation for Mrs. McIntyre to approach Father Flynn about getting some refugees on her farm. Consciously she tells herself that her dealings with the priest are strictly business, and she complains about his religious instruction, but she clearly anticipated and apparently desired the priest's troubling instruction: "After he had got her the Pole, he had used the business introduction to try to convert her—just as she had supposed he would" (*CS*, 225). If Mrs. McIntyre did not go to see a priest because she unconsciously expected to make him a new Judge, she soon learns to associate Father Flynn with the Judge because of their similar attitude toward peacocks. When the priest admires the peacock's spread tail, Mrs. McIntyre seems to sense some of the Judge's affection for the bird. Looking at the bird, the priest stands "transfixed, his jaw slack," and then "Mrs. McIntyre wondered where she had ever seen such an idiotic old man" (p. 226). The answer, of course, is that the Judge was just such an old man. Because of these associations, Mrs. McIntyre probably does have some unconscious expectation that Mr. Guizac will be disruptive in a manner that she associates with both the Judge and the priest. When Mrs. McIntyre discovers that Mr. Guizac is an excellent worker, she blissfully insults Mrs. Shortley by saying, "That man is my salvation!" (p. 203). Of course, this statement is consciously motivated by her desire for financial success, but Mrs. McIntyre also unconsciously associates Mr. Guizac with forces that could bring about her redemption.

Mrs. McIntyre's conscious attitude to Mr. Guizac shifts when she learns of his plan to marry his niece to the black worker Sulk. At this point the previously ungrotesque Guizac becomes fully grotesque in her eyes: "Monster! she said to herself and looked at him as if she were seeing him for the first time. His forehead and skull were white where they had been protected by his cap but the rest of his face was red and bristled with short yellow hairs. His eyes were like two bright nails behind his gold-rimmed spectacles that had been mended over the nose with haywire. His whole face looked as if it might have been patched together out of several others" (p. 222). From one point of view, of course, Mr. Guizac's grotesquerie is potentially positive. Mrs. McIntyre sees in him a disruptive force that shocks her but that she also desires, and in a very significant passage at the end of her confrontation with Mr. Guizac in the cornfield, Mrs. McIntyre senses that her problems with the Displaced Person would delight the Judge: "By nightfall, the Displaced Person would have worked his way around and around until there would be nothing on either side of the two hills but the stubble, and down in the center, risen like a little island, the graveyard where the Judge lay grinning under his desecrated monument" (p. 224). The diction here is probably the narrator's, but the notion that the Judge is grinning is surely Mrs. McIntyre's, and the verb tense ("would have worked") indicates that the thought is formulated as Mrs. McIntyre is leaving the field. It is somewhat surprising, perhaps, that Mrs. McIntyre should imagine her idealized Judge to be grinning about her misfortune, but I would suggest that on some level she has always considered the Judge grotesque, and that unconsciously she realizes that such a disruption of the farm is precisely what the Judge would want for her.

Readers who consider the Judge banal or demonic may feel that the imagined grin indicates Mrs. McIntyre's realization that the Judge was right: she should have stuck with the devils she knows. But such a view ignores the fact that Mrs. McIntyre has just decided that Mr. Guizac is the sort of devilish white-trash worker she has been tolerating for years. Before confronting Mr. Guizac, whom she had considered "a kind of miracle," she desecrates him by likening him to all the white-trash workers she has had: "They're all the same. It's always been like this. . . . Twenty years of being beaten and done in . . ." (p. 220). She even seems to consider Mr. Guizac a participant in the desecration of the Judge's grave (the Herrins stole the granite angel), and before she confronts Mr. Guizac, she strengthens herself by visiting the back hall, which she associates with the Judge and which she has idealized; the hall is "dark and quiet as a chapel," with a safe like a "tabernacle" (p. 221) on the Judge's desk. After her confrontation with Mr. Guizac, she reinforces her demotion of the Displaced Person: " 'They're all the same,' she muttered, 'whether they come from Poland or Tennessee' " (p. 224). Mr. Guizac is now set up in her mind to be both the representative and disrupter of the Judge's values. One could say that she approaches a state like Mrs. Cope's in "A Circle in the Fire," in which everything promises the desired destruction that allows the recapturing of ideals.

The sense in which Mr. Guizac becomes connected with that

most disruptive of figures—Christ—is fairly problematic, however. Although a number of critics consider Mr. Guizac a very effective Christ symbol, the scene in which the Displaced Person and Christ are first connected has received considerable negative response, primarily because neither the priest nor Mrs. McIntyre seems aware of the connection. When she says, "He didn't have to come in the first place" (p. 226), she is talking about Mr. Guizac, but when Father Flynn says, "He came to redeem us," he is talking about Christ. As Carol Shloss says, this passage fails to make clear that either character realizes what is going on.[3] But in the relation of Mrs. McIntyre's dream, it becomes clear that Mrs. McIntyre does indeed associate the Displaced Person with Christ. Earlier she had said to the priest that "Christ was just another D.P." (*CS, 229*) in order to irritate Father Flynn, but in the dream we learn that she takes the comparison seriously. In the dream, the priest refers to the "thousands" of displaced persons, to "the ovens and the boxcars and the camps and the sick children and Christ Our Lord" (p. 231). As Mrs. McIntyre rejects the suffering community, she goes beyond her assertion that Christ is merely a Displaced Person. In this dream, she knows that in rejecting Mr. Guizac (and, I might add, the oven), she rejects Christ.

As soon as the connection between Mr. Guizac and Christ is established, it takes over. Nothing more is said of Mr. Guizac's error in relation to racial custom. Even money ceases to be a problem; it too fits into a plan for redemption. At a certain point everyone realizes that the Guizacs' financial welfare has nothing to do with the issue of whether they will be kept on the McIntyre farm. As Mr. Shortley knows, if Mrs. McIntyre were to dismiss Mr. Guizac, "in three years he would own his own house and have a television aerial sitting on top of it" (p. 228), and Mr. Shortley predicts to Mrs. McIntyre that "one of these days he'll be able to buy and sell you out" (p. 230). She uses this prediction to set up the final step for her transformative displacement. In another dream, she imagines the Guizacs taking her place and imagines herself becoming Mrs. Shortley (p. 231). In Mrs. McIntyre's unconscious plan, she will make Guizac, whom she confuses with Christ, into her master, and she will join the ranks of the displaced simply by allowing the forces she observes in action to continue. She expects Mr. Guizac to displace her just as the Herrins displaced the granite angel. She protests that she does not want such a thing to happen, but her hesitation in getting rid of the Guizacs suggests that unconsciously she desires this displacement. Her feeling that she must discuss matters with the priest before she can dismiss Guizac (p. 228), and her delays even after the discussion with Father Flynn, indicate a strong desire to avoid dismissing Mr. Guizac.

From one point of view, it seems that Mrs. McIntyre finally achieves the sort of displacement she desires. When she cooperates with Mr. Shortley and Sulk to allow the tractor to crush Mr. Guizac, she certainly brings about the destruction of the farm; the workers scatter and she soon loses her health. But ultimately the disruption of her life carries a meaning nearly the opposite of redemption. Having unconsciously defined the inaction of not firing Guizac as the way in which she will cause the Displaced Person/Christ to redeem her, she is suddenly faced with a situation in which inaction has an opposite meaning. Her conscious refusal to act to save the Displaced Person, her willingness to let him "die off" like the peacocks, is on some level a rejection of self-victimization, a rejection of Christ. In siding momentarily with the selfishness of Mr. Shortley and Sulk, she fails to carry through on her personal vision. Unlike Mrs. Shortley, whose extreme individuality makes her succeed in carrying out eccentric plans for redemption, Mrs. McIntyre's ties to a corrupt community weaken her just enough to bring about her betrayal of both Guizac and herself. She frees herself from the narrator's treatment of her (she demonstrates an ability to bring about her redemption), but not from her consciousness. In the end, Mrs. McIntyre is left with clear representatives of the ideal: Father Flynn and the peacock. But neither is of any use to her; the priest can feed the peacock when he visits, but she probably can understand nothing of Father Flynn's discussions of Catholic doctrine. The juxtaposition of the stories of Mrs. Shortley and Mrs. McIntyre leads to the paradoxical conclusion that the illusion of individuality, tenaciously pursued, is a surer path to communal freedom than is self-conscious attention to one's place in an earthly community.

The biggest difference between The Misfit and Mrs. McIntyre is that he seems as active as she is passive. Although The Misfit appears in only half of one of O'Connor's shorter stories, he is perhaps her most famous character, and his meeting with the grandmother provides O'Connor's most thematically significant comparison of redemption controlled by the self and redemption forced upon the self from outside. O'Connor shows both characters to be capable of redemption, but the rules according to which redemption can come about are different for the two characters, and The Misfit's failure to complete his grotesque self-redemption is at least in part a result of his own refusal.

Whereas the grandmother achieves enlightenment because it is forced upon her, The Misfit inclines toward taking control of his redemption, and to some readers, that is what is wrong with The Misfit. Others feel that he knows he cannot save himself, and according to these readers, this realization is responsible for whatever nobility or chance for redemption The Misfit has. Actually, however, The Misfit's statements of helplessness make apparent his turning away from the self-redemptive path he has set for himself. When The Misfit and his henchmen come upon the scene of the family's accident, The Misfit engages in conversation with his victims before they are killed. Initially The Misfit seems a polite fellow, ill-suited to the role of murderer, but one senses that, at least at first, The Misfit is following a routine that he has followed with other victims. The narrator consistently inserts qualifiers that undercut the apparent politeness of The Misfit's actions and statements. When The Misfit gathers the family together in the ditch after implying that they are all to be killed, "he *seemed* to be embarrassed *as if* [my emphases] he couldn't think of anything to say" (*CS*, 127). And when The Misfit answers the grandmother's suggestions that The Misfit is "not a bit common" (p. 128) and could "settle down and live a comfortable life" (p. 129), The Misfit looks "*as if* [my emphasis] he had considered her statement carefully" (p. 128) and "*as if* he *were* [my emphases] thinking about it" (p. 129).

The fairly objective narration of the story at this point seems not to place constraints on The Misfit so much as it reveals the rigid constraints he has placed on himself. Martha Stephens complains about this story's "notion of the essential moral superiority of The Misfit over his victims,"[4] but he does not start to reveal his perverse morality at all until one of his victims, the grandmother, brings it out. When the grandmother frantically says to him, "I know you're a good man" (*CS*, 127), The Misfit begins to reveal the sources of the ideals that he is trying to redeem: "God never made a finer woman than my mother and my daddy's heart was pure gold." The Misfit's father is especially important to him; the father's ideal authority is suggested by The Misfit's statement that the father "never got in trouble with the Authorities" (p. 129).

Part of what makes redemption difficult for The Misfit is that he has been told that he needs to desecrate the image of his father. A prison psychiatrist told The Misfit that he has an Oedipus complex, but The Misfit has not become fully conscious of using the grotesque, because he has misunderstood the psychiatrist: "It was a head-doctor at the penitentiary said what I had done was kill my daddy but I known that for a lie. My daddy died in nineteen ought nineteen of the epidemic flu and I never had a thing to do with it. He was buried in the Mount Hopewell Baptist churchyard and you can go there and see for yourself" (p. 130). One of the few things that The Misfit is sure of is that he did not literally perform the ultimate attack on authority that his crimes suggest: patricide. He is generally very confused about his past. When the grandmother asks what he did to be sent to the penitentiary, he says he cannot recall, but he also says he is sure that it was no mistake he was imprisoned, for "they had the papers on me" (ibid.). On the other hand, he questions his guilt because, when memory is fallible, there seems to be no connection between crime and punishment: "I found out the crime don't matter. You can do one thing or you can do another, kill a man or take a tire off his car, because sooner or later you're going to forget what it was you done and just be punished for it" (pp. 130–31). He goes so far as to make himself a grotesque Christ, based on the absence of proof of his own crimes: " 'It was the same case with Him as with me except He hadn't committed any crime and they could prove I had committed one because they had the papers on me. Of course,' he said, 'they never shown me my papers' " (p. 131). In placing this emphasis on papers as a substitute for memory, The Misfit sets a redemptive trap for himself, but a trap he can easily escape. Consciously, The Misfit tells himself that papers allow one to "hold up the crime to the punishment and see do they match and in the end . . . prove you ain't been treated right." Unconsciously, The Misfit believes that by establishing reliable records of his crimes, he can perform a redemptive self-victimization.

When The Misfit adds that he chose his name "because I can't make what all I done wrong fit what all I gone through in punishment" (p. 131), most readers assume that he feels he has been punished excessively. However, the immediate context of The Misfit's explanation calls this reading into question. As soon as The Misfit explains his choice of the name, we hear "a piercing scream from the woods, followed closely by a pistol report." His response to the murders he has ordered suggests not only that he considers himself overly punished, but also that, unconsciously, at least, he considers himself insufficiently punished: "Does it seem right to you, lady, that one is punished a heap and another ain't punished at all?" It is The Misfit who is not being punished at all at this moment, while the children's mother, June Star, and the baby join the growing heap of dead bodies in the woods. On an unconscious level, The Misfit hopes that by using records to affirm his guilt, he can make himself truly penitent, and although his plan may sound absurd, it almost works. He is determined to place a signature upon his actions: "I sign myself now. I said long ago, you get you a signature and sign everything you do and keep a copy of it" (ibid.). Thus he tries to establish an authority outside himself, to create for himself standards he need not recognize as his own creation.

But in fact one cannot sign an act, it may seem, and thus The Misfit's plan would apparently be sure to worsen matters, to make gaps grow between action and record and between action and punishment. However, it turns out that The Misfit does succeed in signing his acts, and the opening of "A Good Man Is Hard to Find" shows, on a trivial level, the grandmother as authority offering Bailey such "signed acts" as proof of guilt: " 'See here, read this,' and she stood with one hand on her thin hip and the other rattling the newspaper at his bald head. 'Here this fellow that calls himself The Misfit is aloose from the Federal Pen and headed toward Florida and you read here what it says he did to these people. Just you read it' " (p. 117).

Consequently, when The Misfit meets the grandmother, who recognizes him and his crimes from the newspaper,[5] he is presented with just the sort of authority figure, armed with knowledge of his crimes, that he has unconsciously desired, and he has only to admit his guilt. His parental authority stands before him in the grand-mother. But The Misfit avoids his own trap. When he insists, just before the grandmother's gesture which provokes him to shoot her, that he does not know for sure whether Jesus raised the dead, he reveals the objection with which he avoids completing his transfor-mation. In order to be sure whether Jesus raised the dead, he says he would have to have been there to see those miracles: "It ain't right I wasn't there because if I had of been there I would of known. . . . and I wouldn't be like I am now" (*CS*, 132). Thus when The Misfit is faced with the opportunity to accept the grandmother as an avatar of his father, he refuses to accept anything but personal experience preserved by his own memory. The Misfit is in many ways a fundamentalist, certain that "Jesus was the only One that ever raised the dead" (ibid.) and that the Bible is a reliable record. Faced with the opportunity to complete his grotesque maneuver, however, he simply refuses. What finally seems to disturb him is that he cannot pin down Christ in a text. What finally accounts for The Misfit's feeling that "Jesus thown everything off balance" (p. 131) is Christ's freedom from any fixed, reliable, deadening text, and it is just such freedom that The Misfit refuses for himself. It is tempting to speculate that because the narrator of "A Good Man Is

Hard to Find" changes in the course of the story and becomes less
authoritarian in treating The Misfit, The Misfit's redemption becomes more difficult.

As Miles Orvell says, The Misfit insists at the crucial moment
that the possibility of his redemption depends upon something that
happened in the past rather than in the present.[6] And The Misfit
also seems to insist that any lapse of memory about the basis of
one's redemption will invalidate it; he refuses to believe that the
grandmother was a good woman, because there was not someone
beside her throughout her life who was always about to shoot her
and who was thus, apparently, keeping her aware. The sudden
enlightenment of the scatterbrained grandmother, of course, shows
him that he may be wrong; even though his plan for redemption
requires that he reject doubts about records and assert the veracity
of his memory, the grandmother's awakening indicates to The
Misfit that he is not a hopeless case, and O'Connor herself held out
the possibility that The Misfit could become a "prophet" (*MM*,
113). The final point to be made about The Misfit and the grandmother for the purposes of this analysis is that the contrast between
The Misfit's potential awakening-from-within and the grandmother's awakening-from-without is not crucially significant; I
would not say that in "A Good Man Is Hard to Find," O'Connor
argues against self-redemption. Despite his refusal and her near-
refusal of enlightenment, both characters achieve the opportunity
for redemption.

As we saw in relation to both Mrs. McIntyre and The Misfit,
O'Connor's stories typically sketch out the main characters' tracks
to the oven even when the characters do not complete the journey
as planned. The two stories discussed in the rest of this chapter—
"The Life You Save May Be Your Own" and "Good Country
People"—also make clear the protagonists' plans for self-redemption, and each story investigates a brand of failure.[7] The failure of
the protagonists to complete the grotesque process in a fairly large
number of stories is significant in several ways. O'Connor repeatedly works against the common association of the grotesque with a
certain inevitability. Considering O'Connor's emphasis on the unconscious and the strong relationship she reveals between the grotesque and the unconscious, one might expect more psychological
determinism in O'Connor's works than there is. Another point
about the recurrence of failures in the grotesque process is that
careful analysis of almost any character's psyche reveals the grotesque process at work. What at first appears to be the peculiarity of
one protagonist almost seems to become a basic mental feature for

O'Connor's characters. Some of her most wrongheaded characters make plans to enlighten themselves, a surprising circumstance when one considers the frequency with which critics describe her characters as the product of a misanthropic or at least uncompassionate vision. A final point about failed uses of the grotesque is that they introduce more subtlety of psychological analysis than O'Connor is generally attributed. O'Connor was for some time a cartoonist, and to many readers still, her most mature works are theological cartoons.

"The Life You Save May Be Your Own" has, in fact, been made into a sort of cartoon for television. With the elimination of the troublesome ending, O'Connor's story became a segment on "Playhouse of Stars" in 1957, starring Gene Kelly, Agnes Moorehead, and Janice Rule.[8] And without the "unhappy" ending to indicate the story's seriousness, "The Life You Save May Be Your Own" may indeed seem to be little more than a caricature. Critical opinion of Mr. Shiftlet has generally seen him as grotesque in a totally negative fashion; Josephine Hendin, for example, sees him as afraid of sex and able to love only a car.[9] The story is filled, moreover, with images of the negative grotesque. The world is almost rotten, as the title for an early version of the story puts it, and not much of the rot seems potentially rejuvenative. But most critical comments about "The Life You Save May Be Your Own" resemble those made about the rest of O'Connor's work; little has been written to demonstrate the story's uniqueness.

The most controversial part of "The Life You Save May Be Your Own" is the ending; critics have often debated whether it provides a sufficient conclusion. O'Connor's insistence that the story is complete (*MM,* 94–95) is apparently belied by the multitude of attempts in O'Connor's typescripts to expand the story.[10] But insofar as the goal of the story is to reveal the process by which Mr. Shiftlet attempts to bring about his self-transformation, the story is complete. What is gained in keeping the story short and more ambiguous is that Shiftlet becomes a unique protagonist, caught between positive and negative grotesquerie.

Like other O'Connor protagonists who use the grotesque for positive ends, Mr. Shiftlet degrades the spiritual into the physical so that he can force himself to accept a rejuvenated sense of the spiritual. At the same time, however, he seems to reverse the process, inappropriately equating the physical with the spiritual. Mr. Shiftlet's positive, unconscious use of the grotesque involves his association of the spirit with a car, as he explains to Mrs. Crater: "The body, lady, is like a house: it don't go anywhere; but the spirit, lady, is like a automobile: always on the move . . ." (*CS*, 152). The car is more rationally associated with the body, however, as he surely knows; that the car involves a decline by Shiftlet into the physical is made clearer by the fact that in order to get the car, he has to marry Lucynell Crater, who, whatever her ultimate spiritual significance, initially impresses Mr. Shiftlet as being all body. When he marries Lucynell, he is in the perfect position to use her grotesque embodiment of ideals to achieve a new sense of spiritual values. As the boy in the eatery called The Hot Spot notices, Lucynell "looks like an angel of Gawd" (p. 154), and Shiftlet could decide, as O. E. Parker of "Parker's Back" does, that his marriage forces him toward spiritual enlightenment. Of course, no such breakthrough occurs. He leaves Lucynell after she falls asleep on the counter in The Hot Spot, and he races off in the car with no plans to return. His action suggests not only that it is possible for an O'Connor character to refuse the enlightenment toward which the positive grotesque leads, but also that his plan for redemption may be flawed. The latter possibility is indicated by his feelings about Mrs. Crater's car. Unlike Hazel Motes, Mr. Shiftlet does not have clearly religious motives when he decides he wants a car; rather, he seems to give spiritual value to the car primarily to justify wanting the car. When he has obtained the car and abandoned Lucynell, we get a sense of how his philosophizing serves his hypocritical purposes. He picks up a hitchhiker who he thinks has run away from home, and he lectures the boy about mothers in a manner that idealizes mothers completely: he says, "It's nothing so sweet" as a mother, because "she taught him his first prayers at her knee, she give him love when no other would, she told him what was right and what wasn't, and she seen that he done the right thing" (p. 155). But such idealization seems inevitably connected with loss: "I never rued a day in my life like the one I rued when I left that old mother of mine" (ibid.). And his next statement suggests that his idealization of the angelic Lucynell, like his idealization of his mother, provides a rationale for abandonment: " 'My mother was a angel of Gawd,' Mr. Shiftlet said in a very strained voice. 'He took her from heaven and giver to me and I left her' " (p. 156). The hitchhiker, however, expresses more honestly the resentment that underlies such idealization: "My old woman is a flea bag and yours is a stinking pole cat!" By the story's end, Mr. Shiftlet is partially aware that he is a hypocrite and that while his body moves about, his spirit is stuck on the verge of a breakthrough. When he finally calls on the Lord to "break forth and wash the slime from this earth!" (ibid.), he realizes that he himself is slimy. The most important effect of the story's openendedness is to help maintain his partial freedom from the caricatured role the narrator assigns him.

"Good Country People," like "The Life You Save May Be Your Own," concerns a confrontation between farm women and a man from outside, and both stories at first seem simple because they are examples of the traditional story in which a traveling salesman takes advantage of a farmer's daughter. Hulga/Joy Hopewell is not a typical farmer's daughter, of course, and when she decides to seduce Manley Pointer, the apparently innocent Bible salesman, the story threatens to break with convention. But when Manley Pointer turns out to be even more of a nihilist than Hulga and runs off with her glasses and wooden leg, we are surprisingly brought back to a conventional conclusion. Several critics have taken the ending of this story as an indication that Hulga is despicable. Constance Pierce says that all the characters have "a mechanistic way of dealing with the world, a façade that covers their underlying 'neutrality,' or 'nothingness.' "[11] Certainly the narrator of "Good Country People" is a demon of consistent moralism, who reduces Mrs. Freeman to a truck in the opening paragraph, but O'Connor herself sees the story in a more conventionally religious manner; she equates Hulga's wooden leg with a "wooden part of her soul" (*MM*, 99) and says that the loss of the artificial leg shows "her deeper affliction to her for the first time."

Few critics have considered the possibility that Hulga desires her betrayal by Manley. John F. McCarthy does note that her attempt to seduce him is motivated in part by a "strong, if subconscious, desire to return to the innocence that the young man represents,"[12] and Hulga also desires the role of captured lover as the climactic step in her plan for redemption. The key to understanding Hulga's plan for enlightening herself is her choice of the name "Hulga." While she is conscious of the fact that the name is appropriate because of its ugly sound and because it reminds her of Vulcan's powers, Hulga also knows on a deeper level that in making herself into Hulga, she sets a trap. Hulga thinks of Vulcan as one "to whom, presumably, the goddess had to come when called" (*CS*, 275). The key word here is "presumably," a word that hides and reveals a slip in Hulga's thought with which she will trap herself. The notion of a goddess having to come when summoned refers to Vulcan/Hephaistos and his wife Aphrodite. Aphrodite repeatedly deceived her husband with Ares; she "presumably" had to come to her husband, but, as Hulga knows, she often did not.

In Book 8 of the *Odyssey,* a singer relates the story of Hephaistos/Vulcan's use of a very fine net to capture his adulterous wife with

Ares. He leaves the couple trapped in the net until the gods arrive to see the two caught in the act. Mixed with the viewers' laughter and condemnation is a considerable portion of desire, however; Apollo and Hermes agree that they would like to be caught in bed with Aphrodite.[13] The entire story is relevant to Hulga's choice of her name; the trap that Hulga sets for herself leads to just such an enviable capture. In her relationship with Manley Pointer, Hulga plays two roles: consciously she is Vulcan, and unconsciously she is the captured Aphrodite. Hulga is at once the victimizer and the willing victim. The value to Hulga in making herself grotesque is that the grotesque process always involves a return to the ideal, in this instance her identity as her mother's good daughter, Joy. The myth on which Hulga bases her choice of her grotesque name is an illustration of this necessary connection between the grotesque and the ideal. It may be true that Hulga's shock at the end indicates that she is not aware of what she has done, but unconsciously she expects that in the barn she will become Joy as a captured goddess.

One obstacle to the notion that Hulga controls her own capture is our sense that the characters in this story are quite different from one another and that Hulga does not understand the others well enough to control anything about them. However, a set of puns encourages us to investigate the possibility that they are all bound to each other very closely. The key to these puns is the name of the philosopher that Hulga quotes approvingly—Malebranche. This name suggests a connection to each of the characters and brings them together. Hulga's wooden leg is a "mal branch" or bad limb, the addition of which seems to make her "male." Manley Pointer's name suggests a "male branch" and is certainly one of the most phallic names in fiction. Mrs. Freeman's name connects with the notion of detachableness in Hulga's bad limb as well as containing the word "man." And even Mrs. Hopewell joins in the wordplay when Manley mistakenly calls her Mrs. Cedars, a name suggesting wood. It is also interesting that "Malebranche" is the name of the demons in the eighth circle, fifth pouch of the *Inferno* (Cantos 21–23). In Canto 22 the Malebranche try to tear a Barrator apart (by tearing his limbs off), but the story ends in a manner that suggests a connection to O'Connor's story. The Barrator tricks the demons, and, as he escapes, the Barrator makes the demons fall into a stream of pitch.

The function of these connections seems to be to suggest that the story's characters share much more than they, and most readers, initially realize, and that Hulga in particular may have a latent knowledge of what to expect from the others. The most important similarity for Hulga's purposes is that between Manley Pointer and Mrs. Freeman; if she sees the similarity, she will have some idea of what will happen in the hayloft. There is reason to believe that Hulga ought to see a similarity in Manley's and Mrs. Freeman's fascination with her and with the grotesque, but Hulga seems slow to make the connection. When she meets Manley outside the house and makes plans for a picnic, Hulga thinks, "His gaze seemed somehow familiar but she could not think where she had been regarded with it before" (*CS,* 283). She has been regarded in this manner by Mrs. Freeman, of course, but there is little indication that Hulga actually expects to experience in the hayloft the aggressive unmasking she might expect from Mrs. Freeman.

Hulga is nevertheless able to see the similarity among the other characters as they trade trite expressions, and the most significant quality that the characters share, and that Hulga must tap, is banality. The banal serves several functions in this story, more or less as we saw in "The Displaced Person" and in "A Circle in the Fire." It licenses the expression of radical ideas under the cloak of conventionality; the literal meaning of a cliché always threatens to break through the conventional meaning. When Mrs. Hopewell affirms the differences among people, for example, she presents a partial rationale for the grotesque. More generally, the mind frame necessary for operating on the level of cliché implies that everything that can be known is already known. The idea that new knowledge is impossible suggests that the most profound insights, such as Hulga's, are always present in some form before the events in which they reach consciousness. And to some extent, Hulga does succeed in tapping her group's well of banality. In remaining conscious only of the trite reasons for naming herself Hulga, she allows her unconscious to use the profound implications of the myth associated with that name. It is nevertheless difficult to see a successful transformation in Hulga's "churning" face at the end (*CS,* 291). Some critics see Hulga's fall as the preparation for conversion, but I am inclined to agree with Louise Westling that the sexual issues in this story conflict with such a religious interpretation.[14] It may be true, as Josephine Hendin points out, that, like the other lovers of deformity in this story, Hulga is attracted to the "deformity" she sees in Manley, namely Christianity.[15] And when she last sees Manley, he appears Christlike to her weak eyes in that he is "struggling successfully over the green speckled lake" (*CS,* 291). But it is difficult to see that Christianity is what Hulga has prepared herself to return to, and even the reactionary, ideal notion of herself as goddess or dutiful daughter seems too closely related to a sexual role for

Hulga's final state—she is psychically, if not physically, raped—to indicate spiritual success. Like Asbury Fox, of "The Enduring Chill," Hulga goes through the maneuvers to bring about her transformation, but in the end she seems as shocked by the experience as Julian, of "Everything That Rises Must Converge."

1. Hassan, *Contemporary American Literature 1945–1972*, p. 69.

2. Orvell, *Invisible Parade*, p. 147.

3. Shloss, *O'Connor's Dark Comedies*, p. 77.

4. Stephens, *Question of O'Connor*, p. 33.

5. The sources for The Misfit are articles in the Atlanta *Constitution* and the Atlanta *Journal*. See Tate's "Good Source Is Not So Hard To Find."

6. Orvell, *Invisible Parade*, p. 133.

7. Two other stories that I do not discuss here—"A View of the Woods" and "The Comforts of Home"—also feature protagonists similar to those discussed in this chapter.

8. Farmer, *Flannery O'Connor*, p. 117.

9. Hendin, *World of O'Connor*, p. 68.

10. See O'Connor, "The Shiftlet Fragment." Portions of early drafts from Files 156–57, O'Connor Collection, are also available in Hegarty, "A Man Though Not Yet a Whole One."

11. Pierce, "The Mechanical World of 'Good Country People,'" p. 30.

12. McCarthy, "Human Intelligence Versus Divine Truth," p. 1144.

13. Anneliese Smith, in "O'Connor's 'Good Country People,'" uses Vulcan's failures to argue that Hulga's "understanding is deficient." Smith asks, "When in classical mythology was Vulcan ever successful as an autonomous figure?" I would argue that Hulga knows that Vulcan is sure to fail.

14. Westling, "O'Connor's Mothers and Daughters," pp. 519–20. Compare Westling's *Sacred Groves and Ravaged Gardens*, pp. 149–53.

15. Hendin, *World of O'Connor*, p. 74.

7

THE EYE
AND THE BODY
Wise Blood

The martyrs do not underestimate the body; they cause it to
be elevated on the cross. In that they are at one with their
enemies.

—Kafka,
"Reflections on Sin,
Pain, Hope, and the True Way"

UNLIKE MOST O'CONNOR CRITICS, I consider *Wise Blood* O'Connor's
most interesting and challenging text. Frederick Asals probably has
been *Wise Blood*'s most outspoken defender, but his view of the
novel understates its relation to the rest of O'Connor's works: "It
could not have been predicted from the stories that precede it, nor
does it have any real successors in her work."[1] I believe that *Wise
Blood* actually presents a typical dramatization of a character's unconscious laying of tracks toward the oven of redemption, and that
the sections of the novel on Mrs. Flood and Enoch Emery show
those characters to be following paths comparable to Hazel's.

Examining the novel's composition will help us understand the
role of O'Connor's narration in making *Wise Blood* a religious
novel. Caroline Gordon, in an early study pointing to the seriousness of the novel's treatment of religion, emphasizes that it is
the "theological framework"[2] in *Wise Blood* that separates it from
novels by other modern writers. Comparing *Wise Blood* to Truman
Capote's *Other Voices, Other Rooms,* Gordon says that Capote's
novel lacks "moral judgment" and "a frame of reference larger than
that of the individual action."[3] Gordon could feel confident that
O'Connor's novel contained such a theological frame of reference

because Gordon had helped get it into *Wise Blood*. Early in 1951, Robert Fitzgerald sent a draft of the novel to Gordon, who responded positively to it but said that "certain technical imperfections deprive it of its proper frame of reference and actually limit its scope."[4] Gordon advised O'Connor during the final revisions of *Wise Blood,* and one might assume that these revisions brought the novel in line with Gordon's intentions. When one examines the advice that Gordon gave O'Connor and compares O'Connor's revisions with that advice, however, the effect of the revisions seems ambiguous. The nine-page letter that contains the bulk of Gordon's advice recommends a number of specific changes as well as a series of more significant changes of tone, pacing, and foreshadowing. O'Connor accepted and used much of the advice in some fashion: she made Hazel Motes's eyes more significant in the first chapter; she put more emphasis on Enoch Emery's "wise blood" when Hazel first meets him; she eliminated colloquial expressions from the narrator's language; she elaborated the characterization of a number of minor characters. But in several instances, O'Connor either rejected Gordon's advice or made changes in the novel that accomplish something other than what Gordon advised.

Sally Fitzgerald has found "two sections of what probably is a draft"[5] of O'Connor's letter replying to Gordon's nine pages of advice. After mentioning several ways in which she used Gordon's advice, O'Connor pointed to her major difficulty: "The business about making the scenery more lyrical to contrast with [the characters'] moods will be harder for me to do. I have always been afraid to try my hand at being lyrical for fear I would only be funny and not know it."[6] This difficulty relates to Gordon's primary piece of advice having to do with a frame of reference. Gordon said that "the whole book would gain by not being so stripped, so bare, by surrounding the core of action with some contrasting material."[7] Gordon illustrated what the novel needed with the opening of the third chapter, where Hazel meets Enoch and Sabbath Lily Hawks. Gordon advised, "If the night sky were beautiful, if the night were lyrical the sordid roles the characters have to play would seem even more sordid."[8] Later in her letter, Gordon again mentioned this problem; at the beginning of the sixth chapter, when Hazel starts preaching, Gordon said she would "like to know what kind of night it was."[9]

Despite O'Connor's difficulty with such advice, she did add passages contrasting the sky to the characters' actions. At the beginning of the third chapter, she inserted the following:

> The black sky was underpinned with long silver streaks that looked like scaffolding and depth on depth behind it were thousands of stars that all

seemed to be moving very slowly as if they were about some vast construction work that involved the whole order of the universe and would take all time to complete. No one was paying any attention to the sky. The stores in Taulkinham stayed open on Thursday nights so that people could have an extra opportunity to see what was for sale. Haze's shadow was now behind him and now before him and now and then broken up by other people's shadows, but when it was by itself, stretching behind him, it was a thin nervous shadow walking backwards. (*WB,* 37)

Near the beginning of the sixth chapter, when Hazel parks his car in front of a theatre to start preaching, O'Connor added a sentence that produces something of the same effect: "The lights around the marquee were so bright that the moon, moving overhead with a small procession of clouds behind it, looked pale and insignificant" (pp. 103–4). The typescript on which O'Connor inserted the long passage about the stars[10] also contains several other insertions about the sky. At the beginning of the seventh chapter, where Hazel and Sabbath Lily drive out to the country, Gordon recommended that the scene be "broken up" to show the "feeling of tension"[11] between Hazel and Sabbath Lily. Part of O'Connor's response to this advice was to add several brief passages about the clouds, some on this typescript and some later. At the beginning of the chapter, as Hazel starts his drive, O'Connor inserted, "The sky was just a little lighter blue than his suit, clear and even, with only one cloud in it, a large blinding white one with curls and a beard" (*WB,* 117). As Hazel and Sabbath Lily drive on, "The blinding white cloud was a little ahead of them, moving to the left" (p. 120), and when they turn onto a dirt road, "The white cloud was directly in front of them." At the end of the chapter, as Hazel and Sabbath Lily head back to the city, "The blinding white cloud had turned into a bird with long thin wings and was disappearing in the opposite direction" (p. 127). Another important insertion is in the scene where Hazel's car is pushed over an embankment by a patrolman, a scene which Gordon believed needed more details about "how Hazel's face looked then."[12] O'Connor expanded the passage on Hazel's moment of insight by saying that Hazel's face reflected the depths of the sky. O'Connor's final version of the passage differs only slightly from this revision; the novel reads, "His face seemed to reflect the entire distance across the clearing and on beyond, the entire distance that extended from his eyes to the blank gray sky that went on, depth after depth, into space" (*WB,* 209).

A few critics have claimed that these related revisions succeed in making the characters "more sordid" and providing the novel a clear theological framework. Sally Fitzgerald considers the description of the stars "a prophetic passage" that makes clear O'Connor's "own real point of view,"[13] while Leon V. Driskill and Joan T. Brittain describe the changing cloud as "God the Father" becoming "the Holy Ghost."[14] Critics have occasionally proposed non-religious interpretations for these passages or wondered about their seriousness,[15] but the most important effect of these insertions seems to me to be almost the opposite of what Gordon wanted. The descriptions of stars and sky make the narrator's larger frame of reference ridiculous in relation to the lives of the characters. Although it is possible to connect the star passage to other lines in the novel—Asa Hawks has "streaked" cheeks (*WB*, 39), and Hazel is found dying at the end of the novel "near an abandoned construction project" (p. 229)—only the narrator sees these connections; the characters never notice the stars or clouds or moon at the moment of such a passage. The fancifulness of these passages suggests that the narrator is imposing a set of standards on the novel's content that is at once oppressive and misleading. The cloud passage, in particular, recalls the scene in "A Good Man Is Hard to Find" where the grandmother and the children play a game with the skies: "When there was nothing else to do they played a game by choosing a cloud and making the other two guess what shape it suggested. John Wesley took one the shape of a cow and June Star guessed a cow and John Wesley said, no, an automobile, and June Star said he didn't play fair, and they began to slap each other over the grandmother" (*CS*, 120). The "meaning" of a cloud can only be imposed on it, and one implication of this passage is that the O'Connor narrator sometimes imposes meaning like a child in a game. The narrator does not say that the cloud was one that John Wesley thought suggested a cow; the narrator says John Wesley's cloud was cow-shaped. One might indeed wonder, then, about a narrator who sees "curls and a beard" on a cloud.

But perhaps I am claiming too much in calling these passages completely ridiculous. For my purposes, the point to be made here about the passages concerning stars and clouds is that the banality of their religious symbolism requires us to question the theological standards of the narrator who is responsible for them, a narrator who has been called O'Connor's "most baldly intrusive."[16] This narrator's frame of reference is so clichéd that it cannot be directly meaningful to the characters until it has literally been brought down to earth. It is just such authoritarian, individualistic standards as the narrator's that the characters must escape to find redemption. To see how ideals are brought down to earth and redemption found in *Wise Blood*, we must consider the grotesquely inverted theological standards the characters set for themselves.

I do not mean to imply that every character's standards are inherently the equal of every other character's standards. In a draft of a letter to Gordon, O'Connor paraphrased Truman Capote to the effect that "private worlds" are "never . . . vulgar," and added, "I can think up plenty of vulgar private ones myself."[17] O'Connor's Taulkinham, the setting for most of *Wise Blood,* is a capital of the negative grotesque. The citizens of Taulkinham are natives of the wasteland, and many of them seem to have no theology at all. Although much of the talk in "Talking-ham" sounds religious, one must have money and/or social status to be significant in the city, and it is by this standard that people respond to others and order their lives. Even in the train on its way to Taulkinham, Mrs. Hitchcock feels that she has "placed" Hazel and "fortified" herself against him upon discovering that his "suit had cost him $11.98" (*WB,* 10). Similarly, the steward and the women in the dining car humiliate Hazel for his manners. The Taulkinham policeman ridicules Hazel-the-country-boy for not knowing about stoplights, and virtually all of the people Hazel meets in Taulkinham—Leora Watts, Enoch Emery, Asa and Sabbath Lily Hawks, Hoover Shoats, Solace Layfield, Mrs. Flood—initially take an interest in Hazel because they think he can bring them money.

The only major characters whose values are merely vulgar, however, are the prostitute and two of the preachers. Mrs. Leora Watts is a thoroughly grotesque body with no complexity of mind: "Mrs. Watts's grin was as curved and sharp as the blade of a sickle. It was plain that she was so well-adjusted that she didn't have to think any more. Her eyes took everything in whole, like quicksand" (p. 60). Mrs. Watts's most obvious counterpart in the religion business is Hoover Shoats, alias Onnie Jay Holy, for whom religion is junk food: "If you want to get anywheres in religion, you got to keep it sweet" (p. 157). Onnie feels that Hazel's idea of a new jesus is a good idea simply in need of "a little promotion" by an "artist-type" like himself. Asa Hawks, the sham blind man with whom Hazel is obsessed, is more complex. Hawks had apparently at one time been a genuine preacher, but he had despaired of his religion. He tried "to blind himself to justify his belief that Christ Jesus had redeemed him" (p. 112), but just as he was ready to do it, the narrator says, the "devils" that "were necessary to do it" all "disappeared, and he saw himself standing there as he was" (p. 114). Unable to deal with this revelation of his falsity, he could go on only by pretending to be what he knows he is not. When Hazel meets him, he is making money by preaching and, more significantly, by *not* preaching: "Help a blind preacher. If you won't repent, give up a nickel. . . .

Wouldn't you rather have me beg than preach?" (p. 40). Apparently he takes an interest in Hazel because he thinks he can get Hazel to preach for him, and perhaps because he thinks Hazel will relieve him of Sabbath Lily, his daughter.

As for Sabbath Lily Hawks and Solace Layfield, who accompany the two false preachers, their economic motivation is not enough to corrupt them completely. Sabbath Lily may seem at first to be driven by lust, but ultimately it is economic necessity that drives her. After Asa deserts her, she goes straight to Hazel's bed although she expects to be beaten. And Solace, who dresses up like Hazel Motes and says what Hoover Shoats tells him to say about the Holy Church of Christ Without Christ, is not malicious or intentionally deceitful. Solace's attitude is made clear when the narrator says that "he had consumption and a wife and six children and being a Prophet was as much work as he wanted to do" (p. 201). Solace's main concern is economic, and where conventional religion is already thoroughly corrupt, little harm remains to be done. In Taulkinham, where religion is totally a matter of money, even a potato-peeler salesman is a kind of preacher; his "pyramid of green cardboard boxes" forms an "altar" behind which the salesman sells the machines that will make potatoes white (p. 38). Perhaps the best indication that economic motivation does not make a character hopelessly corrupt is found in Mrs. Flood, Hazel's landlady; at once the greediest person in the novel and the closest thing to a normal citizen of Taulkinham, she still manages something of a spiritual awakening at the novel's end, as we shall see later.

The two major characters of *Wise Blood,* Hazel Motes and Enoch Emery, follow complex but parallel paths. The relationship between the plots of Hazel and Enoch is one of the major critical issues—perhaps I should say major complaints—about *Wise Blood.* The usual view of Enoch is that he illuminates by contrast Hazel Motes's religious transformation. Most readers, I think, would agree that at least on a first reading of the novel Enoch's story seems to play something like this role of contrast; certainly the narrator takes Hazel more seriously than Enoch. It is only later that the Enoch story may begin to seem superfluous. On the other hand, the Enoch story may seem to become the equal of the Hazel story. Martha Stephens says, "The distinction the novel is trying to develop between the true quest of Hazel Motes and the false—and therefore merely comic?—quest of the miserable Enoch, is a distinction a good many readers have not been able to appreciate."[18] My solution to the problem of Enoch's "uppity" plot is to extend and reverse the process by which most readers have understood *Wise Blood*. After using Enoch to make ourselves take seriously the religiosity of Hazel Motes, we must work backwards; once we understand how Hazel uses the grotesque to redeem himself, we are ready to understand that the gorilla-suited Enoch uses a similar strategy.

Not all critics consider Hazel's transformation positive, of course. Josephine Hendin sees Hazel "engulfed in a sense of nothingness, a mental emptiness broken by ambiguous, irrelevant symbols."[19] And several critics have argued that by the end, Hazel has merely been defeated by his Oedipus complex.[20] But like many of O'Connor's other protagonists, Hazel Motes uses his negative grotesquerie to facilitate a positively grotesque transformation. The negative, individualistic side of Hazel's grotesquerie should be fairly apparent, and it is that side that has received most of the critical attention: he is to some extent a corrupt, weak, disturbed character. One particularly interesting indication of Hazel's individual grotesquerie is the novel's emphasis on the strangeness of his eyes, which Mrs. Hitchcock first notices on the train to Taulkinham and which Mrs. Flood is obsessed by at the novel's end. Hazel's eyes, his "vision," make him physically and philosophically peculiar. One might therefore feel that Hazel's eyes make him a poor candidate for participation in the positive grotesque; to Mikhail Bakhtin, the eyes are parts of the body that are unrelated to the positive, communal grotesque: "They express an individual . . . self-sufficient human life, which is not essential to the grotesque."[21] The source of Hazel's extreme individualism is also clear. Haunted by the harsh criticism he received from his fundamentalist grandfather and mother, Hazel attempts throughout *Wise Blood* to destroy and escape from principles he was taught as a child. What makes Hazel's isolation and destructiveness most interesting, however, is the way in which they blend into more positive, communal possibilities. Careful attention to Hazel's early life shows that his determination to destroy his past includes a desire to recapture and redeem that past.

Even as Hazel's upbringing was making him rebellious and obsessively individualistic, Hazel was also constructing a system of associations and equations that would eventually lead him out of his isolation, back toward the familial community, toward a redeemed Jesus, and toward salvation. One part of his past that Hazel is attracted to is his grandfather, a circuit preacher "with Jesus hidden in his head like a stinger" (*WB*, 20). Hazel inherited his grand-

father's face and in many instances played the double to his grandfather, who taught Hazel to place a heavy emphasis on the physical.
Consequently, when Hazel considered shooting himself in the foot
to stay out of the army, he put the issue to himself in totally
physical terms: "He was going to be a preacher like his grandfather
and a preacher can always do without a foot. A preacher's power is
in his neck and tongue and arm" (p. 21). Hazel learned this lesson so
well, in fact, that abstractions became a torment to him; even a
concept as important to Hazel as sin remained incomprehensible
until it became understood, through physical imagery, as a material
condition. And in making the personal associations through which
he achieved such an understanding, Hazel again depended upon his
upbringing. His grandfather led Hazel to associate sin with Jesus,
and his mother taught Hazel to associate sin with sex. Hazel vividly
remembers the time he saw a naked woman at a carnival and went
home to face his mother's chilling question—"What you seen?"—
and her reminder that "Jesus died to redeem you" (p. 63). These
associations may seem quite traditional, but Hazel unconsciously
created grotesque versions of them. For one thing, Jesus became a
threatening figure, so threatening, in fact, that Hazel considered
living the life of a sinless preacher in order to *escape* Jesus. Hazel
developed "a deep black wordless conviction . . . that the way to
avoid Jesus was to avoid sin" and decided that the predictable, static
life of a preacher—a situation comparable in some ways to that of
the O'Connor narrator—would allow him to avoid both the stain
of sinful actions and Jesus: "Where he wanted to stay was in Eastrod
[his hometown] with his two eyes open, and his hands always
handling the familiar thing, his feet on the known track, and his
tongue not too loose" (p. 22). In other words, he considers the sort
of retreat that Mr. Head and Nelson accomplish at the end of "The
Artificial Nigger." For Hazel to return to Jesus and to those
positive, communal possibilities which he associates with his
home, past, and family, he has to depend on the association he
learned from his mother: the equation of sin with sex. Although he
cannot submit consciously to Jesus—he spends most of the novel,
in fact, spouting blasphemies—he is able to bring himself to recapture a version of Jesus by extending his unconscious, distorted logic
about Jesus and sin. The absurd connections he makes are as follows: if the way to avoid Jesus is to avoid sin, and sin equals sex,
then the way to return to Jesus is to fornicate. It is only by such
extreme indirection, by not knowing what he is doing, that Hazel
can bring himself to recapture ideals that frighten him.

Several of the most interesting studies of *Wise Blood* have emphasized Hazel's relationship with his mother. As Thomas LeClair points out, Hazel associates Jesus with his mother, and consequently, any approach to Jesus causes Oedipal fears in Hazel.[22] James C. McCullagh, who also sees the connection in Hazel's mind between his mother and Jesus, notices Hazel's peculiar logic equating fornication and salvation as well. Furthermore, McCullagh says, "The more [Hazel] attempts to reach Christ through sin . . . the more he is tied to his mother."[23] Whereas McCullagh sees Hazel's fornication as an "Oedipal chain" that must be "forcefully broken" before Hazel can truly be "ready for Christ,"[24] I believe that the sex/sin equation is Hazel's path to redemption more than it is an obstacle, and I would say that Hazel faces more obstacles than an Oedipus complex. Hazel does eventually stop his sexual sinning, but he does so because it has served its purpose. And at the end of the novel, Hazel has not freed himself of his mother; rather, he has rejoined a rejuvenated community that includes his entire family. Another way of putting all of this is to say that Hazel wants to learn to die, and to die more willingly than his family did. As a child, Hazel could not deal with the idea of death, as his reaction to the deaths of relatives showed. He opened his brother's coffin because "he had thought, what if he had been in it and they had shut it on him" (*WB*, 20), and he was surprised that his grandfather, father, and mother allowed themselves to be buried. What Hazel does in the course of the novel, then, is to pile up his sinful acts—fornications and religious blasphemies—until he feels that he can no longer resist Jesus. The philosophical stages he seems to go through are actually ploys to make sinning easier and to bring about what he has desired since childhood: his union with a group of familial bodies, at once rejuvenated and dead.

At one point Hazel seemed almost conscious of his individual, grotesque set of standards. When he was in the army, he thought that he would "tell anyone in the army who invited him to sin that he was from Eastrod, Tennessee, and that he meant to get back there and stay back there, that he was going to be a preacher of the gospel and that he wasn't going to have his soul damned by the government or by any foreign place it sent him to" (p. 23). When he was invited to go to a brothel, however, his voice cracked in the middle of his rehearsed refusal. That crack of the voice reveals Hazel's real desires; it occurred not because he really wanted to go to a brothel, but because he feared that if he succeeded in returning uncorrupted to Eastrod and staying there, he might succeed in avoiding Jesus. It is typical of Hazel that a movement into word-lessness should say more about his unconscious desires than his conscious statements do. Hazel then decided to tell himself that he was "converted to nothing" (p. 24), to tell himself that he believed he had no soul and that "the misery he had was a longing for home; it had nothing to do with Jesus." Hazel's "conversion" to nothing is significant, but not because Hazel no longer cares about Jesus; on the contrary, Hazel knows that once he has started to tell himself that his sins do not matter, he can sin more easily and therefore can find Jesus more easily.

When Hazel returns home, all the people of Eastrod have moved away or died. As he approaches Taulkinham, he is the last representative of Eastrod, so his sense of his background is something he can easily control. In light of the deterministic readings some critics have presented, it is important to note that the train carries evidence that the Eastrod mythos is not inescapable. The porter, who Hazel believes is "a Parrum nigger from Eastrod" (p. 12), has apparently rewritten his past:

> "I'm from Chicago," the porter said in an irritated voice. "My name is not Parrum."
> "Cash is dead," Haze said. "He got the cholera from a pig."
> The porter's mouth jerked down and he said, "My father was a railroad man." (Pp. 18–19)

It is true that the porter may really be from Chicago, but this possibility does not change the significance of Hazel's confrontation with him. Hazel uses the porter to convince himself of his *own* freedom by imagining that the porter has freed himself from Eastrod. Consequently, I would say that Hazel's allegiance to Eastrod values is the result of a free choice. When he returns to his seat, "Eastrod filled his head and then went out beyond and filled the space that stretched from the train across the empty darkening fields" (p. 12). Here Hazel treats the entire landscape as an extension of Eastrod, just as he will apply his Eastrod values to the city, but in the light of Hazel's belief in the porter's ability to change, one should not conclude that Hazel was forced to embarrass the porter in order to demonstrate allegiance to Eastrod. If Hazel is a puppet—he is described as looking "as if he were held by a rope caught in the middle of his back and attached to the train ceiling"—he also controls the strings.

By the time Hazel enters Taulkinham, near the beginning of *Wise Blood,* he is on a quest for sin, and at this point he is clearly beginning to participate in the positive, bodily, communal grotesque. When he visits Mrs. Leora Watts, the prostitute, he thinks that "he should have a woman, not for the sake of the pleasure in her, but to prove that he didn't believe in sin since he practiced what was called it" (p. 110). But in going to visit Mrs. Watts, Hazel takes an important step toward Jesus, because he manages to trick himself into the sexual sin that will eventually make him unable to avoid Jesus. Consequently, his blasphemous assertion that he does not need Jesus because he has Leora Watts (p. 56) is grotesquely accurate. Having made of sex a pathway to the fearsome Jesus, Hazel can unconsciously equate his sexual partners with Jesus. The women with whom Hazel sleeps grotesquely embody Him.

The citizens of Taulkinham may not share Hazel's values, but they all sense that Hazel desires religion. The taxi driver who takes Hazel to the home of Mrs. Watts calls him a preacher on the basis of his hat and face (p. 31). Enoch tells Hazel that he has "nobody nor nothing but Jesus" (p. 59). And Sabbath Lily, after Hazel destroys the mummy that Enoch has stolen and that Enoch considers the "new jesus," furiously says, "I seen you wouldn't never have no fun or let anybody else because you didn't want nothing but Jesus!" (p. 188). In fact, Hazel labels himself a preacher even in denying it. After changing his face and tilting his hat to convince the taxi driver that he is not a preacher, he "put his head in at the window, knocking the hat accidentally straight again. He seemed to have knocked his face straight too for it was now completely expressionless" (p. 32). When he meets Mrs. Watts, he again insists on the preacher label by saying, "What I mean to have you know is: I'm no goddam preacher" (p. 34). Most of the time, however, Hazel and the people of Taulkinham find it very difficult to communicate, as when Hazel attempts to preach blasphemously. The people who listen to Hazel's blasphemies apparently cannot tell that his ideas are unusual. While Hazel assumes that his audiences consider themselves "redeemed," the narrator compares groups of Taulkinham citizens to an unraveling spread (p. 55) and to draining fluid (p. 103). There are also a number of instances in which Hazel engages in conversation with a citizen of Taulkinham, but in which the two understand things quite differently. The waitress at the Frosty Bottle tells Hazel that he is a "clean boy," unlike Enoch, whereupon Hazel, in accordance with the reverse theology of his Church Without Christ, leans toward her and says, "I AM clean" (p. 91). This assertion so flusters the waitress that she is soon screaming, "What do you think I care about any of you filthy boys?" (p. 92).

After Hazel begins to practice sin with Mrs. Watts, his next important move is to meet Asa Hawks, whom Hazel expects to badger into saving him, into forcing Hazel to submit to Jesus. He begins his Church Without Christ to annoy Hawks, he moves into Hawks's apartment house, and he even plans to seduce Sabbath Lily. That this planned seduction is merely part of a religious struggle is shown when the narrator says that Hazel had never been interested in Sabbath Lily until he found out that she was her father's bastard (p. 118). When Asa Hawks is not pleased to learn that Hazel is in his apartment house, Hazel is stunned: "Haze had expected a secret welcome. He waited, trying to think of something to say. 'What kind of a preacher are you?' he heard himself murmur, 'not to see if you can save my soul?'" (p. 108). Hazel's experience with his car is another important episode in his journey toward Jesus. He decides to buy the car on the morning after he first meets Hawks, although he does not admit to himself why he wants it: "The thought was full grown in his head when he woke up, and he didn't think of anything else. He had never thought before of buying a car; he had never even wanted one before" (p. 67). He even tells the used car salesman, "I wanted this car mostly to be a house for me" (p. 73), but it is not long before Hazel has "climbed up on the nose of it" (p. 104), like his grandfather, to preach. Thus his car seems to be chiefly a means to set up a church that will provoke Hawks.

Upon his discovery that Hawks is not blind, one senses his awareness increasing in a way that anticipates his insight when he loses his car: "Haze's expression seemed to open onto a deeper blankness and reflect something and then close again" (p. 162). But when he realizes that Hawks is a sham, Hazel loses what he had planned to use to force himself toward Jesus. As a result, he has to work on himself more directly, although he preaches against the conscience that he is soon to begin using: "'Your conscience is a trick,' he said, 'it don't exist though you may think it does, and if you think it does, you had best get it out in the open and hunt it down and kill it, because it's no more than your face in the mirror is or your shadow behind you!'" (p. 166). Throughout the rest of the novel, Hazel, rather than waiting for Hawks to work on him, finds various ways to exercise his Jesus-haunted conscience on himself.

Hazel first uses this revived conscience on himself when he rejects the new jesus, which he had earlier blasphemously asked for, and which Enoch Emery brings him in the form of a mummy stolen from a museum. This mummy presents something of a puzzle, for it is the most important link between Enoch and Hazel, but it is never specifically identified in Hazel's presence as the new jesus. And O'Connor's comment on Hazel's rejection of the mummy—he throws it against the wall as soon as he sees it—makes the puzzle seem very important. In a letter dated 23 July 1960, O'Connor wrote, "That Haze rejects that mummy suggests everything. What he has been looking for with body and soul throughout the book is suddenly presented to him and he sees it has to be rejected, he sees it ain't really what he's looking for" (*HB*, 404). Hazel's response to the mummy makes it representative of a new jesus whether or not Hazel is told that that is what Enoch considers the mummy to be. Hazel sees the mummy carried in the arms of Sabbath Lily as if it were the child produced by their fornication (*WB*, 187). Insofar as he unconsciously equates Jesus with the women with whom he sleeps, Hazel could consider the mummy the son of Jesus, in which case the name "new jesus" would be appropriate. It has puzzled many readers that after pages of buildup, the new jesus is destroyed and forgotten in an instant, but when one recognizes the full significance of the mummy for Hazel, no other response seems possible.

Hazel's rejection of the new jesus, then, is part of his preparation to reject the pseudofaith he concocted to lead him toward Jesus, much as his realization that a bastard like Sabbath Lily could not be saved, that "her case was hopeless" (p. 122) regardless of the teaching of Hazel's church, perhaps starts Hazel's conscious questioning of the Church Without Christ. Hazel's next act of conscience is the murder of Layfield, the prophet and Hazel's double. Hazel rams Layfield's car and makes him undress, accusing Layfield of something of which Hazel is much more guilty: " 'You ain't true,' Haze said. 'You believe in Jesus' " (p. 203). Then Hazel runs down Layfield. At this point Hazel is almost playing the role of his own authority figure, and as Layfield is dying, Hazel becomes more aware of his own sinfulness: he tells Layfield not to confess, but Hazel does so as he is "leaning his head closer to hear the confession" (p. 205). In playing the authority to his double, and almost encouraging Layfield to confess by maintaining the conversation, Hazel approaches the moment of his return to Jesus.

After Hazel has tricked himself into the sexual sins that lead him toward Jesus, the rest of his actions in the novel serve to prepare Hazel for his final revelation to himself that, because of his sins, he cannot avoid Jesus. Near the end of the novel he tells himself that he is leaving Taulkinham for another city in which to spread his Church Without Christ, but on his way he virtually stops himself:

"He drove very fast out onto the highway, but once he had gone a few miles, he had the sense that he was not gaining ground." And soon "he had the sense that the road was really slipping back under him" (p. 207). Then a patrol car appears, as if Hazel had called it up from deep in his psyche, and the patrolman pushes his car over an embankment. It seems important that the patrolman stops him not because he broke a law but because of his physical characteristics: the patrolman explains why he stopped Hazel by saying, "I just don't like your face" (p. 208). This most unlikely of characters allows Hazel to bring about a transformation that would be extremely difficult if Hazel were fully conscious of the fact that he is transforming himself. Rather than using a religious figure or a symbol of home to transform himself, Hazel uses a representative of secular Taulkinham authority, in relation to whom Hazel is merely a hick from Eastrod.

When Hazel loses his car, he has the controversial vision in which his face reflects the depths of space. For some critics, Hazel's vision causes a conversion that is too sudden to be compatible with free will.[25] For others, the passage implies that Hazel "receives no revelation."[26] My view—that the "blank, gray sky that went on, depth after depth, into space" (*WB*, 209) is a void upon which Hazel now must impose meaning himself—is reinforced, I believe, by a pattern of imagery appearing throughout the novel. The characters of *Wise Blood* search constantly for a valid level of meaning in the physical world. The potato-peeler salesman presents the peeled potato as magically more valid than the unpeeled. Many characters think that peeling off clothes reveals some special reality. Onnie Jay Holy says that your natural sweetness is hidden deep inside you. These searches for the level of real meaning are always in danger of ending up like Enoch's chair, which, after several cleanings reveal a variety of layers of dirt, collapses. When Hazel looks at the sky, he does not see the narrator's version of the divine plan of creation or a representative of a deity—he sees layers upon layers of space.

Having sensed that he must be responsible for the meaning of his life, then, Hazel returns to his apartment, blinds himself with lime, and starts wearing barbed wire around his chest and walking with rocks in his shoes. Thus he appears to have achieved the relation to Jesus that he learned to value in his childhood. From one perspective, Hazel is most negatively grotesque and most isolated at this point; certainly he seems unaware of his landlady and of his neighbors in the boarding house. But if we recall Bakhtin's notion that grotesque death is related to birth, we see more than isolation in

Hazel's death. By the time he dies, he has joined the familial community from which he had rebelled. In unconsciously choosing the grave, Hazel joins the dead family members (his mother, father, brothers, and grandfather) whose casketed bodies he had studied so intently as a child. By the end, Hazel has joined what is, at least for him, a community of the rejuvenated dead, a community of souls whose dead bodies suggest spiritual wholeness. He tells his landlady, Mrs. Flood, that "my people are all dead" (p. 217), a line which Mrs. Flood takes to refer to Hazel's isolation, but which also makes apparent Hazel's belief that the dead can still be his people. And the eventual wholeness of his community makes Hazel's decision to blind himself more significant. That *Wise Blood,* a novel with a wealth of eye imagery, should end in the destruction of eyes, is a final sign of the movement of Hazel Motes from his individual grotesque vision into the community. In Hazel's war between the eye (or "I") and the body, it is the body, which is both dead and alive, that wins.

This conclusion may seem to understate the complexity of Hazel's self-blinding, however, for when he destroys his eyes, he does not merely destroy the peculiarities of his personal vision. The connection between sin and sight implied by his mother's question—"What you seen?"—suggests a relationship between the eye and Hazel's sexual sins, between the eye and the penis. The loss of the eyes in *Wise Blood* is of course a form of suicide, but it is also specifically a castration, a rejection of sexual contact, as Mrs. Flood learns; one of the causes of his death is her proposal of marriage. The blinding, then, may seem to be a rejection of the communal body, a final retreat into bodiless abstraction. There are several indications, however, that Hazel's actions at the end do not completely reject the body. On the simplest level, one could argue that mortification "saves" through the body as much as it rejects the body. One could say that Hazel's redemption, like the redemptive death of Mrs. Shortley or Mrs. May, is supremely physical. Another reason for believing that Hazel's blinding is not a rejection of the body is to be found in the comparison of Hazel to Oedipus, who, as Freud says, performs a similar blinding/castration,[27] and who is never so much a part of his community as when he becomes the scapegoat. Hazel knows nothing of Oedipus—he blinds himself to carry through with the act that Asa Hawks tried to perform and failed—but like Oedipus, Hazel has an effect upon his living community; there are people in Taulkinham who are affected by Hazel and his reformation of religion despite his lack of awareness of them.[28] To some extent, Hazel does retreat into an ideal, but we also see Mrs. Flood and Enoch using the grotesque; in them Hazel retains a link to the living and becomes a new Jesus.

The primary sign that Hazel continues to have an influence upon the living world after he dies is his transformation into a pinpoint of light. Mrs. Flood invents this image when she tries to figure out what the inside of his head looks like:

> She could only imagine the outside in, the whole black world in his head and his head bigger than the world, his head big enough to include the sky and planets and whatever was or had been or would be. How would he know if time was going backwards or forwards or if he was going with it? She imagined it was like you were walking in a tunnel and all you could see was a pin point of light. She had to imagine the pin point of light; she couldn't think of it at all without that. She saw it as some kind of a star, like the star on Christmas cards. She saw him going backwards to Bethlehem and she had to laugh. (Pp. 218–19)

At the novel's end, as Mrs. Flood stares into Hazel's eye sockets after he dies, she has a more elaborate vision:

> The outline of a skull was plain under his skin and the deep burned eye sockets seemed to lead into the dark tunnel where he had disappeared. She leaned closer and closer to his face, looking deep into them, trying to see how she had been cheated or what had cheated her, but she couldn't see anything. She shut her eyes and saw the pin point of light but so far away that she could not hold it steady in her mind. She felt as if she were blocked at the entrance of something. She sat staring with her eyes shut, into his eyes, and felt as if she had finally got to the beginning of something she couldn't begin, and she saw him moving farther and farther away, farther and farther into the darkness until he was the pin point of light. (Pp. 231–32)

Some critics see in this complex final passage Mrs. Flood's conversion. While it is inspired by Hazel, it is also in part the product of Mrs. Flood's extremely materialistic mind. Mrs. Flood feels that she owns everything: "She felt justified in getting anything at all back that she could, money or anything else, as if she had once owned the earth and been dispossessed of it" (p. 214). She raises Hazel's rent for putting up with the way his face looks, raises his rent for letting Sabbath Lily stay with him, raises his rent when she finds out how much he gets from the government, and proposes marriage to get his money when he dies. When Hazel leaves and she wants him back, she calls the police and says Hazel owes her rent. Furthermore, there are several indications that the pinpoint of light substitutes for Hazel as much as it shows an understanding of him. The fact that she "had to imagine the pin point of light," that she "couldn't" think about Hazel's head without it (pp. 218–19), suggests that the reality of Hazel is too much for her. And in the final vision, it is not until Mrs. Flood's eyes are shut, until she quits looking at him, that she sees the pinpoint of light. Near the end of the next-to-last chapter, Mrs. Flood tells herself, "She was not religious or morbid, for which every day she thanked her stars" (p. 211), and one might conclude that the pinpoint of light is a device by which she keeps herself from becoming religious.

I believe that at the end Mrs. Flood is beginning a grotesque process of transformation. She uses her materialism to bring herself toward an understanding of what Hazel mysteriously says he is "paying" for (p. 222), and, in the pinpoint of light, she constructs an idealized, unapproachable version of Hazel (she feels she is "blocked at the entrance"—p. 232), which she may later desecrate and then return to. The first sign that she is going to idealize Hazel occurs as she begins to realize that she is fascinated by the grotesquerie of his eyes. Part of her fascination, of course, involves her connection of Hazel with his money; the effect of his eyes "irritated her with him and gave her the sense that he was cheating her in some secret way" (p. 213). Her greed is so strong that "she couldn't look at anything steadily without wanting it, and what provoked her most was the thought that there might be something valuable hidden near her, something she couldn't see" (p. 214). As she comes up with more devices for getting away from Hazel the money he receives from the government, she becomes more convinced that there is something else of value that he is hiding from her. And as she extends her desire for his money into a sexual desire, she becomes similar to other O'Connor characters who use sex for redemption, although her sexual role, interestingly, seems masculine: "Her plan had become to marry him and keep him. Watching his face had become a habit with her; she wanted to penetrate the darkness behind it and see for herself what was there" (p. 225). The other O'Connor character she most resembles is Mrs. May, startled by the religiosity of Mrs. Greenleaf but finally adopting it. More than Mrs. May, however, Mrs. Flood achieves affection for another. When Hazel rejects her offer of marriage and leaves the house, she manages to produce one of the few expressions of love in O'Connor's works: "Lying in her bed, awake at midnight, Mrs. Flood, the landlady, began to weep. She wanted to run out into the rain and cold and hunt him and find him huddled in some half-sheltered place and bring him back and say, Mr. Motes, Mr. Motes, you can stay here forever, or the two of us will go where you're going, the two of us will go" (pp. 228–29).

Earlier in the novel, Mrs. Flood had imagined that when she and Hazel sat on the porch, she looked as if she "was being courted by a corpse" (p. 217); and by its end, she is courting a dead man, using Hazel to start her own grotesque journey. That Hazel himself is in a sense forgotten in the beginning of the process is not a sign of his meaninglessness, but of his idealization, his transformation into a new jesus. Hazel becomes not only a pinpoint of redeemed, communal freedom, but also a point of departure. He is free of Mrs. Flood's vision of him, but he can also serve as a version of the ideal for her.

Although it may seem that Hazel gains a disciple only when he stops looking for one, he has had another disciple throughout the novel, in Enoch Emery. Mrs. Flood inadvertently suggests the link between Hazel and Enoch when she reacts to Hazel's mortification: "He might as well be one of them monks, she thought, he might as well be in a monkery" (p. 218). Her substitution of "monkery" for "monastery" raises the question whether Hazel-as-monk and Enoch-as-monkey share related values. As I mentioned earlier, I believe the two follow complementary paths toward redemption, but many critics have argued that Enoch is merely corrupt, his religion merely monetary. I consider Enoch at once an apostate and a disciple. At times, critics point out the bases for another view of Enoch even as they condemn him. Donald Gregory says that Enoch "never acts consciously" because his behavior is "utterly predetermined" by his wise blood.[29] Claire Kahane says that Enoch "carries the burden of the negative exemplum" in the novel because he is "locked into the physical."[30] Frederick Asals feels that Enoch's religion "parodies the true purposes of worship," but he also considers Enoch an "ur-Catholic."[31] Asals argues that Hazel is the opposite of Enoch on the basis of Hazel's spirituality and Enoch's physicality, but if Hazel redeems himself through the physical, Enoch is even better prepared to do so.

O'Connor's own statements about Enoch often imply that she does not take him seriously. She sometimes treated Enoch as an alter ego—see her undated 1950 letter to Robie McCauley (*HB*, 21), for example—but she could also say that Enoch "is a moron and chiefly a comic character. I don't think it is important whether his compulsion is clinical or not" (*MM*, 116–17). Perhaps she was not inclined to take Enoch seriously because she had so little trouble composing his parts of the novel; in letters dated 25 November 1955 and 21 September 1957 (*HB*, 117, 241) she said that Enoch was one of the easiest characters for her to write about. There is considerable evidence, however, that Enoch is more important than O'Connor said. Stuart L. Burns criticizes the structure of *Wise Blood* for its emphasis on Enoch, but as he does so, he suggests a reason to take

Enoch seriously. Burns points out that if one reads "The Heart of the Park" and "Enoch and the Gorilla"—sections of *Wise Blood* about Enoch that were published before the novel—without knowing about the revisions of those sections, one would assume that Enoch is the protagonist of the upcoming novel.[32] In both of these "stories," Enoch is much more of a religious seeker than Hazel Motes is in "The Heart of the Park" or in "The Train," an M.F.A. thesis story later revised by O'Connor into the first chapter of *Wise Blood*. Although Burns says that "O'Connor never successfully solved the problem of Enoch's importance,"[33] I think that O'Connor's struggle with this early material—in contrast to her struggle with "The Geranium"—makes *Wise Blood* a better novel.

Although critical opinion of Enoch is overwhelmingly negative, one can occasionally discover critics relating Enoch to Mrs. Shortley and Mrs. Greenleaf, two of the clearest examples of participants in the positive grotesque. I consider Enoch another member of the group of characters who are not quite willing to remain in the margins of O'Connor's works. If one agrees to evaluate Hazel's experience according to the rules of his personal world view, it seems proper to do the same for Enoch. Although Enoch may seem as absurd as Mrs. Shortley at first seems, the narrator's dismissal of him ultimately encourages us to see the necessity for his desperately conceived personal system.

The standards necessary for considering Enoch's experience religious are not radically different from the standards we apply to Hazel Motes. Like Hazel, Enoch degrades his oppressive religion to a physical level. His sense of religion comes from time spent with a "Welfare woman" who "didn't do nothing but pray" (*WB*, 46) and time spent at the Rodemill Boys' Bible Academy. Further, Enoch, like Hazel, associates Jesus with a relative: "My daddy looks just like Jesus," Enoch says, apparently because "his hair hangs to his shoulders" (p. 51). And Enoch's father is a much more threatening figure than Hazel's family are to Hazel. Enoch's father differs from Jesus in having "a scar acrost his chin" (ibid.), and he has very little use for Enoch; he traded Enoch to the Welfare woman and, two months before Enoch met Hazel, forced Enoch to go to Taulkinham. Enoch seems to feel that he might return to his father, but even as he suggests why he might be able to return, he gives another indication that his father is an unpleasant person: "He done gone off with a woman and made me come but she ain't going to stay for long, he'll beat hell out of her before she gets herself stuck to a chair" (p. 57).

Like Hazel, Enoch uses sex to return to the family member he associates with Jesus. Enoch explains how he escaped the Welfare woman: "I scared hell out of that woman, that's how. I studied on it and studied on it. I even prayed. I said, 'Jesus, show me the way to get out of here without killing thisyer woman and getting sent to the penitentiary,' and durn if He didn't. I got up one morning at just daylight and I went in her room without my pants on and pulled the sheet off her and giver a heart attact. Then I went back to my daddy and we ain't seen hide of her since" (p. 48). That Enoch substitutes sex for religion is shown again during the argument when Hazel tries to get rid of him. Enoch says he doubts that Hazel has "got wiser blood than anybody else" (p. 59), and the reason for this doubt is that Hazel seems stuck on Jesus rather than on a woman: "You ain't got no woman nor nothing to do. I knew when I first seen you you didn't have nobody nor nothing but Jesus" (p. 58).

The fifth chapter of *Wise Blood* focuses on Enoch's grotesque personal religion. Each day when he gets off work, he enters the park and hides on a slope above the swimming pool to watch women. Hiding in the bushes, Enoch seems almost aware of himself as a participant in an antireligion: "Anyone who parted the abelia sprigs at just that place, would think he saw a devil and would fall down the slope and into the pool" (p. 82). The next step in his ritual is a trip to a hotdog stand, where he orders a milkshake and makes "suggestive remarks" to the waitress. Then, after a visit to the zoo to insult the animals, he goes to the park museum to see the mummy at the heart of his religion: "It was a mystery, although it was right there in a glass case for everybody to see and there was a typewritten card over it telling all about it. But there was something the card couldn't say and what it couldn't say was inside him, a terrible knowledge without any words to it, a terrible knowledge like a big nerve growing inside him" (p. 81). One of O'Connor's most explicit analyses of a character's psyche separates Enoch's unconscious from his conscious mind in a manner that shows Enoch to be well equipped to use the grotesque positively. The narrator says of Enoch's mind that "the part in communication with his blood" (p. 87)—that is, the unconscious—"never said anything in words" but did the "figuring" to get Hazel to go through Enoch's ritual. The conscious part of Enoch's mind, on the other hand, is completely trivial, "stocked up with all kinds of words and phrases" that Enoch ridiculously spouts throughout the novel.

Enoch's blood tells him he must present the mummy to someone, and Enoch shows it to Hazel. Hazel forgets the mummy quickly and hits Enoch on the head with a rock to get rid of him, but Enoch is determined to believe that he has had a religious experience. When he catches up with Hazel outside the museum, Hazel grabs Enoch, who feels "weak and light as a balloon" (p. 99); when let go, Enoch "fell backward and landed against one of the white-socked trees. He rolled over and lay stretched out on the ground, with an exalted look on his face." Recovering from the blow to the head, Enoch decides that "whatever was expected of him was only just beginning" (p. 100). We next see Enoch when his unconscious—his wise blood—is starting to tell him to refurbish his room, steal the mummy from the museum, and install the mummy in his room. Consciously, Enoch considers all these actions "a mystery beyond his understanding," something "awful" (p. 129). When he realizes that the day has arrived for him to act, "he decided not to get up. He didn't want to justify his daddy's blood, he didn't want to be always having to do something that something else wanted him to do, that he didn't know what it was and that was always dangerous" (pp. 134–35). The fact that he consistently spends money on things he does not consciously want during this section of the novel indicates a transformation of Enoch's materialism into religion. He finds himself buying materials to make his room a sanctuary for the mummy instead of buying himself new clothes (p. 134), and he later obeys his blood in spending money on a triple feature he does not want to see (p. 138).

When Enoch hears Hazel Motes preaching about the new jesus, he decides that the museum mummy is the new jesus, and after he has stolen it, he expects "one of the supreme moments in his life" (p. 175), his transformation into "an entirely new man, with an even better personality than he had now." Soon he is consciously opposed to his involvement with the mummy; he decides to take the new jesus to Hazel and tells himself, "One jesus was as bad as another" (p. 176). On his way to Hazel's apartment, however, Enoch regains some respect for the new jesus when he encounters Gonga, the Jungle Monarch (a man in an ape suit), in front of a movie house. Gonga is important because Enoch feels that "an opportunity to insult a successful ape came from the hand of Providence" (p. 178). And although the man in the ape suit responds to Enoch's sudden friendliness by saying, "You go to hell" (p. 182), Enoch does not despair. Even after he gives the new jesus to Sabbath Lily, he "couldn't get over the expectation that the new jesus was going to do something for him in return for his services" (p. 191); he imagines his reward is to be his transformation into "THE young man of the future, like the ones in the insurance ads." His reward, however, turns out to be an ape suit; rather like Hazel

forcing Solace Layfield to undress, Enoch steals the costume of
Gonga. As Gonga, Enoch achieves—or thinks he does—his long-
desired acceptance into the community, and he desires to shake
everyone's hand. However, he horrifies the first two people he
approaches, and, when we last see him, it is not clear what will
become of Enoch.

From one point of view, the ending of Enoch's story may seem to
refute his personal grotesque religion. Enoch does achieve some of
what he unconsciously desires, however. Although the narration
encourages the reader to disapprove of Enoch, there is little reason
to prefer Hazel's experience to Enoch's. The narrator abandons
Enoch before his story ends, but the abrupt termination of Enoch's
story, like the terminations of several other of O'Connor's characters' stories, may contribute to the positive quality of Enoch's
experience. It may be premature to say that Enoch has achieved
everything he desires—can he equate Gonga with his daddy and
with Jesus? Although some critics feel that Enoch's story is indeed
over when the narrator abandons him, I think that the end of
Enoch's story, his confrontation with Gonga, whom he may have
killed, corresponds to Hazel's murder of Solace Layfield. In any
case, it is not necessary for us to see Enoch complete the grotesque
process. He is subordinate to Hazel in the novel: his story serves
primarily to complement Hazel's. For that purpose, we need only
to see that Enoch's religion incorporates his eccentric interpretation
of Hazel. We need not claim that Enoch is a co-protagonist to
consider him an embodiment of Hazel's indirect but continuing
connection to the physical world. Enoch's story, like Mrs. Flood's,
succeeds in reminding us that Hazel's death is not the end of the
grotesque process.

1. Asals, *Flannery O'Connor*, p. 5.
2. Gordon, "O'Connor's *Wise Blood*," p. 9.
3. Ibid., p. 6.
4. Quoted by Sally Fitzgerald in "A Master Class," p. 828.
5. Ibid., p. 844.
6. Quoted in ibid., p. 846
7. Quoted in ibid., p. 833.
8. Quoted in ibid., p. 834.
9. Quoted in ibid., p. 842.
10. The sentence about the marquee lights does not appear on this typescript; it
was added later. The typescript is in File 151, O'Connor Collection.
11. Quoted by Sally Fitzgerald in "A Master Class," p. 842.
12. Quoted in ibid., p. 835.
13. Sally Fitzgerald, "Rooms with a View," p. 14. Fitzgerald discusses the star
description on p. 15; she considers it a fulfillment of Gordon's request.

14. Driskill and Brittain, *Eternal Crossroads*, p. 122.

15. Josephine Hendin, in *World of O'Connor*, sees the passage as a description of "a city under construction" (p. 47). Asals, in *Flannery O'Connor*, discusses the clouds as follows: "Surely the 'curls and a beard' are more than a little absurd, the neat metamorphosis deflatingly comic, the tone here a humorous mocking of the hero's obsessions? Or is it?" (p. 59).

16. Stephens, *Question of O'Connor*, p. 52.

17. Quoted by Sally Fitzgerald in "A Master Class," p. 846.

18. Stephens, *Question of O'Connor*, p. 57.

19. Hendin, *World of O'Connor*, p. 54.

20. Thomas LeClair, in "O'Connor's *Wise Blood*," says that Hazel finally accepts the "inescapable dominance of his mother" (p. 203). André Bleikasten, in "Heresy of O'Connor," says that "Hazel's backward journey is essentially a return to the mother" (p. 63).

21. Bakhtin, *Rabelais and His World*, p. 316.

22. LeClair, "O'Connor's *Wise Blood*," pp. 199–200.

23. McCullagh, "Symbolism and the Religious Aesthetic," p. 48.

24. Ibid., p. 56. Stuart Burns also argues, in "Evolution of *Wise Blood*," but from a different point of view, that Hazel's feelings about his mother interfere with the religious theme. Burns notes that the sections of *Wise Blood* published before the novel's publication put more emphasis on Hazel's attraction to his mother. Burns considers such passages in the published novel to be mere carryovers from an earlier, abandoned conception of the novel. He notes, however, that there are revisions in which O'Connor made the mother more important and her significance more religious (p. 151).

25. Kellogg, *The Vital Tradition*, p. 192. J. O. Tate, in "The Essential Essex," suggests the car's importance for Hazel's conversion. If "nobody with a good car needs to be justified" (*WB*, 113), it follows, as Tate points out (pp. 50–51), that anyone without a good car *does* need justification.

26. Asals, *Flannery O'Connor*, p. 53.

27. *The Basic Writings of Sigmund Freud*, trans. A. A. Brill (New York: Modern Library, 1938), p. 393. According to several scholars, O'Connor owned this book by 1947: Getz, *Flannery O'Connor: Her Life, Library and Book Reviews*, p. 95; Feeley, *Flannery O'Connor*, p. 110; and Kinney, *O'Connor's Library*, p. 86. In his introduction to *Everything That Rises Must Converge*, Robert Fitzgerald reports that O'Connor read the Oedipus plays for the first time in the summer of 1950 and decided to have Hazel blind himself (p. 13). It is also interesting that in one draft of the eleventh chapter of *Wise Blood*, in File 135, O'Connor Collection, O'Connor specifically compares both Hazel and Enoch to Oedipus.

28. Jonathan Culler's reading of *Oedipus* in *The Pursuit of Signs*, pp. 172–76, suggests more of the play's similarity to *Wise Blood*. The logic of the play, from one point of view, is that events determine meanings; the crimes of Oedipus produce meaning regardless of his intentions. From a contrary perspective, however, the revelation of the crimes is ambiguous, for Oedipus decides that he is guilty before evidence of his guilt is complete. From this contrary perspective, it is Oedipus's conception of the meaning of his life on the basis of what is necessary for the coherence of the play that determines events. For Culler, these two perspectives "put in question the possibility of a coherent, noncontradictory account of narrative" (p. 175). I see a similar contrast in *Wise Blood* between the notion that Hazel is forced into redemption and the notion that he unconsciously brings it about.

29. Gregory, "Enoch Emery," p. 52.

30. Kahane, "Comic Vibrations and Self-Construction in Grotesque Literature," pp. 115, 117.

31. Asals, *Flannery O'Connor*, pp. 45, 44.

32. Burns, "Evolution of *Wise Blood*," pp. 152–56.

33. Ibid., pp. 155–56.

8

THE "DEMONIC" O'CONNOR

The Violent Bear It Away and "The Lame Shall Enter First"

> Whatsoever thy hand is able to do, do it earnestly; for neither work, nor reason, nor wisdom, nor knowledge shall be in hell, whither thou art hastening.
>
> —Ecclesiastes 9:10

The Violent Bear It Away, O'Connor's second novel, is at once her most consistently religious work and the work that has inspired the most comments about her so-called devilishness. As in *Wise Blood,* the protagonist of *The Violent Bear It Away,* Francis Marion Tarwater, takes a difficult path toward the religious role that an ancestor has defined for him, but several aspects of *The Violent Bear It Away* make Tarwater's trek more difficult than Hazel Motes's. Both Hazel and Tarwater resent their ancestors, but Tarwater's great-uncle, Old Mason Tarwater, is a more oppressive force than is Hazel's family. And unlike Hazel Motes, who is allowed consciously to forget the terms of the process by which he transforms himself, Tarwater cannot forget. He constantly has before him reminders of the choice he has to make: in the internal, devilish voice he considers his "friend"; in Rayber; and in the idiot Bishop, Tarwater's cousin, whom Old Tarwater had enjoined Tarwater to baptize. Tarwater does not practice mortification, as Hazel does, but he is still almost destroyed by his trials. In fact, to some critics, Tarwater's torture is inconsistent with a religious reading. To understand the relationship between the demonic and the religious in *The Violent Bear It Away,* we must pay particular attention to

142

O'Connor's narration in this novel. And because "The Lame Shall Enter First" presents a significant variation on O'Connor's second novel, I shall consider that story here as well.

The most famous critic to write that there is a devilish side to Flannery O'Connor's fiction is the novelist John Hawkes. In his article "Flannery O'Connor's Devil," Hawkes says that O'Connor uses the voice of the devil to destroy man's belief he is "rational"; when an O'Connor character is compared to an inanimate object and/or made to seem meaningless, says Hawkes, O'Connor fully agrees with the demonic spirit of her satire.[1] As an example of O'Connor's demonic treatment of a character, Hawkes refers to her "wonderfully unsympathetic portrait"[2] of Rayber, Tarwater's uncle, a portrait I shall discuss at some length later.

Some critics, following Hawkes's ideas about O'Connor's narration, make O'Connor's vision seem even bleaker. Claire Katz Kahane describes the O'Connor narrator as a "sadistic" figure trapping the characters.[3] Josephine Hendin says, "I think O'Connor is best when writing like a devil of reduction, most convincing when most literal and least convincing when consciously symbolic."[4] Such an attitude leads Hendin to the conclusion, "Demanding neither hope nor salvation, O'Connor's heroes need only certainty. And all they can know absolutely, 'know for sure,' is isolation, rage, and death."[5] Another result of this attitude is suggested by Melvin J. Friedman, who discusses at length the relationship between O'Connor and Hawkes. Surprisingly, Friedman says that the literary "methods" of O'Connor and Hawkes "could not be less alike,"[6] but he believes that they share "a fascination with the surface of objects," a fascination that Friedman thinks might link O'Connor and Hawkes to the engrossment with physical objects of the New Novelists.[7] The idea that O'Connor and Hawkes emphasize surfaces implies that the two writers do not concern themselves with the psychology of characters.

To some extent, O'Connor responded predictably to the critical approach of Hawkes and his followers. O'Connor read Hawkes's article before it was published, and in a letter of 12 January 1962, she said that "there are some quite wild things in it" (*HB*, 461). By 27 January 1963, she wrote in a letter to T. R. Spivey that Hawkes's view of the devil was quite different from her own: she explained, "His devil is an impeccable literary spirit whom he makes responsible for all good literature. Anything good he thinks must come from the devil. He is a good friend of mine and I have had this out with him many times, to no avail" (p. 507).

When she wrote to Hawkes himself on 5 April 1962 and explained her disagreement, however, she also told him not to have doubts about the piece, that she liked the article in spite of her disagreement, and that she hoped the article would be read (pp. 470–71). This letter may seem hypocritical, but O'Connor had had time to discover some value in Hawkes's approach, because she and Hawkes had been discussing each other's fiction ever since Hawkes stopped at O'Connor's house in 1958 to introduce himself and give her two of his books (pp. 291–93). By 1959, when O'Connor was writing *The Violent Bear It Away* and Hawkes was writing *The Lime Twig,* O'Connor was sending parts of her manuscript to Hawkes for his suggestions. Despite their disagreements about the devil, O'Connor often indicated to Hawkes that she felt he understood her work. In a letter dated 13 September 1959, responding to Hawkes's comments on her novel's opening, O'Connor wrote, "It's not every book that gets itself understood before it has been read" (p. 351), and she later gave him credit for improving the prose in the middle of the novel (p. 368).

It is interesting to note in this regard that Hawkes's suggestions about the Rayber section, which appear on a typescript of *The Violent Bear It Away* at Georgia College, generally encourage O'Connor to take a harsher attitude toward Rayber and to produce a novel more like what Hawkes's famous article says it is.[8] Along with certain technical suggestions, Hawkes recommended that O'Connor make Rayber's opinions more pronounced and less reasonable; he encouraged her to make Rayber less likable, and he singled out for special praise the grotesque description of Rayber's head as having a "pie-shaped hairline" (*V,* 105). O'Connor took some of Hawkes's advice, but in a letter dated 20 November 1959 she explained to Hawkes why she did not make Rayber more devilish: "I had in mind that Rayber would echo all [Tarwater's] friend's sentiments in a form that the reader would identify himself with. With trial and error I found that making Rayber pure evil made him a caricature and took away from the role of the old prophet since it left him nothing worth trying to save" (*HB,* 359). It is true, as O'Connor suggests here, that in one draft of the novel, Tarwater has never seen Rayber until he goes to the city to live with him, and in this draft Tarwater discovers a remarkable resemblance between his personal devilish "friend" and his uncle.[9] However, this resemblance is almost completely absent from the published version of the novel.

Equally interesting are O'Connor's indications that she felt her works and Hawkes's were similar. O'Connor wrote to Hawkes on 6 October 1959 that she agreed with him that their artistic visions were alike: "As you say, your vision, though it doesn't come by way of theology, is the same as mine" (p. 352). And O'Connor responded enthusiastically to *The Lime Twig*; she wrote on 9 October 1960, "This one I might have been dreaming myself" (p. 412). Of course O'Connor's opinions prove nothing about the critical approach of Hawkes, but as one reads the statements of critics who have attacked Hawkes's ideas about O'Connor, it is important to remember that O'Connor was not entirely opposed to his approach.

One wonders, still, how O'Connor and Hawkes found common ground. I would suggest that an answer is to be found by examining a major problem that remains in the approach of Hawkes and of others who discuss O'Connor's devilishness. None of these critics define clearly what they mean by the term "devil." Clearly they do not mean what O'Connor meant: an actual being, God's antagonist, Satan. Generally, Hawkes and his followers seem to consider the devil a spokesman for nihilism or determinism. For the purposes of this study, it should suffice to say that these critics locate O'Connor's devilishness primarily in the voice of her narrators and that what makes these narrators devilish is their emphasis upon the negative grotesque. I have found Hawkes and his followers inspiring, and I believe that what O'Connor approved of in Hawkes's approach was his delight in the grotesque. But when one gets beyond the perverse thrill of calling O'Connor demonic and looks carefully at what Hawkes is saying, one discovers that he and many of his followers make the same basic mistake that many of O'Connor's religious critics make: equating O'Connor with her narrators. Surely part of what she rejected in Hawkes's approach was the notion that she was directly, personally, morally responsible for every word, every grotesque comparison, every nuance produced by her narrators.

My emphasis upon the positive grotesque also provides an answer to the suggestion by Hawkes and others that O'Connor's characters are determined, reduced, destroyed by her. Much of Hawkes's argument about O'Connor's devilishness depends upon his citation of her use of the negative grotesque; and, as I have sought to demonstrate, most of O'Connor's characters are capable of directing negative grotesquerie toward positive ends. O'Connor's characters achieve redemption not because they submit to the narrator, but because they free themselves from the narrator. The notion that O'Connor explores surfaces rather than psychology involves a misunderstanding of the split in her works between consciousness and unconsciousness, and the frequent extension of Hawkes's approach to deny O'Connor's characters free will ignores the evidence that these characters contribute to and modify the rules according to which they achieve redemption. In "The Lame Shall Enter First," O'Connor comes close to producing the sort of work that Hawkes and his followers describe; but in *The Violent Bear It Away,* all the negative, "demonic" forces lead toward rejuvenation.

All three of the major characters in O'Connor's second novel construct plans for their redemption. In fact, Old Tarwater has read an analysis of his self-redemption in a journal article written by Rayber, and of course Old Tarwater must not and cannot accept Rayber's interpretation, as he explains to Tarwater: "From time to time, the old man would spit out of his mouth, like gobbets of poison, some of the idiotic sentences from the schoolteacher's piece. Wrath had burned them on his memory, word for word. 'His fixation of being called by the Lord had its origin in insecurity. He needed the assurance of a call, and so he called himself' " (*V,* 19). Much more than Tarwater, Old Tarwater is comfortable with his religious role, a quality that makes him comparable to the characters discussed in chapter 4. Old Tarwater is obsessed with his own death, but not because he fears death; he simply wants to make sure that Tarwater buries him properly. When Old Tarwater climbs into a coffin he built for himself, he announces "with satisfaction" that "this is the end of us all" (*V,* 14). His plans for death include the promise that "as soon as I hear the summons, I'm going to run downstairs. I'll get as close to the door as I can." Then it will be up to Tarwater to put his great-uncle into a deep grave.

Despite O'Connor's frequent praise for Old Tarwater, a few critics have questioned his value as a model for Tarwater. Such comments show why Tarwater must redeem his conception of Old Tarwater, the old man's religion, and the role of prophet. The oppressiveness of Old Tarwater's ideals becomes clear as he tells Tarwater he was

> "born into bondage and baptized into freedom, into the death of the Lord, into the death of the Lord Jesus Christ."
> Then the child would feel a sullenness creeping over him, a slow warm rising resentment that this freedom had to be connected with Jesus and that Jesus had to be the Lord.
> "Jesus is the bread of life," the old man said.
> . . . In the darkest, most private part of his soul, hanging upsidedown like a sleeping bat, was the certain, undeniable knowledge that he was

not hungry for the bread of life. Had the bush flamed for Moses, the sun stood still for Joshua, the lions turned aside before Daniel only to prophesy the bread of life? Jesus? He felt a terrible disappointment in that conclusion, a dread that it was true. The old man said that as soon as he died, he would hasten to the banks of the Lake of Galilee to eat the loaves and fishes that the Lord had multiplied.

"Forever?" the horrified boy asked. (Pp. 20–21)

Tarwater seems inclined to reject the vision of heaven as a communal feast, but when the old prophet dies, Tarwater is forced into actions that show he has learned from his great-uncle's example. Still, Tarwater is unwilling to admit that he is obeying anyone's orders.

Tarwater's first step in grotesquely transforming himself into a prophet is his refusal to bury his great-uncle. Because the old man had talked constantly about Tarwater's obligation to put him properly in the ground, Tarwater refuses to. Instead he burns the house and runs away, but these actions are significant in ways Tarwater cannot admit. First, his apparent flight from responsibility in his home is actually a flight toward the city, where his quest for prophethood will have to take place. The sign that Tarwater is running *toward* responsibility as well as away from it is his confusion of the city's lights with the fire of the burning cabin (p. 51). Second, Tarwater's refusal to bury his great-uncle may be motivated by a desire to feel guilt, to ensure his continuing feeling of obligation toward Old Tarwater.

Several critics have emphasized the novel's first paragraph as a clear indication from the narrator that Tarwater's conscious rebellion is destined to fail. Tarwater leaves Powderhead thinking that he has burned his great-uncle, but we are told in the novel's first sentence that "the boy got too drunk to finish digging his grave and a Negro named Buford Munson, who had come to get a jug filled, had to finish it and drag the body from the breakfast table where it was still sitting and bury it in a decent and Christian way, with the sign of its Saviour at the head of the grave and enough dirt on top to keep the dogs from digging it up" (p. 3). This passage, which apparently reflects Buford Munson's perspective, has been taken as proof that Tarwater's actions are determined. For Joyce Carol Oates, the opening implies a "classic predestination,"[10] and Claire Katz Kahane goes so far as to say:

> The circle of completed action has closed on Tarwater from the start. In a sense, this is a metaphor for the state of being of all O'Connor's characters, precluding free choice. Although critics have called *The*

> *Violent Bear It Away* an exploration of freedom, they ignore the novel's
> structure, the inevitability of Tarwater's destiny. . . . *The Violent Bear It
> Away* shows us that the more Tarwater thinks he is going forward in
> time, the more he is carried backward to the point where he began.[11]

However, the novel's opening paragraph is more complicated than
this reading makes it. If, before going to the city, Tarwater had
known that his great-uncle had been buried, he would have been
relieved of part of the burden Old Tarwater placed upon him. In
fact, before Tarwater abandons his digging, he tells himself that "he
would have to bury the old man before anything would begin. It
was as if there would have to be dirt over him before he would be
thoroughly dead" (*V,* 12). If Tarwater had known about the burial,
he might have been freed from Old Tarwater. Consequently, in
setting the fire and running off toward the city, Tarwater simultaneously expresses his conscious rebellion against Old Tarwater
and his unconscious desire not to allow the old man to be thoroughly dead. The point here is that as Tarwater chooses his destination, he frees himself from the narrator's implication of helplessness.

The voice that Tarwater hears is another device by which Tarwater pushes himself toward becoming a prophet without admitting that that is what he is doing. In other words, Tarwater's devil is
an assailant of Tarwater's own creation, with whom Tarwater cooperates for his own ends. By expressing his rebellion in a second
voice, Tarwater is able to deal with those thoughts that threaten his
becoming a prophet without having to realize that they are his own
thoughts, and when Tarwater is ready to dismiss his rebelliousness,
all he has to do is set a fire and imagine that "his adversary would
soon be consumed in a roaring blaze" (p. 238). It is worth noting
that one of the first pieces of advice that this devilish voice gives
Tarwater is, "Bury him first and get it over with" (p. 13). The fact
that Tarwater does not follow this advice reinforces the idea that his
trip to the city begins his grotesque transformation.

The status of Tarwater's "friend," the voice that urges him away
from the role of prophet, has produced considerable controversy.
Some critics follow O'Connor's lead, labeling the friend as the
Devil. Most critics assert that to some extent the friend expresses
Tarwater's desires, but they seldom cite evidence to show that
Tarwater controls the voice. I find several such indications. At one
point we are shown Tarwater "softening the stranger's voice so that
he could stand it" (p. 25). At another point the friend asks Tarwater
what he knows about "whores" (p. 40), and although Tarwater
vaguely repeats from the Bible something that shows his inno-

cence, the voice later agrees that "you know what one of them is" (p. 42). Kathleen Feeley asserts that the voice is the Devil, but her evidence also supports an opposite interpretation. Feeley points to the passage in the novel where the stranger insists that Tarwater demand a sign from God before baptizing Bishop, and she argues that the voice must be the Devil's because the voice, in accordance with the Devil's inability to read minds, does not know that Tarwater is also tempted to drown Bishop.[12] I would argue, rather, that Tarwater is using the friend's voice to make the baptism easier; while telling himself that he is going to drown Bishop, and using the stranger's voice to assure himself that he will not perform a baptism, he brings himself closer to the moment of baptism.

Throughout Tarwater's time in the city, he leads himself toward redemption by telling himself that he is doing the opposite. Unlike Hazel Motes, who tries unsuccessfully for a long time to convince the sham preacher Asa Hawks to redeem him, Tarwater brings his adversary with him—in the friend—and, once in the city, finds two people whom he justly considers participants in his redemptive struggle—Rayber and Bishop. As Buford Munson had told Tarwater about the city, if "nobody going to bother you," then "that going to be your trouble" (*V,* 48). Consequently, Tarwater's consistent hostility toward Rayber and Bishop is useful to him, because it increases the conflict he is trying to resolve while it hides from Tarwater the fact that he intends to follow his great-uncle's order to baptize Bishop. The tensions between Tarwater and Rayber ultimately allow Tarwater to tell himself that he is performing the drowning/baptism in a spirit of hatred.

Another of the interesting differences between *Wise Blood* and *The Violent Bear It Away* is that whereas Hazel starts several false paths toward redemption, Tarwater consciously realizes that his path to redemption requires a baptism and the adoption of the role of prophet. But while Hazel seems absolutely certain that the loss of his car marks the turning point in his life, Tarwater has a very difficult time accepting any action or moment as crucial. Tarwater undergoes a series of apparent turning points, and it is not clear that they are all necessary. The first of these turning points is the baptism, a necessary step, but one which does not commit Tarwater to becoming a prophet; while Tarwater drowns Bishop, he says, the words of baptism "just come out of themselves" by "accident" (p. 209). Tarwater claims that the baptism is meaningless, and although he recalls that at the moment of baptism he heard "the sibilant oaths of his friend fading away on the darkness" (p. 216), Tarwater is not transformed by the baptism.

The next apparent turning point for Tarwater is his rape in the woods. Most critics consider Tarwater's rape by a driver resembling Tarwater's friend—who picks up the hitchhiking Tarwater, drugs him, and carries him into the woods—to be the appropriate result of Tarwater's abandonment of his calling. To some extent, the rape also appropriately symbolizes Tarwater's acceptance of his calling, for he equates his friend with the rapist—for whom Tarwater feels absolute disgust—and as he burns the area where the rape occurred, Tarwater seems close to dismissing his reluctance to be a prophet.

Tarwater's inclination to see his rape in religious terms has been carefully prepared for. Old Tarwater had told him repeatedly that after he was baptized as a child by Old Tarwater, Rayber had blasphemously baptized Tarwater's buttocks, saying, "Now Jesus has a claim on both ends" (p. 73). And Old Tarwater had prepared him to believe that anyone who treats him as the rapist does will be devilish: " 'You are the kind of boy,' the old man said, 'that the devil is always going to be offering to assist, to give you a smoke or a drink or a ride, and to ask you your bidnis' " (p. 58). Despite these preparations for Tarwater to understand his rape in spiritual terms, the sudden appearance of the rapist, like the sudden appearance of the trooper near the end of *Wise Blood,* is critically controversial. Martha Stephens discusses Tarwater's friend as a figure in an allegory constructed by Tarwater,[13] but she objects when Tarwater's friend suddenly seems to exist outside Tarwater's mind. It seems clear, as Stephens points out, that the rapist exists, for he is described returning to his car while Tarwater is unconscious, and as Stephens says, such a description is outside the bounds of a mental allegory.[14] But Stephens makes two mistakes in her attack on this passage. First, the allegorizing of events and characters by O'Connor's protagonists is not a device limited to a few passages; it is an essential feature of the way O'Connor characters view the world. The extremity of the example of Tarwater's rape should make clear the extent to which O'Connor characters impose personal interpretations upon everything. Once one realizes the extent to which Tarwater and other characters unconsciously allegorize to exercise control over what happens to them, they seem less like victims of chance events and more like self-determining figures able to make even chance events operate within their unconscious plans for self-redemption. The second problem with Stephens's attack is that it mistakes an effect for a cause. Tarwater does not become a prophet because he is raped; rather, he interprets his rape theologically because he is in the process of making himself into a prophet.[15] One effect of having Tarwater realize his transformation slowly, during a series of apparent turning points—even the friend reappears, surprisingly, and Tarwater sets another fire to banish him again—is to emphasize that no external force is capable of transforming him. The transformation occurs when Tarwater is ready.

To some extent, one could say that Tarwater's redemption starts from the moment he begins his trek toward prophethood, so that the series of apparent turning points is of little significance. However, Tarwater's conscious acceptance of the role of prophet occurs only when he returns to Powderhead, at which point I believe that Tarwater's freedom is clear.[16] Most critics assume that when Tarwater returns to Powderhead and discovers that Old Tarwater has been buried after all, he suddenly realizes that he cannot defeat the old man. But from another perspective, it is only at this point that Tarwater realizes that his original obligation to Old Tarwater has been fulfilled, and that if he wishes to go off on a path different from the one Old Tarwater wants him to follow, *now* is the time to start. Tarwater treats his return as if he has no choice but to become the prophet, but there is no particular reason why the return to Powderhead necessitates Tarwater's capitulation. In one typescript of the novel, Tarwater returns to Powderhead, discovers his great-uncle's grave well before the novel's end, and returns to the city, still intending to drown Bishop.[17]

However, when Tarwater discovers his great-uncle's grave in the published novel, he takes the discovery as the occasion for a revelation. In a field by the cabin he sees what Clinton W. Trowbridge calls "the country of the redeemed dead,"[18] a more explicit version of what I referred to in the last chapter as a community of the rejuvenated dead:

> Everywhere, he saw dim figures seated on the slope and as he gazed he saw that from a single basket the throng was being fed. His eyes searched the crowd for a long time as if he could not find the one he was looking for. Then he saw him. The old man was lowering himself to the ground. When he was down and his bulk had settled, he leaned forward, his face turned toward the basket, impatiently following its progress toward him. The boy too leaned forward, aware at last of the object of his hunger, aware that it was the same as the old man's and that nothing on earth would fill him. (*V*, 241)

Unlike Hazel Motes, Tarwater does not merely rejoin this community, which resembles Old Tarwater's description of heaven. He hears the command of his prophecy and heads back to the city, "where the children of God lay sleeping" (p. 243).

The most problematic character in *The Violent Bear It Away* is Rayber, who, like Enoch Emery in *Wise Blood*, strikes some critics

as a character who "arrogates attention."[19] Rayber is generally
considered a stereotype of the aspects of modern intellectuality for
which O'Connor had the most contempt, but his role in the novel
is considerably more complicated than this view implies. Miles
Orvell adequately describes the problems involved in understanding Rayber when he says that O'Connor "makes Rayber's absurdity
too patent a premise of her authorial viewpoint."[20] On the one
hand, we are supposed to take Rayber seriously as an attractive
alternative to Old Tarwater in the eyes of Tarwater, but, as Orvell
points out, the narrator's negative attitude toward Rayber—the sort
of characterization John Hawkes encouraged O'Connor to use—
makes it difficult to see how Rayber could attract Tarwater. Although O'Connor did not always follow Hawkes's advice, Rayber
is in many ways a negatively grotesque figure, and he has more
trouble than Enoch Emery does in turning his negative grotesquerie into positive grotesquerie. One major instance of Rayber's
grotesquerie is his hearing aid; as Orvell explains it, "when Rayber
initially appears at the door to greet Tarwater, he is without his
hearing aid and so cannot hear the boy; in capital letters, we
imagine the message: Rayber is deaf to Tarwater."[21] Orvell concludes, "The cumulative effect of this simplistically satirical characterization is that our very last view of the man (when his feelings
are supposedly in tragic conflict) seems oddly jarring—prepared for
but not quite convincing."[22] It may be true that many readers are
unable to take Rayber as seriously as Tarwater does, but when one
looks carefully at Rayber's psyche, one finds that he is far from a
caricature of the modern intellectual. A more reasonable criticism
of the characterization in *The Violent Bear It Away* is that of Walter
Sullivan, who complains that the novel's characters are "too much
alike."[23]

    As I mentioned earlier, O'Connor explained to Hawkes that she
had to make Rayber less of a caricature as she revised her novel.
Stephen Gause Driggers concludes on the basis of O'Connor's
typescripts that "O'Connor never intend[ed] to make him a
prophet"[24] and that she failed to revise Rayber's character successfully.[25] However, as I have argued throughout this study, the
meaning of a character's experience depends less on the narrator's
treatment of that character, however harsh, than on the way the
character's own mind works. Rayber is actually a budding prophet,
who, like Enoch Emery in *Wise Blood,* borders on duplicating the
experience of his novel's primary character.

    Like Tarwater, Rayber was kidnapped as a child by Old Tarwater
and given religious training at Powderhead. Rayber rebelled against

Old Tarwater's influence, moreover, at about the age when Tarwater rebels. And although Rayber tells Old Tarwater that he has
overcome the old man's harmful influence, it is clear that Rayber
continues to be drawn to him: " 'You're too blind to see what you
did to me. A child can't defend himself. Children are cursed with
believing. You pushed me out of the real world and I stayed out of it
until I didn't know which was which. You infected me with your
idiot hopes, your foolish violence. I'm not always myself, I'm not
al . . .' but he stopped. He wouldn't admit what the old man knew.
'There's nothing wrong with me,' he said" (V, 73). Rayber lives the
life of an ascetic, and he recognizes that he still faces the issues he
sees Tarwater struggling with, but Rayber also recognizes that
Bishop embodies and contains his religious struggle: "He had not
conquered the problem of Bishop. He had only learned to live with
it and had learned too that he could not live without it" (p. 112).
Bishop becomes Rayber's one link to the positive grotesque, and
even as Rayber ridicules the idea of God, he links God to Bishop:
"He did not believe that he himself was formed in the image and
likeness of God but that Bishop was he had no doubt" (p. 113).
Rayber realizes, in fact, that he is constantly on the verge of
returning to religious belief, to the purposeless, "horrifying" (ibid.)
love that Bishop inspires, and that what would force his crucial
decision would be the loss of Bishop.

   Within the context of these assumptions, Rayber's treatment of
Tarwater seems crucially influenced by a desire to have Tarwater's
confrontation with the unbaptized Bishop take place. In fact,
Rayber rejects opportunities to gain Tarwater's acceptance. As
Rayber and Tarwater walk home after witnessing the sermon of
Lucette Carmody, for example, the narrator reports that "at any
point along the way, he could have put his hand on the shoulder
next to his and it would not have been withdrawn, but he made no
gesture" (p. 136). Louis D. Rubin, Jr., treats this complicated passage as Rayber's failure to save Tarwater from Old Tarwater's nox-
ious influence.[26] Preston M. Browning, Jr., interprets the passage
as reflective of Rayber's refusal of love, a reaction to his identification with and rejection by Lucette Carmody, whom Rayber momentarily associates with Old Tarwater.[27] I suggest that we consider what the result would be if Rayber did establish a loving
relationship with Tarwater. Rayber might succeed in producing a
relationship something like the one he had with Bishop or with Old
Tarwater, but he might also draw Tarwater out of the antagonistic
relationship that Rayber senses might eventually plunge him into
transformation. I think that Rayber's motives at this point are as

complex as they ever are in the novel, and that any valid reading of
his behavior must take into account Rayber's unconscious sense that
Tarwater is going to destroy Rayber's ability to avoid the religion
and love he associates with Old Tarwater.

Later in the novel, Rayber recognizes more explicitly that the loss
of Bishop could plunge him into love:

> His own stability depended on the little boy's presence. He could control
> his terrifying love as long as it had its focus in Bishop, but if anything
> happened to the child, he would have to face it in itself. Then the whole
> world would become his idiot child. He had thought what he would
> have to do if anything happened to Bishop. He would have with one
> supreme effort to resist the recognition; with every nerve and muscle
> and thought, he would have to resist feeling anything at all, thinking
> anything at all. He would have to anesthetize his life. He shook his head
> to clear it of these unpleasant thoughts. After it had cleared, they
> returned one by one. He felt a sinister pull on his consciousness, the
> familiar undertow of expectation, as if he were still a child waiting on
> Christ. (*V*, 182)

When Tarwater takes Bishop out in the boat and drowns him,
Rayber is ready to cooperate with Tarwater's action and force
himself toward a final decision about religion and love: "What had
happened was as plain to him as if he had been in the water with the
boy and the two of them together had taken the child and held him
under" (p. 203). The drowning of Bishop has a religious meaning
for Rayber even if no baptism accompanies it; in losing Bishop,
Rayber will be forced to confront the ideals for which Bishop has
substituted. Long before Tarwater's arrival, Rayber had tried to
drown Bishop, and it was at this point that Rayber discovered that
Bishop was what was keeping him from religion. Once Rayber
made this discovery, he could not let Bishop go. But in allowing
Tarwater to drown the child, Rayber relieves himself of the crutch
that prevents his collapse toward religiosity.

Like Enoch Emery, Rayber is abandoned before the conclusion of
his story is clear, and there is a variety of opinion about whether
Bishop's death brings Rayber toward or away from Old Tarwater.
We can say confidently that Rayber redeems himself from the status
of the narrator's caricature, but Rayber's lack of feeling at the end
makes most critics agree with John F. McCarthy that Rayber "experiences no recognition."[28] However, as with Enoch, it is very
difficult to justify a negative verdict on Rayber. Our one indication
of what happens to Rayber after he allows Bishop's drowning is
that he begins to "question" his initial theory about Tarwater, the
theory that the boy "was held in bondage by his great-uncle, that he
suffered a terrible false guilt for burning and not burying him, and

. . . that he was engaged in a desperate heroic struggle to free himself from the old man's ghostly grasp" (*V,* 106). Could this character, whom Hawkes says O'Connor has devilishly destroyed, have questioned this theory if his final leap had been toward nothingness?

In "The Lame Shall Enter First" we are much closer to the sort of purely destructive story predicted by Hawkes's analysis of O'Connor. This story, closely patterned after O'Connor's novel, appeared in the Summer 1962 issue of the *Sewanee Review,* which also features Hawkes's famous article; and in a letter to Hawkes dated 6 February 1962, O'Connor wrote that in "The Lame Shall Enter First" she would "admit that the Devil's voice is my own" (*HB,* 464). But like one of her characters who has heard the workings of the unconscious explained, O'Connor worked differently when she became more analytic about what she was up to. "The Lame Shall Enter First" is even more disquieting than most of O'Connor's works, and her protagonist's maneuverings for redemption are thoroughly skewed.

The major characters in "The Lame Shall Enter First"—Sheppard, Rufus Johnson, and Norton—are clearly alternate versions of Rayber, Tarwater, and Bishop in *The Violent Bear It Away,* although Rufus as well as Tarwater appears in early drafts of the novel. The two major differences between the story and the novel are that Sheppard, a more secularized character than Rayber, is the story's protagonist, and that the place of Old Tarwater is filled in the story by Sheppard's dead wife. Although Sheppard is a believable character who is uniquely sincere among O'Connor's intellectuals, he is nearly destroyed, for his unconscious maneuvers are consistently self-serving rather than self-redeeming.

The story's narration is of course where we would expect to see Sheppard unmasked. Frederick Asals compares O'Connor's narration to the actions of the devilish Rufus Johnson, who claims to be in Satan's power and whose sole motivation throughout the story seems to be to show up Sheppard.[29] And it is true that O'Connor gave Rufus one of her most famous lines; O'Connor says she writes because she is "good at it" (*MM,* 81), and Rufus says, "I lie and steal because I'm good at it!" (*CS,* 480). It may be surprising to note, then, that Sheppard's flaws are revealed subtly; "The Lame Shall Enter First" has more narrated monologue than most of O'Connor's other works, so that Sheppard's point of view is almost always before the reader. It should not be surprising that this narrative technique can have a devilishly reductive effect. In most of O'Connor's works, the authoritarian narration leaves room for the reader to discover ways in which characters are less negatively grotesque than they at first appear. The narration of "The Lame Shall Enter First" is almost entirely authoritative, and one effect of this authoritative narration is to make Sheppard's faults seem less escapable.

Our sense that Sheppard has many faults is not entirely the result of the narration, however, for Sheppard's unconscious maneuverings are among the most corrupt in O'Connor's works. Sheppard, a counselor at a reformatory, tells himself that his invitation of Rufus into his home and his plan to buy a new shoe for Rufus's clubfoot are fully well-intentioned attempts to help an unfortunate boy. Sheppard's dealings with Rufus are actually part of an unconscious strategy for returning to an ideal. The "ideal" to which Sheppard wishes to return, however, is his dead wife, and Rufus is to be her replacement, a circumstance which becomes most apparent when Sheppard is buying Rufus a shoe. After the shoe salesman says that the new shoe will allow Rufus to ride instead of walk, the narrator focuses on Sheppard "staring straight in front of him at a leather corset with an artificial arm attached" (p. 471). The reference to riding and the leather corset connects with the dead mother's corset, which Rufus puts on when he first enters Sheppard's house, saying, "Thisyer must be her saddle" (p. 456). These associations provide an answer to the question why Rufus tells the police at the story's end that Sheppard made "immor'l suggestions" (p. 480) to him. Sheppard's interest in Rufus is in part a result of his desire to find a replacement for his dead wife, a woman corseted, controlled, abstracted, killed. Sheppard's explanations of his reasons for wanting Rufus to stay with him and Norton—in the dead wife's room, significantly—fool only Sheppard. Rufus accuses him of believing he is Christ (p. 459), and throughout the story, Rufus tries repeatedly to show the falsity of Sheppard's conscious motivations and his basic selfishness; Rufus refuses the offered shoe, constantly insults Sheppard, and commits acts of vandalism around the neighborhood. When the police accuse Rufus after his first act of vandalism, the narrator describes Sheppard as uncompassionate in his refusal to defend Rufus. As his "sense of injury" increases, "Sheppard's face became harder" (p. 465), and instead of worrying about Rufus, Sheppard concentrates on an object: "All his regret turned suddenly on the shoe; his irritation at the sight of Johnson doubled." As Sheppard tells Rufus that he "did have" confidence in him up to now, the narrator describes Sheppard's face as "wooden" (ibid.). In a moment that foreshadows the ending, Sheppard feels guilt over wanting to be liked by Rufus. But before he sends Rufus off with the police, Sheppard realizes that he will make the youth angrier if he enforces rules strictly. He seems fully aware that his treatment of Rufus will make him more determined in his opposition. The fact that Sheppard hears "an appeal in his voice that Sheppard had not heard there before" (ibid.) makes his refusal to defend Rufus seem an even greater betrayal.

Once one has discovered the illusions Sheppard has about himself, one can return to passages which at first seem generous to Sheppard and find additional signs of his corruption. In the story's opening the narrator generally describes Sheppard positively, although one can also find bits of description that will reinforce the negative view of Sheppard we are later to accept; Sheppard has "intense blue eyes" and a "sensitive face," and he wants his son to be "good and unselfish" (p. 445). Sheppard's negative comments on his son are reported in narrated monologue so that it is easy to agree with them. But the narrator also describes Sheppard as eating "mechanically" and labels Sheppard's desire for his son to have a virtuous character as "all he wanted" for the child (ibid.). As he watches his son eat, Sheppard makes a lecture for his son out of the fact that he saw Rufus eating garbage the day before. Sheppard accuses his son of selfishness, a fault he considers more serious than "a violent temper, even a tendency to lie" (p. 446). Sheppard tells himself that "he could not allow himself to bring [Norton] up on a lie" (p. 461) about heaven and the boy's dead mother, but Sheppard feels that on some level he lies constantly. The "kindness and patience" he shows Rufus is "armor," and although Sheppard believes that there are no cracks in this armor, he also knows that he could be wounded if "a successful shaft could be driven" (ibid.) into him.

At the end of the story, as Rufus finally allows himself to be caught by the police, Sheppard appears to experience a recognition:

> "I did more for him than I did for my own child." He heard his voice as if it were the voice of his accuser. He repeated the sentence silently.
> Slowly his face drained of color. It became almost gray beneath the white halo of his hair. The sentence echoed in his mind, each syllable like a dull blow. His mouth twisted and he closed his eyes against the revelation. Norton's face rose before him, empty, forlorn, his left eye listing almost imperceptibly toward the outer rim as if it could not bear a full view of grief. His heart constricted with a repulsion for himself so clear and intense that he gasped for breath. He had stuffed his own emptiness with good works like a glutton. He had ignored his own child to feed his vision of himself. He saw the clear-eyed Devil, the sounder of hearts, leering at him from the eyes of Johnson. His image of himself shrivelled until everything was black before him. He sat there paralyzed, aghast.

He saw Norton at the telescope, all back and ears, saw his arm shoot up and wave frantically. A rush of agonizing love for the child rushed over him like a transfusion of life. The little boy's face appeared to him transformed; the image of his salvation; all light. He groaned with joy. He would make everything up to him. (Pp. 481–82)

While Sheppard does realize his error, in part—he never admits that he has tried to make a wife of Rufus—he also translates his guilt into pride: he will be the thorough, ideal penitent. As Joyce Carol Oates says, "Even at this dramatic point Sheppard is deluded. It is still *his* salvation he desires, *his* experience of the transformation of his son's misery into joy."[30] At the end of his story, then, we agree with the narrator's apparent conclusion: Sheppard is a negatively grotesque character who believes, inaccurately, that he has redeemed himself. The story's climax is chilling, not only because we see Sheppard further tangling himself in illusions, but because we see that Sheppard's unconscious maneuverings have led him away from redemption. Rufus and the narrator are right: Sheppard, including his unconscious, is thoroughly corrupt. Like Julian of "Everything That Rises Must Converge," Sheppard does not really maneuver himself toward redemption, but whereas Julian is finally pushed toward "the world of guilt and sorrow" (*CS,* 420), there is little indication that Sheppard is forced toward genuine enlightenment.

The emphasis is so thoroughly upon Sheppard that many readers miss, as Sheppard himself does, the redemptive experience of Norton's death. Norton has a good instinctive understanding of the positive grotesque, especially as it relates to food. Like his father's ideas, the cake Norton eats is "stale" (p. 446) and needs to be made grotesque; Norton puts peanut butter and catsup on the cake, and he listens eagerly when Rufus turns Sheppard's views upside down. But Norton is more like Harry Ashfield in "The River" than he is like other characters. Faithful and unintellectual, Norton works out his redemptive reunion with his dead mother on the story's margin; Sheppard ignores him, while Rufus uses him to attack Sheppard. Like Harry, Norton takes over his own redemption when the other characters leave him alone. While the other characters are ending their stories, Norton hangs himself in order to launch his "flight into space" (p. 482) toward the mother he sees in the heavens. Like Harry Ashfield, Norton achieves redemption without using the grotesque. Norton ultimately serves to reconcile "The Lame Shall Enter First" with the rest of O'Connor's works. If this story consisted entirely of the battle between Sheppard and Rufus, one could easily decide that the story attacks the entire notion of self-redemption. And it is true that these characters are guilty of being overly conscious of their plans to redeem themselves. Only Norton reminds us in "The Lame Shall Enter First" that self-redemption is possible no matter how impressive the obstacles.

1. Hawkes, "O'Connor's Devil," pp. 26, 32–33.
2. Ibid., p. 28.
3. Katz [Kahane], "O'Connor's Rage of Vision," p. 57.
4. Hendin, *World of O'Connor*, p. 20.
5. Ibid., p. 37.
6. Friedman, "Hawkes and O'Connor," p. 44.
7. Ibid., pp. 42–43.
8. This typescript is in File 181, O'Connor Collection.
9. This typescript is in File 180, O'Connor Collection.
10. Oates, *New Heaven, New Earth*, p. 153.
11. Katz [Kahane], "O'Connor's Rage of Vision," p. 63.
12. Feeley, *Flannery O'Connor*, pp. 168–69.
13. Stephens, *Question of O'Connor*, pp. 136–38.
14. Ibid., p. 138.
15. Tarwater's interpretation of the rapist seems ultimately responsible for our perception of the rapist as devilish. As a consequence, this most devilish of O'Connor characters should not be considered a personification of the Devil.
16. Nancy Barcus, in "Psychological Determinism and Freedom in O'Connor," also argues that Tarwater becomes free only at the novel's end.
17. This typescript is in File 180 on *The Violent Bear It Away*, O'Connor Collection.
18. Trowbridge, "Symbolic Vision of O'Connor," p. 313.
19. Pearce, "O'Connor's Ineffable 'Recognitions,'" p. 303.
20. Orvell, *Invisible Parade*, p. 120.
21. Ibid.
22. Ibid., p. 121.
23. Sullivan, "O'Connor, Sin, and Grace," p. 25.
24. Driggers, "Imaginative Discovery in the O'Connor Typescripts," p. 76.
25. Ibid., p. 78.
26. Rubin, "O'Connor and the Bible Belt," p. 63.
27. See Browning, *Flannery O'Connor*, pp. 90–94.
28. McCarthy, "Human Intelligence Versus Divine Truth," p. 1145.
29. Asals, *Flannery O'Connor*, pp. 158–59.
30. Oates, *New Heaven, New Earth*, p. 163.

OCCASIONS OF GRACE?

What shall we say, then? Shall we continue in sin, that grace
may abound?

—Romans 6:1

IN THIS STUDY I have examined the paths toward redemption followed by O'Connor's major characters. The characters discussed
here fall into five groups, the most important of which includes
Mrs. Shortley, Mrs. Turpin, Asbury, Mrs. Cope, Mrs. May, the
child in "A Temple of the Holy Ghost," Calhoun, Hazel Motes, and
Tarwater. All of these characters unconsciously use the grotesque to
redeem themselves despite narratorial bias, and one is tempted to
include Enoch Emery, Mrs. Flood, and Rayber in this group as
well. Two other groups of characters achieve qualified versions of
redemption. O. E. Parker, Mr. Head, and Tanner also redeem
themselves, but the narratorial bias from which they free themselves is slight; other characters free themselves from the role that
the narrator assigns them, but without completing the redemptive
course they have planned: Mrs. McIntyre, The Misfit, Mr. Shiftlet,
and Hulga/Joy. All of the characters in these three groups participate in a strategy for redemption that I believe has not previously
been adequately described. Another group of characters follows a
redemptive pattern described frequently in O'Connor criticism. If
the grandmother, George Poker Sash, Ruby Hill, Julian, or Sheppard is redeemed, an outside force causes it. Whatever attempts
these characters make to save themselves are ineffectual. The final
group, small but significant, consists of Harry/Bevel, Norton, and
perhaps Bishop, innocents who redeem themselves without using
the grotesque.

O'Connor repeatedly investigated the process for achieving redemption. Her repetitiousness transformed the moments in which

her characters achieve redemption into the object of her constant contemplation. Redemption itself in O'Connor's works, however, remains an abstract, idealized moment, the specifics of which never quite become clear. To some extent redemption is a recapturing and reforming of ideals; from another perspective, redemption lies in the characters' freedom from the role assigned them by the narrator. Insofar as the O'Connor narrator combines the ideals and strictures toward which the characters feel attraction and repulsion, the narrator would seem to hold the key to an understanding of O'Connor's view of redemption. Insofar as her implications about redemption remain ambiguous, one may take her descriptions of redemption as evidence of her reluctance to define the most sacred of subjects. Or it might be argued that O'Connor did not consider the state of redemption interesting in itself: that she used the grotesque because the cyclical nature of the grotesque demotes redemption from a conclusion to a moment in an ongoing process. Another possibility is that the precise nature of redemption remained problematic for O'Connor, and that the repetitiousness of her art was part of a strategy to capture and understand redemption.

I will conclude this study by assessing the significance of the groupings of characters and by discussing some of the broader questions about the goals of O'Connor's fiction. When she dramatized a traditional version of redemption, as with the grandmother, the source of redemption (if it occurs) seems to be supernatural. The grandmother herself does almost nothing to cause redemption. One of the problems with such a scenario, however, is that it leaves little room for the character's good works to operate; as a result, "A Good Man Is Hard to Find" can be taken as a tale of Protestant election.[1] O'Connor needed a way to dramatize characters' ability to foster their own redemption, and she found two approaches toward a solution. The less intriguing involved characters such as Harry/Bevel, innocents who, once they learn of it, unhesitatingly grasp religion. The more intriguing and difficult story to tell involved more sophisticated and corrupt characters, and O'Connor found in the grotesque a way for these characters to use their weaknesses to bring about redemption.

Although O'Connor used this last scenario in most of her fiction, it also raises problems. One problem is that the institution of the Catholic Church may seem irrelevant. As O'Connor said in a letter dated 5 July 1958, "Writers like myself who don't use Catholic settings or characters, good or bad, are trying to make it plain that personal loyalty to the person of Christ is imperative, is the structure of man's nature, his necessary direction, etc. The Church, as institution, doesn't come into it one way or another" (*HB,* 290). Through her handling of the grotesque and of narration, O'Connor avoided making the isolated individual the source of redemption. The grotesque often involves the further degradation of some tired ideal shared by the character's community, and O'Connor's narrator in these stories typically reminds the reader why the character needs to use the grotesque as a response to the community. The similarity of O'Connor's typical narrator to Sarah Ruth Cates in "Parker's Back" suggests a sense in which O'Connor's narrator helps bring about grotesque behavior by her characters.

Another problem in this scenario is the continuing ambiguity of the undegraded ideals from which characters originally fell away. Characters are conscious only of that form of the ideal by which they feel oppressed, and the stories so consistently focus upon achieving freedom and upon *reforming* ideals that the original ideals themselves are difficult to pinpoint. In *Wise Blood* and *The Violent Bear It Away,* we can identify relatives of Hazel Motes and Tarwater, with whose pronounced ideas the protagonists struggle throughout their novels. As to other characters, however, the word *ideal* may seem inappropriate because of its emphasis on the characters' ideas, and, with some characters—Mrs. Shortley or Enoch Emery, for example—ideas seem almost irrelevant. Nonetheless, the word *ideal* seems appropriate, finally, precisely because it suggests the interplay between the characters and their community, an interplay basic to the grotesque even when it is difficult to detail.

In linking characters to their community and focusing on their ability to bring about redemption, O'Connor brings her fiction toward the Catholic art she said it was. Almost all her characters are Protestant, however, and the emphasis on private religious experience in her works is also associated with Protestantism. The pattern that emerges is that the brand of Protestantism practiced by many O'Connor characters (and, for that matter, the atheism of Asbury or Hulga/Joy) functions as a grotesque form of Catholicism. In O'Connor's statements about her art, we find evidence that she regarded her fiction as linking Catholicism and Protestantism. Although she called the South's religion a "do-it-yourself religion" (*HB,* 350), she was interested in the ways her Protestants find their way back to religious states like those of Catholicism. She considered Old Tarwater of *The Violent Bear It Away* very individualistic, but she also saw him as a Catholic (p. 517). Part of O'Connor's message is that the most individualistic religious experience can bring people back to Catholicism. She even suggested that Protestantism is especially likely to produce the grotesque; she once explained that "the fact of the Word made flesh" is for her "the fulcrum that lifts my particular stories. I'm a Catholic but this is in orthodox Protestantism also, though out of context—which makes it grow into grotesque forms" (p. 227). Another of her goals was to link the Catholic emphasis on works with the Protestant emphasis upon grace. Throughout this study I have avoided the term *grace,* to further my point that when we examine O'Connor's characters' psyches, we discover that the characters work to bring about their own redemption. The concept of grace is usually used in the criticism to argue the opposite, to show that O'Connor characters are redeemed in spite of themselves. Some characters believe that they themselves are recipients of grace, suggesting that the term need not be ignored, however. If we use the word *grace* in describing O'Connor's works, we must redefine it so that grace comes under the control of characters through its link to sin, which the characters do control. Just as in Catholicism there are "occasions of sin"—situations likely to increase temptation—one might say that O'Connor's characters invent for themselves "occasions of grace," moments in which sins bring about redemption. Once grace is understood as being caused by sin, it becomes a useful term for understanding O'Connor's works, although some may object to redefinition of the term.[2]

O'Connor herself always contrasted her religious explanations of behavior to psychological ones, but I would suggest that psychological and theological approaches to her works are compatible. Psychology in O'Connor's works exists in a grotesque relation to dogma; as characters live out their religious conflicts, they produce grotesque and enlivened versions of religious formulae. The relationship between characterization and narration also resembles that between religious formula and personal psychology. As the representative of an authoritarian religious outlook, the narrator treats character as static and narration as a matter of disclosure. The character, however, uses narration—that is, the events of the story—to counter the narrator's treatment of character.

In studying O'Connor one constantly confronts a tension between the individualistic and the communal, but O'Connor generally balances satiric judgment and romantic admiration of the individual. Bakhtin's theories perhaps overemphasize the ability of individuals to overcome their community,[3] so one might ask whether O'Connor's works avoid such an overemphasis. D. A. Miller has argued that Bakhtin overemphasizes the freedom possible in the novel, and that one means by which the novel maintains control over characters is to pretend to be freed of its policing power.[4] I believe that O'Connor succeeds in dramatizing her characters' liberation without underestimating the forces that oppress them, but the possibility of an argument such as Miller's has caused me to emphasize those instances in which characters reform ideals.[5] Hazel Motes's alteration of his ancestors' religion is probably the most detailed example of such reformation, although Enoch Emery's and Mrs. Flood's eccentric interpretations of Hazel provide more striking examples.

The reactions of Enoch and Mrs. Flood to Hazel provide metaphors for readers' reactions to O'Connor's works. O'Connor is often interpreted as scolding her audience, and she frequently made a point of refusing to write trivially "uplifting" literature. It is certainly worthwhile to ask what sorts of effects O'Connor's works produce for readers, and the answer is complicated. The characters' grotesquerie challenges and reforms the ideals of their society. At the same time, however, many O'Connor characters have a very limited, fragile sense of their community; in addition to renouncing a dead, abstract version of their community, most of the characters renounce most of the rest of the world. The reader of one of O'Connor's texts, then, is in a sense never a part of the world redeemed by the protagonist. The reader can, however, like Enoch and Mrs. Flood, use the experiences of O'Connor's protagonists and their idealization as part of another grotesque cycle. Mrs. Flood's and Enoch Emery's grotesque misunderstandings of Hazel Motes are basically affirmed by the novel; apparently if one can achieve conviction, one can achieve redemption, and one purpose for O'Connor's defamiliarization of religious experience could be to give the reader a new start toward such conviction.

Extending this observation, we derive a contribution to the debate over the relation between reader and text in the production of interpretations. While the notion of freely endorsing subjective interpretations seems to be anathema to most theorists, we find just such an endorsement in *Wise Blood*. Even Enoch Emery and Mrs. Flood, characters who interpret Hazel Motes in eccentric ways, are discovered finally to be part of an interpretive community, one which ultimately may include even the most authoritarian of O'Connor's narrators. If the reader of her works is encouraged to follow an individual path, we have a rationale for the variety of readings her works receive. Surely O'Connor as reader found in the variety of her characters' experiences a series of reinforcements for her own religious quest. Even when her characters, and narrators, are willfully distorting religious ideals, there is a sense in which their unconscious quests succeed; as Johan Huizinga puts it in describing "the nature and essence of ritual and mystery," it seems that their activity, "by representing a certain desired cosmic event, compels the gods to effect that event in reality."[6] We may conclude that the reader of O'Connor is encouraged to produce an extremely personal reading. Perhaps it was O'Connor's greatest act of faith as a writer to assume that "misreadings" of her work might turn out to be so many more paths to redemption.

1. See Bellamy, "Everything Off Balance"; and Milder, "Protestantism of O'Connor."

2. Although she arrives at conclusions quite different from mine, Lorine Getz discusses varieties of grace in O'Connor while analyzing differences among the works. See her *Nature and Grace in O'Connor's Fiction.*

3. See Michael Holquist's discussion of Bakhtin's work on Freud, "The Politics of Representation," especially pp. 177–82.

4. Miller, "The Novel and the Police."

5. Paul Ricoeur says that such a notion of reform is compatible with religion, for, in Romans 5:12–21, grace is described as providing more than a "restoration" of the human state before sin: "The gift is the establishment of a new creation." See *The Symbolism of Evil,* trans. Emerson Buchanan (New York: Harper, 1967), p. 272.

6. Huizinga, *Homo Ludens: A Study of the Play-Element in Culture* (1950; reprint, Boston: Beacon, 1955), p. 15.

SELECT BIBLIOGRAPHY

I. WORKS BY FLANNERY O'CONNOR

The Complete Stories. New York: Farrar, 1971.
"The Displaced Person." *Sewanee Review* 62 (1954): 634–54.
Everything That Rises Must Converge. New York: Farrar, 1965.
"An Exile in the East." *South Carolina Review* 11 (1978): 12–21.
The Habit of Being. Edited by Sally Fitzgerald. New York: Farrar, 1979.
Mystery and Manners. Edited by Sally Fitzgerald and Robert Fitzgerald. New York: Farrar, 1969.
O'Connor Collection, Georgia College, Milledgeville. File numbers for the collection are now in the process of being changed, but the numbering system followed here, which was designed by Robert J. Dunn, may still be used to locate typescripts.
   File 12, on "The Geranium." [Quoted in part in Driggers, "Imaginative Discovery in the O'Connor Typescripts"; and in part in May, *The Pruning Word.*]
   File 135, on *Wise Blood.*
   File 151, on *Wise Blood.*
   File 154, on "A Good Man Is Hard to Find."
   Files 156–57, on "The Life You Save May Be Your Own." [Quoted in part in Hegarty, "A Man Though Not Yet a Whole One." Published in part as "The Shiftlet Fragment."]
   File 158, on "The Artificial Nigger." [Quoted in part in May, *The Pruning Word.*]
   Files 180–81, on *The Violent Bear It Away.* [Quoted in part in Driggers, "Imaginative Discovery in the O'Connor Typescripts."]
   File 189, on "Revelation." [Quoted in part in May, *The Pruning Word.*]
   File 194, on "Getting Home." [Quoted in part in May, *The Pruning Word.*]
The Presence of Grace and Other Book Reviews. Compiled by Leo J. Zuber. Edited by Carter W. Martin. Athens: University of Georgia Press, 1983.
"The Shiftlet Fragment." *Flannery O'Connor Bulletin* 10 (1981): 78–86.
The Violent Bear It Away. New York: Farrar, 1960.
Wise Blood. 2d ed. New York: Farrar, 1962.

II. BIBLIOGRAPHICAL, BIOGRAPHICAL, AND CRITICAL STUDIES

Allen, Suzanne. "Memories of a Southern Catholic Girlhood: Flannery O'Connor's 'A Temple of the Holy Ghost.' " *Renascence* 31 (1979): 83–92.
Asals, Frederick. *Flannery O'Connor: The Imagination of Extremity.* Athens: University of Georgia Press, 1982.

166

Bakhtin, Mikhail Mikhailovich. "Discourse in the Novel." In *The Dialogic Imagination: Four Essays,* edited by Michael Holquist and translated by Caryl Emerson and Michael Holquist, pp. 259–422. Austin: University of Texas Press, 1981.

————. *Problems of Dostoevsky's Poetics.* Edited and translated by Caryl Emerson. Minneapolis: University of Minnesota Press, 1984.

————. *Rabelais and His World.* Translated by Hélène Iswolsky. Cambridge, Mass.: MIT Press, 1968.

Barcus, Nancy B. "Psychological Determinism and Freedom in Flannery O'Connor." *Cithara* 12, no. 1 (1972): 26–33.

Bellamy, Michael O. "Everything Off Balance: Protestant Election in Flannery O'Connor's 'A Good Man Is Hard to Find.'" *Flannery O'Connor Bulletin* 8 (1979): 116–24.

Bleikasten, André. "The Heresy of Flannery O'Connor." In *Les Américanistes: New French Criticism on Modern American Fiction,* edited by Ira D. Johnson and Christiane Johnson, pp. 53–70. Port Washington, N.Y.: Kennikat, 1978.

Browning, Preston M., Jr. *Flannery O'Connor.* Carbondale: Southern Illinois University Press, 1974.

Bryant, Hallman B. "Reading the Map in 'A Good Man Is Hard to Find.'" *Studies in Short Fiction* 18 (1981): 301–7.

Burns, Stuart L. "The Evolution of *Wise Blood.*" *Modern Fiction Studies* 16 (1970): 147–62.

————. "Freaks in a Circus Tent: Flannery O'Connor's Christ-Haunted Characters." *Flannery O'Connor Bulletin* 1 (1972): 3–23.

Cassill, R. V. *The Norton Anthology of Short Fiction: Instructor's Handbook for the Complete and Shorter Editions.* 2d ed. New York: Norton, 1981.

Cohn, Dorrit. *Transparent Minds: Narrative Modes for Presenting Consciousness in Fiction.* Princeton, N.J.: Princeton University Press, 1978.

Coles, Robert. *Flannery O'Connor's South.* Baton Rouge: Louisiana State University Press, 1980.

Coulthard, A. R. "From Sermon to Parable: Four Conversion Stories by Flannery O'Connor." *American Literature* 55 (1983): 55–71.

Culler, Jonathan. *The Pursuit of Signs: Semiotics, Literature, Deconstruction.* Ithaca, N.Y.: Cornell University Press, 1981.

Denham, Robert D. "The World of Guilt and Sorrow: Flannery O'Connor's 'Everything That Rises Must Converge.'" *Flannery O'Connor Bulletin* 4 (1975): 42–51.

Desmond, John F. "Flannery O'Connor, Henry James and the International Theme." *Flannery O'Connor Bulletin* 9 (1980): 3–18.

————. "The Lessons of History: Flannery O'Connor's 'Everything That Rises Must Converge.'" *Flannery O'Connor Bulletin* 1 (1972): 39–45.

Doxey, William S. "A Dissenting Opinion of Flannery O'Connor's 'A Good Man Is Hard to Find.'" *Studies in Short Fiction* 10 (1973): 199–204.

Driggers, Stephen Gause. "Imaginative Discovery in the Flannery O'Connor Typescripts." Ph.D. diss., Indiana University, 1981.

Driskill, Leon [V.]. " 'Parker's Back' vs. 'The Partridge Festival': Flannery O'Connor's Critical Choice." *Georgia Review* 21 (1967): 476–90.

Driskill, Leon V., and Joan T. Brittain. *The Eternal Crossroads: The Art of Flannery O'Connor.* Lexington: University Press of Kentucky, 1971.

Eggenschwiler, David. *The Christian Humanism of Flannery O'Connor.* Detroit: Wayne State University Press, 1972.

Farmer, David. *Flannery O'Connor: A Descriptive Bibliography.* New York: Garland, 1981.

Feeley, Kathleen. *Flannery O'Connor: Voice of the Peacock.* 2d ed. New York: Fordham University Press, 1982.

Fitzgerald, Robert. "The Countryside and the True Country." *Sewanee Review* 70 (1962): 380–94. Reprinted in *Flannery O'Connor,* edited by Robert E. Reiter, pp. 69–82. St. Louis: Herder, 1968.

———. Introduction to *Everything That Rises Must Converge,* by Flannery O'Connor, pp. 5–30. New York: Farrar, 1965.

Fitzgerald, Sally. "A Master Class: From the Correspondence of Caroline Gordon and Flannery O'Connor." *Georgia Review* 33 (1979): 827–46.

———. "Rooms with a View." *Flannery O'Connor Bulletin* 10 (1981): 5–22.

Fowler, Roger. "Anti-Language in Fiction." *Style* 13 (1979): 259–78.

Friedman, Melvin J. "John Hawkes and Flannery O'Connor: The French Background." *Boston University Journal* 21, no. 3 (1973): 34–44.

Getz, Lorine M. *Flannery O'Connor: Her Life, Library and Book Reviews.* New York: Mellen, 1980.

———. *Nature and Grace in Flannery O'Connor's Fiction.* New York: Mellen, 1982.

Golden, Robert E., and Mary C. Sullivan. *Flannery O'Connor and Caroline Gordon: A Reference Guide.* Boston: Hall, 1977.

Gordon, Caroline. "Flannery O'Connor's *Wise Blood.*" *Critique* 2, no. 2 (1958): 3–10.

———. "Rebels and Revolutionaries: The New American Scene." *Flannery O'Connor Bulletin* 3 (1974): 40–56.

Gordon, Caroline, and Allen Tate. *The House of Fiction.* 2d ed. New York: Scribner's, 1960.

Gossett, Louise Y. *Violence in Recent Southern Fiction.* Durham, N.C.: Duke University Press, 1965.

Gregory, Donald. "Enoch Emery: Ironic Doubling in *Wise Blood.*" *Flannery O'Connor Bulletin* 4 (1975): 52–64.

Grimshaw, James A., Jr. *The Flannery O'Connor Companion.* Westport, Conn.: Greenwood, 1981.

Harpham, Geoffrey Galt. *On the Grotesque: Strategies of Contradiction in Art and Literature.* Princeton, N.J.: Princeton University Press, 1982.

Hassan, Ihab. *Contemporary American Literature 1945–1972: An Introduction.* New York: Ungar, 1973.

Hawkes, John. "Flannery O'Connor's Devil." *Sewanee Review* 70 (1962): 395–407. Reprinted in *Flannery O'Connor,* edited by Robert E. Reiter, pp. 25–37. St. Louis: Herder, 1968.

Hawkins, Peter S. *The Language of Grace: Flannery O'Connor, Walker Percy, and Iris Murdoch.* Cambridge, Mass.: Cowley, 1983.

Hegarty, Charles M., S.J. "A Man Though Not Yet a Whole One: Mr. Shiftlet's Genesis." *Flannery O'Connor Bulletin* 1 (1972): 24–38.

Hendin, Josephine. *The World of Flannery O'Connor.* Bloomington: Indiana University Press, 1970.

Hines, Melissa. "Grotesque Conversions and Critical Piety." *Flannery O'Connor Bulletin* 6 (1977): 17–35.

Holquist, Michael. "The Politics of Representation." In *Allegory and Representation: Selected Papers from the English Institute, 1979–80,* edited by Stephen J. Greenblatt, pp. 163–83. Baltimore: Johns Hopkins University Press, 1981.

Howe, Irving. "Flannery O'Connor's Stories." *New York Review of Books,* 30 September 1965, pp. 16–17.

Humphries, Jefferson. *The Otherness Within: Gnostic Readings in Marcel Proust, Flannery O'Connor, and François Villon.* Baton Rouge: Louisiana State University Press, 1983.

Hyman, Stanley Edgar. *Flannery O'Connor.* Minneapolis: University of Minnesota Press, 1966.

Ireland, Patrick J. "The Place of Flannery O'Connor in Our Two Literatures: The Southern and National Literary Traditions." *Flannery O'Connor Bulletin* 7 (1978): 47–63.

Kahane, Claire [Katz]. "The Artificial Niggers." *Massachusetts Review* 19 (1978): 183–98.

———. "Comic Vibrations and Self-Construction in Grotesque Literature." *Literature and Psychology* 29 (1979): 114–19.

———. "Gothic Mirrors and Feminine Identity." *Centennial Review* 24 (1980): 43–64.

Katz [Kahane], Claire. "Flannery O'Connor's Rage of Vision." *American Literature* 46 (1974): 54–67.

Kayser, Wolfgang. *The Grotesque in Art and Literature.* Translated by Ulrich Weisstein. 1963. Reprint, Gloucester, Mass.: Peter Smith, 1968.

Kellogg, Gene. *The Vital Tradition: The Catholic Novel in a Period of Convergence.* Chicago: Loyola University Press, 1979.

Kinney, Arthur F. *Flannery O'Connor's Library: Resources of Being.* Athens: University of Georgia Press, 1985.

Klevar, Harvey. "Image and Imagination: Flannery O'Connor's Front Page Fiction." *Journal of Modern Literature* 4 (1974): 121–32.

LeClair, Thomas. "Flannery O'Connor's *Wise Blood:* The Oedipal Theme." *Mississippi Quarterly* 29 (1976): 197–205.

Martin, Carter [W.] "The Genesis of O'Connor's 'The Partridge Festival.'" *Flannery O'Connor Bulletin* 10 (1981): 46–53.

———. *The True Country: Themes in the Fiction of Flannery O'Connor.* Nashville, Tenn.: Vanderbilt University Press, 1969.

May, John R. *The Pruning Word: The Parables of Flannery O'Connor.* Notre Dame, Ind.: University of Notre Dame Press, 1976.

McCarthy, John F. "Human Intelligence Versus Divine Truth: The Intellectual in Flannery O'Connor's Works." *English Journal* 55 (1966): 1143–48.

McCullagh, James C. "Symbolism and the Religious Aesthetic: Flannery O'Connor's *Wise Blood*." *Flannery O'Connor Bulletin* 2 (1973): 43–58.

Milder, Robert. "The Protestantism of Flannery O'Connor." *Southern Review* 11 (1975): 802–19.

Miller, D. A. "The Novel and the Police." *Glyph* 8 (1981): 127–47.

Muller, Gilbert H. "The City of Woe: Flannery O'Connor's Dantean Vision." *Georgia Review* 23 (1969): 206–13.

———. *Nightmares and Visions: Flannery O'Connor and the Catholic Grotesque*. Athens: University of Georgia Press, 1972.

Murphy, George D., and Caroline L. Cherry. "Flannery O'Connor and the Integration of Personality." *Flannery O'Connor Bulletin* 7 (1978): 85–100.

Nisly, Paul W. "The Prison of the Self: Isolation in Flannery O'Connor's Fiction." *Studies in Short Fiction* 17 (1980): 49–54.

Oates, Joyce Carol. *New Heaven, New Earth: The Visionary Experience in Literature*. New York: Vanguard, 1974.

Orvell, Miles. *Invisible Parade: The Fiction of Flannery O'Connor*. Philadelphia: Temple University Press, 1972.

Pearce, Howard D. "Flannery O'Connor's Ineffable 'Recognitions.'" *Genre* 6 (1973): 298–312.

Pierce, Constance. "The Mechanical World of 'Good Country People.'" *Flannery O'Connor Bulletin* 5 (1976): 30–38.

Rubin, Louis D., Jr. "Flannery O'Connor and the Bible Belt." In *The Added Dimension: The Art and Mind of Flannery O'Connor*, 2d ed., edited by Melvin J. Friedman and Lewis A. Lawson, pp. 49–72. New York: Fordham University Press, 1977.

———. "Flannery O'Connor's Company of Southerners: or, 'The Artificial Nigger' Read as Fiction Rather Than Theology." *Flannery O'Connor Bulletin* 6 (1977): 47–71.

Ryan, Steven T. "The Three Realms of O'Connor's 'Greenleaf.'" *Christianity and Literature* 29, no. 1 (1979): 39–51.

Schleifer, Ronald. "Rural Gothic: The Stories of Flannery O'Connor." *Modern Fiction Studies* 28 (1982): 475–85.

Shloss, Carol. *Flannery O'Connor's Dark Comedies: The Limits of Inference*. Baton Rouge: Louisiana State University Press, 1980.

Smith, Anneliese H. "O'Connor's 'Good Country People.'" *Explicator* 33 (1974), item 30.

Stephens, Martha. *The Question of Flannery O'Connor*. Baton Rouge: Louisiana State University Press, 1973.

Sullivan, Walter. "Flannery O'Connor, Sin, and Grace: *Everything That Rises Must Converge*." *Hollins Critic* 2, no. 4 (1965): 1–8, 10. Reprinted in *Death by Melancholy: Essays on Modern Southern Fiction*, pp. 22–35. Baton Rouge: Louisiana State University Press, 1972.

Tate, J. O. "The Essential Essex." *Flannery O'Connor Bulletin* 12 (1983): 47–59.

————. "A Good Source Is Not So Hard To Find." *Flannery O'Connor Bulletin* 9 (1980): 98–103.

Thomson, Philip. *The Grotesque*. London: Methuen, 1972.

Trowbridge, Clinton W. "The Symbolic Vision of Flannery O'Connor: Patterns of Imagery in *The Violent Bear It Away*." *Sewanee Review* 76 (1968): 298–318.

Walker, Alice. "Beyond the Peacock: The Reconstruction of Flannery O'Connor." *Ms.*, December 1975, pp. 77–79, 102, 104–6. Reprinted in *In Search of Our Mothers' Gardens*, pp. 42–59. New York: Harcourt, 1983.

Westling, Louise. "Flannery O'Connor's Mothers and Daughters." *Twentieth Century Literature* 24 (1978): 510–22.

————. *Sacred Groves and Ravaged Gardens: The Fiction of Eudora Welty, Carson McCullers, and Flannery O'Connor*. Athens: University of Georgia Press, 1985.

Wood, Ralph C. "From Fashionable Tolerance to Unfashionable Redemption: A Reading of Flannery O'Connor's First and Last Stories." *Flannery O'Connor Bulletin* 7 (1978): 10–25.

INDEX